Hypnosis for

Weight Loss 2

books in 1

Rapid Weight Loss Hypnosis and Gastric Band. Burn Fat Fast, Rewire your Brain, Stop Emotional Eating and Increase Your Motivation With Chakra Meditation

Copyright © 2020 [Jessica Moon]

Legal & Disclaimer

The information contained in this book and its contents is not designed to replace or take the place of any form of medical or professional advice; and is not meant to replace the need for independent medical, financial, legal or other professional advice or services, as may be required. The content and information in this book have been provided for educational and entertainment purposes only.

The content and information contained in this book have been compiled from sources deemed reliable, and it is accurate to the best of the Author's knowledge, information, and belief. However, the author cannot guarantee its accuracy and validity and cannot be held liable for any errors and/or omissions. Further, changes are periodically made to this book as and when needed. Where appropriate and/or necessary, you must consult a professional (including but not limited to your doctor, attorney, financial advisor or such other professional advisor) before using any of the suggested remedies, techniques, or information in this book.

Upon using the contents and information contained in this book, you agree to hold harmless the Author from and against any damages, costs, and expenses, including any legal fees potentially resulting from the application of any of the information provided by this book. This disclaimer applies to any loss, damages or injury caused by the use and application, whether directly or indirectly, of any advice or information presented, whether for breach of contract, tort, negligence, personal injury, criminal intent, or under any other cause of action.

You agree to accept all risks of using the information presented inside this book.

You agree that by continuing to read this book, where appropriate and/or necessary, you shall consult a professional (including but not limited to your doctor, attorney, or financial advisor or such other advisor as needed) before using any of the suggested remedies, techniques, or information in this book.

Gastric Band

Hypnosis

Burn Fat, Lose Weight, Rewire your Anxious Brain, Stop Food Addiction and Eat Healthy with Rapid Weight Loss Hypnosis and Chakra Meditation. Over 100 Affirmations for Women.

Contents

Rapid Weight Loss

Hypnosis

Natural Weight Loss Hypnosis, Blast Calories, Burn Fat and Stop Emotional Eating. Increase Your Motivation, Self Esteem and Heal Your Body and Soul with 90+ Affirmations

Contents

11

Gastric Band

Hypnosis

INTRODUCTION

You will then learn everything you should know about the common myths and misconceptions associated with obtaining your ideal weight, losing weight, and practicing healthy eating habits. You will learn that you do not should experience common issues brought about by all those meal plans and dieting. You will be able to create a good relationship with food because it is essential to your nourishment.

If you're able to combine intuitive eating, affirmations, visualization, and the hypnotic gastric band, then you will be able to realize your dreams of attaining and maintaining your ideal weight. Also, you will learn how to utilize the hypnotic gastric band as the best choice for your health and resilience.

It does not matter how you feel or what you're suspecting in your body, so long as you see signs that you are losing control of your body weight, then you should be evidence of your physical appearance. Seeing these signs is one thing; understanding what they mean is another thing. This book does not involve practices that you should rush or practices that you should do without a routine and a goal if you mean to change your body weight drastically. Now when it comes to knowing if your body's weight is perfect and if you have full control, then you should make sure that you have used various measures to influence your subconscious mind involved in the practices that will help to keep it in check.

To that end, you will find this book educative, and you will find valuable information meant to keep you as alert as possible in ensuring that you understand how to use this hypnotic gastric band to help to keep your body within the ideal weight and appearance. You will also learn some crucial insights that are related to hypnosis and meditation, and how you can incorporate intuitive eating, powerful affirmations, and visualization aids to achieve your ideal weight and help to improve your relationship with food. Most of the practices that you will carry out might appear impossible, because of the negative thoughts in your subconscious mind.

At this stage, the understanding that you already have is important because you've made it a point to conduct a deep search of the most important aspects of the hypnotic gastric band. The first step to losing your weight is to get started, and that is the obstacle for many people because there is no deadline to complete it. So don't let yourself become complacent. Stop dreaming about doing something and get to work. Get started today by buying this book today!

CHAPTER ONE

HYPNOTIC GASTRIC BAND

A gastric band is a silicone device commonly used to treat obesity. The device is normally placed around the upper part of your stomach to help decrease the food that you're eating. On the upper part of the stomach, the band makes a relatively smaller pouch. It fills up quickly and slows your consumption rate. The band shows you whenever you make healthy food options, reduce appetite, and limit food intake and volume.

However, it leaves you with a difficult option of bariatric surgery, which is a drastic step that carries risks and pains like any other gastrointestinal surgical operation. You should not experience these challenges when you can take a simple and less invasive approach to achieve the same results as in a surgical gastric band.

The gastric band for weight loss

So now you can relax and take this time to wind yourself down, and allow all those tensions to start flowing out and disappearing. So just bring to mind to remember that hypnosis is just self-hypnosis, as you're reading this book now, that this is not something that someone will be able to do for you. Because hypnosis is simply a state of deep relaxation, which successfully helps you to bypasses your critical factors so that the suggestions that are beneficial to your true self will be readily received and accepted by your deeper unconscious mind.

After all, trance is an everyday natural calming experience, and you're entering into that experience easily and effortlessly. So start by asking yourself, if you've ever put yourself in a calm relaxing state before this moment, and if so, you can recall all those calm and relaxing states that you've previously experienced, whether it's via your favorite hobby, an activity, a journey or a holiday.

The most important thing to realize is that you should bring to your mind, relaxation, and protective magical thinking practices each day in your waking state because you know that the practice imprints it in your mind. And as time goes by, it becomes easier for you to be able to gain the benefits of these experiences, which helps to promote self-acceptance.

Once they become permanently fixed into your mind, you will experience some positive changes in your life, and they will become active by helping you to create positive changes in your life that are for your benefit, and they will lead you forward towards a real realization of those changes. And as you speak directly to the deeper inner part of the self that controls your eating habits and weight, you will realize that you have been eating more food than the food that your body wants or needs. And also, you will realize that your mind controls your eating habits.

Now just seeing all those levers that you can adjust, you can then choose which one to use because you know that you have the power over your weight and your eating habits. And also you know what you're eating. The exact time and amount that you choose to eat are controlled in this place, which is the deeper part of your authentic self.

This part of the body is not your stomach or your appetite, but it controls your food, but it is your mind, and you get to ask that aspect of yourself beginning today, to develop new habits for yourself. And set new positive goals for yourself because you are laying a mental foundation for yourself, who is now a cheerful, attractive, positive, and authentic you. The great importance of this new you and your healthy, active, and attractive body is that you are eating less food, and you're happier.

The more you smile, and the more relaxed you are, the better you will look and the better you will feel. Also, you will be able to find satisfaction in eating less and pride yourself in knowing that each time you do so, you are rewarding your slimmer, healthier, and natural self. and you will know that the slimmer you are deep within you as you exercise, this new strength will grow. And as you eat healthily and sensibly, you will find yourself filling satisfied, and you will discover that the exercise makes it more reinforce and more natural towards your authentic identity.

Because it is like using and strengthening your muscles to become stronger and stronger, now eating sensibly becomes easier, easier, in a practical, and the positive way means that you are mentally asking your body the foods it needs, and then you are taking the time to listen to your own body quietly. And always check in with your body on the little food that your body needs from time to time, and you will be able to take time to integrate these ideas on a deeper level.

If you are listening to these and choosing to drift into a deeper sleep, you can just do so. Now just feeling good will allow your body to be able to drift down and go into a deeper and restful sleep. If you want to get up and continue with your activities, then you have to count from one to five, and when you reach five, you can then open your eyes and come back to the fully conscious reality.

And so on counting one, you should allow yourself to come back to full conscious reality with relaxation and ease. Then as you count two, come back slowly to your full conscious reality, and as you count three, take some nice deep relaxing breath. Moreover, as you count four, allow your eyes to open as if you've bathed them with fresh water, and now, as you count five, open your eyes completely and adjust yourself to your environment while getting ready to carry on with your day's activity.

What is the hypnotic gastric band

If you would like to lose some weight without using surgery, then the hypnotic gastric band is the best tool for you. The hypnotic gastric band is the natural healthy eating tool that will help to control your appetite and your portion sizes. In this sense, hypnosis plays a significant role in helping you to lose weight without having to go through the risk that comes with surgery.

It is a subconscious suggestion that you already have, a gastric band comes intending to influence the body to respond by creating a feeling of satiety. It is now available in a public domain that dieting does not help to solve lifestyle challenges that are needed for weight loss and management.

Temporary diet plans are not effective while maintaining continuous plans are difficult. Notably, these plans are going to deprive you of your favorite foods, since they're too restrictive. Deep down within you, you might have a problem with your body's weight since diets have not worked for you in the past.

If you want to try something that will be able to provide a positive edge for you, then you should be able to control your cravings around food hypnotically. By reaching this point, you must try hypnosis, which has proven some results in aiding weight loss.

Benefits of hypnosis vs. surgery

If you would like to lose weight without starvation or yo-yo dieting, then the hypnotic gastric band is the ultimate resort for you. This gastric band does not require surgery but only meditation and hypnosis. Therefore, it offers numerous benefits that make it the solution to rapid weight loss and craving healthy food.

It is pain-free: As opposed to the physical gastric band, the hypnotic gastric band does not require surgery, which is associated with pain and routine follow-ups. Therefore, you do not need to worry about the risks you need to take, as no physical operation will be done on your body. You only need to hypnotize and utilize the hypnosis to work on your body weight.

100% safe: As hypnosis is a non-invasive, non-surgical, and safe technique, so is the hypnotic gastric band whose mechanism is initiated in your subconscious mind. Through the practice, there are no expected dangers, and you learn about self-awareness and the course of your life.

Time-efficient: You do not need to wait for your vacation to acquire a hypnotic gastric band. The tool does not affect your schedule as hypnosis can be combined with most of your day to day activities. You do not need time off to adjust the band or report complications

No meal replacement or dieting: With the hypnotic gastric band, you do not need to stop eating your most enjoyable food. Instead, you develop a principle that makes you feel in control and enable you to lose weight consistently and naturally without dieting. You just exercise and unlock the power in you to make positive changes in life.

No complications: The fact that no surgery is performed in hypnotic gastric surgery puts away the worry about future complications. The ease in your mind plays a significant role in focusing your mind on the things that matter, such as visualization and meditation. This way, you can put off negative thinking and live your life fearlessly and positively.

Helps discover your hidden potential: The use of hypnosis and meditation makes you learn about how to utilize the power of your mind in changing your perception and erasing negative thoughts. Similarly, you become capable of helping not only with weight loss but also with other psychological and social aspects such as confidence. In this case, hypnosis helps plant a subconscious suggestion in your mind making it stick and become a strong idea.

Cost-Effective: Hypnotic gastric band does not snatch away your working time, making you fully productive at your workplace with no deductions. In the same way, there are no costs in hypnosis and meditation as opposed to the physical gastric band. Positively living your life substantially adds to your savings.

Weight loss through hypnosis

Now, as I am walking down the beach, I will come to an area with unpleasant bells written by me in the sand. Those labels have been given to me in the past. Those labels are the labels that have held me back in the past from reaching my true capacity and from reaching my true power. I see those labels in the sand, and I begin to use my leg to clean them and use my legs to wash it off and clean the area with sweeping. With my feet, I erase the words away with every stroke of my feet, and I watch as the water comes to the shore to clear them away and clear all this around me.

Those words mean nothing to me; they do not exist again because I was the only one that saw them. I turn them around, and I work a little way down the beach. I feel more confident and taller. I come to the middle of a large rock sitting in the middle of the sand, and on this rock, there is a little pick. I pick it up, and I begin to write all the things that I want about my life. I begin to write all the things that I want about my weight. I am writing all the things that describe me. I am writing that I am confident, I am talented, and I am accomplished. And that I am a good person. I write as many words as possible that describe me.

I write things like positive, attractive, and capable I look at all the words that I have written on this rock and I know that I am a great person. I begin to recall all the moments whereby I felt confident. I think of the

24

time that I felt confident, and I recall those feelings again. I visualize those convenient moments in my life, and what it felt like, what it sounded like, and I then realize what it smells like. I believe this positive moment in my life. I think of the times where I felt confident in my life.

I feel those feelings. I picture those moments again, and I make the colors brighter and more vivid. I feel those feelings of confidence and pride, and I turn off the sounds and the smells. I get back into those moments where I was feeling so confident and powerful that I was feeling so confident in myself and all the things that I was doing. I am confident in the way I look. I am confident in the way I dress, and I'm confident in the way I act. I am confident in my relationship. I am confident in the relationship that I have with the members of the opposite sex. I am confident in the relationship that I have with my family with my friends and my coworkers.

Things come to me easily, with the way I talk to people. Conversations come out fluently from my mouth, and people respect what I have to say. I am strong and respected, and everyone around me sees me as confident and capable I take a look at myself, and I see that I am full of positive energy. I am the one that is radiating how everyone sees me. Everyone around me sees the positive energy in me, not only the people around me, but I also respect myself. I stand tall and strong. I stand proud of myself. I know that I can accomplish whatever I put my mind to accomplish. All I am seeing are positive things in my life.

I have practical and creative ideas, and I fill my mind with positive energy. I drop the future and go forward with confidence. I imagine myself one year from now, and I imagine the person that I will grow up to be. When I imagine this image, I will not be able to recognize the person that I once was. I have accomplished great things in the past year, great things that will help me to reach my capabilities.

My confidence has enabled others to look at me with great confidence and respect. I enjoy talking with people, and they're interested in what I have to say. My career is going great, and I can voice my ideas and opinions to other people because they value them. The relationship with my friends and families are great. Most of my friends and families come to seek advice from me because they hold me in high esteem. I look at myself, and I see how positive I am. I can point others in the right direction that they should go. I have faith in myself. I have great ideas, and I know that my family and friends respect my ideas, and they know my values too. I hold my head high, and I know that nothing can bring me down. I stand tall and strong because I know that I am an accomplished, beautiful, capable, and confident person.

Why it works

Normally, the conscious mind is receptive to suggestions, because it normally analyzes it.

With hypnosis, you will be able to reach your desired weight, become healthier, and stay in shape for life with the right mindset. You will be able to empower your mind to accept suggestions in a deep and relaxed state. This way, you will be able to reframe your thinking patterns because of all the principles of suggestion and disassociation. With the hypnotic gastric band, you will be able to use suggestions to influence a different response from your body triggered by sensory data to be able to create a new reality. The suggestions will be to provide a guideline for you to follow without questioning or critiquing.

Ultimately, this power will be able to allow you to reframe and reshape your perception regarding a specific behavior. The complex network in your brain has many different interpretations of the world around you, and the most unhelpful and negative thoughts have worked their way into that network.

Thus, you become susceptible to uncontrolled unconscious urges, like overeating and ignoring bodyweight concerns. Hypnotic gastric band will help you to be able to dampen and overcome all those uncontrolled thoughts, believes, and suggestions that are helping you alter your behavior.

PLACING, TIGHTENING, REMOVAL

Placing

In this meditation, you will learn how to walk along a beautiful beach walk, allowing you and deeply relax.

Follow me on this mental vacation as we place an emotional and mental and gastric band around your stomach, which will allow you to feel a full as soon as you eat exactly as much food as you need.

So, get into a comfortable seated position, on your favorite spot, so that you are undisturbed for the rest of this session. As you relax, the gastric band will become more powerful and influential over your life. Take a big deep breath, relax, and then exhale the tension and worry as you close your eyes. Feel your body already slowing down. Take another breath and let to go with a sigh of relief. This moment is for you to practice your new lifestyle, of being full, at the perfect time. Now say to you with faith, "overeating is impossible for me."

Now breathe into the truth of these words as you breathe them out into reality. You are creating a smaller stomach. Relax and breathe and then use the power of your imagination to visualize a beautiful beach with white sand, reflecting in the sunlight. It looks like snow. You can see the turquoise waters fading to a deep blue as the ocean goes deeper.

Look down into the sand where you stand, and notice the beautiful bits of shells with all different colors and textures as you see dried seaweed scattered about something that catches your eye buried into the sand, it is your preferred color. So as you get closer, you will see that it is a small yet thick band that is as big around as your fist, and it just so happens that it is the most vivid version of your favorite color. The brightness of this hue brings you joy. The curious, round band, flashing of your most beloved color choice is called the gastric band

It is placed around the top of your stomach, cinching down the amount your stomach can hold. So, it makes your stomach feel smaller, which gives you that feeling of fullness that you've had enough to eat. This band only exists in the medical world. But, you can get the same results, using the power of your mind, by placing the band within and around your stomach in this relaxing session.

But before you do this, try to walk along a beach (this beach is gorgeous), carrying around your gastric band. Feel and notice the band in your hand and notice the texture, the width, and the weight of the band.

Feel your feet entering the sand and allow yourself on each step to relax more and more. Notice the powdery texture, dispersing under your feet, and allow it deeply soothe you. Feel the ocean breeze, and smell the salty air. As you walk, you will get tired. A perfect chair has appeared just for you, facing the ocean. So have a seat and recline backward with your gastric band in your hand. Familiarize yourself with its shape and size. It is like a small belt that can be tightened and loosened.

Relax backward in the chair, look out upon the horizon, and then notice the ocean melting with the sky. The clouds are gliding along ever so slowly on a bright blue backdrop. No one is around you. Feel it; it is peaceful. It is relaxing. It is gorgeous. Feel the serene sun on your skin, giving you nutrients. Also, notice the warm sand under your feet, soft and grounding. Allow your breaths to become deeper and heavier. Listen to the calming sound of the air coming in and out.it is similar to the sound of the waves crashing on the shore.

Now take a long deep breath through your nose while you imagine the waves. Also, take and a long, deep exhale from your mouth and let it come in and out just like your breath. Focus on the relaxing and calming sound of the waves gazing out upon the ocean is right in front of you. Notice the crystal-clear waters as it's rippling in the beach wind and reflecting the rays of light and as it makes the surface of the water to dance.

If your mind starts wandering and you start noticing some negativity or some doubts about weight loss, just breathe into it. Let the wave come in and take that thought back out to the ocean as you exhale again. Take a deep breath in and feel that you and the waves are the same things.

Exhale your long breath out and feel the sensations of your worries and negativity of your weight been flushed away. Feel it dissolving and becoming less in your mind.

Repeat this beautiful process of letting go of self-doubts again. Now begin to breathe into the waves and then breathe out. Feel the sound of your negative self-talk washing away and letting go. Now deeply breathe into the waves and allow them to recollect all thoughts, negativity, and worries about overeating and then breathe out while you feel them crashing and disappearing going away forever.

Feel how you finally free yourself from all anxiety and stress. Feel as if you're brand new, recharged, rejuvenated, and light. Now take in the positive vibes of this scenario, the lights, the calming water, the warm, reassuring sand, the rhythm of the wave as its cradling you, while you take your powerful gastric band and imagine that you can easily place it upon the stomach, in the perfect spot. Cinch the band and feel your stomach getting smaller. It feels amazing.

Notice your stomach feeling full and firm. Imagine the sensation of having a full and satisfied stomach right now. Imagine what satisfaction feels like when you've had enough. It normally feels healthy, and it also brings your confidence that you only need the right amount or less, then you are full. You cannot take another bite when you've had enough now that you have your brand new gastric band.

This relaxing gastric band session brings you to perfect health and weight through the power of your mind. It brings about a new and improved positive attitude to life with intention, positivity, and knowing when enough is enough. Now bring your hands into the mode of prayer and notice how you feel. Notice your mind and body going back on track, firmly ready to eat the healthy amount.

Take a few calming, relaxing moments before coming back to the present moment. Take a long breath in and feel the gastric band as it's limiting your ability to overeat. Feel the band affecting the weight throughout your body. When you are ready, just gently open your eyes. And then seal this in with a grateful smile.

Tightening

Welcome to this relaxing meditation. This meditation will guide you to a pristine lake that is surrounded by mountains and help you to tighten your gastric band, making for an even smaller stomach that will fill up quickly. Get yourself into a nice seated position where you can easily fully let go, and you will not be disturbed by the surrounding world.

As you get into a powerful state of relaxation, begin to imagine that you are tightening this gastric band, and as you do so, you will find that weight-loss becomes easier and easier by the day. Now begin to breathe deeply while allowing your body to expand. Exhale all of your stress out and take another deep breath in, and as you exhale and allow, let your eyes gently closed.

Now notice how you feel. Notice how your body is settling down, and as it becomes relaxed as we go along. Let go of any current worries or obligations. Enjoying for yourself, and you begin your health and wellness journey from the first session by placing a gastric band near your stomach with the power of your mind. So, appreciate yourself for taking on this amazing opportunity.

Now say to yourself, "I will eat only as much food as I need. I need less food to feel full."

Breath in, and allow these words to become part of every level of your awareness. Breathe out any doubt and breathe in any truth that you are capable of eating just the right amount to have the perfect shape, size, and overall wellness. Now relax, calm down, and be at complete ease. Let your body slow down just a little bit more. Activate your imagination by bringing into your mind the eye, the site of a magnificent lake that is surrounded by mountains. And the sky, which is a crisp turquoise blue dappled with the cloud. And the sun is shining all around you. The waters of this lake are crystal clear, and it's reflecting the blueness of the sky. The water is acting as a mirror for the mountain range.

Now become aware of your stomach and notice it becoming smaller from your wonderful session on the beach when you first found your gastric band. Feel how your stomach is comfortable and happy about its new size and wants to become even smaller.

As you walk toward the lake, notice the soil under your feet, becoming smooth and supportive. As you go near to the water edge, dip your toes in the cool and fresh aqua. Even though your feet are submerged, the waters of this mystical lake relax your entire body.

Notice beside you the small red canoe waiting for you. Enter into this canoe and pick up the beautiful hand-carved oar. The oar signifies the ability to be able to tighten your gastric band. Dip the oar into the water, moving to the bottom of the lake, and push off the shore. Feel as this simple movement helps to tighten your gastric band by a millimeter.

Now start to row into the middle of the lake and captivate the beauty of your surroundings. Hear as the water sloshes against the sides of the boat once you dip them the oar into the water to propel the boat forward that carries you with ease, you are tightening the band around your stomach.

Notice as the weather is perfect, and beautiful birds are flying overhead, chirping a melody for you. This is a delightful sensation, like as if you are working out in the gym trying to build muscle, loosen ligaments and activate the healthy blood flow. And you are rowing a boat in your mind. You've reached the middle of the lake, and the band is getting tightened down to the perfect size. Now stop rowing and let the canoe glide through the water on its own.

Now notice the beautiful mountains surrounding you in all directions. They are protecting this lake from any harsh weather just as they are protecting you from any self-doubt that you are capable of eating only as little as you need at every meal and every day for the rest of your life.

This choice is critical because you care most about your health. You are well passionate about feeling good and moving your body freely with great energy.

Now imagine that you can see this beautiful gastric band, around the top of your stomach, gently squeezing it needing less food to make you full. The band is made up of your favorite color shining brightly. Now fell as the band is hugging your stomach like a hug you normally receive from your favorite grandparent, uncle, or anyone you know that hug you and comfort you. Feel it supporting you and letting you know that this band is here because you asked for its assistance.

Now take a deep breath and smell the clean air. Have a deep inner sense that you can notice the fat cells eliminated from your body. You have the ultimate awareness in the middle of the lake. Therefore, use this opportunity to see your future where you are a perfect size, and you feel better than you've ever sensed in your entire life. Now see yourself clearly and feel how it feels like to be in perfect health.

Also, visualize yourself in your kitchen now preparing your next meal. You will find that when you put the plate on your food, all of your choices are healthy. You will notice that you will only scoop a small amount of each item because you have a good ability to put the right amount of food that you need on your plate, now with your gastric band supporting you. You don't want to waste a bite of food. You should only eat the perfect amount.

See yourself eating this healthy meal, and shocked at the small food that it took for you to feel satisfied. Now, as you rise from this wonderful meditation, allow the image of the canoe and the see-through water to fade away from your mind, as well as the great mountains and along with the visual of your next meal.

Right now, bring yourself back from this experience into reality. Breathe in deeply, and become aware of your surroundings in the present moment. Wiggle around your toes and fingers a little bit and feel the fresh new energy and wisdom coming into you. And then whenever you are ready, open your eyes.

Removal

So far, you have placed this band around your stomach while walking on the relaxing beach and tightening the band while rowing your canoe on a crystal-clear lake. Right now, we will visit an ancient Japanese castle to be able to remove this band and discard it during the beautiful ceremony. Now make sure that you're in a comfortable position, in a place that you can enjoy practicing this relaxing session. This is the final step in your gastric band experience. So take a nice deep breath in and then breathe out while closing your eyes.

Relax your body. Feel it sinking into the chair or bed, soft and supportive underneath you.

Breathe in and then breathe out while noticing the gentle rise and fall of your chest as you breathe in. Now start becoming aware of your abdomen and feel how slim it is as you're, eating less food. You are becoming fuller and making hunger outdated. You know that you're supposed to eat, but eating doesn't consume your day or your mind. You only eat when you should eat and refuse to eat when you don't should eat. It's as simple as that.

Activate your creative mind again. Now imagine that you are standing in a beautiful field with tall grass, blowing in your wind. Now imagine

38

that there's a path in front of you, and that path is made up of smooth stones. As you walk along this path, see yourself coming towards a magnificent Japanese temple that was built hundreds of years ago.

The building is well maintained with a fresh coat made of red paint as well as gold trim surrounding the windows and doors. Now make your way up to the front door and feel like the iron handle in your hand on this door is massive as you open it.

So as you step inside the temple, feel the cool air around you. Also, imagine that the interior of this structure is a work of art, crafted by sheer genius. Now notice that there is a large golden bowl in the center of the room that is set atop a marble column. Now, as you move away from this bowl, it will appear to be illuminated with a ray of sunlight, which is casting down through the window in the rooftop.

As you see, the water in the bowl, reflecting the light like a diamond. Now, you easily remove the gastric band and place it inside the sacred water. So you can see that it is your favorite color, yet it's a bit worn and tired from all the work that it did for your health. Now imagine as the ray of light beaming down and see it begin to dissolve the gastric band until the water is pure. Start to feel lighter than ever, and your stomach smaller, along with your figure, shrinking every day.

Now, notice how you feel right. Breathe in the ultimate health and wellness. Exhale out any last lingering doubts. Extend the gratitude towards yourself for this wonderful transformation and dedication. Say "thank you," out loud. So allow the image of the temple to fade slowly and return the awareness to your present moment, as you feel lighter than ever before. Now slowly open your eyes when you are ready and be truly blessed by this experience.

To achieve these desires, you must be relaxed and focused on what you want and need in your life. It is totally up to you to dedicate much time every single day to make the necessary efforts towards achieving your goals. So say to yourself: "I intend to wake up early, stop eating sugar, and every food that turns converts into sugar remove any blocks behind my business needs. I make plans without feeling they should inconvenience others because I know that this is the recipe for success

So now go into a very comfortable position and make sure that you have not been disturbed. Give yourself time to breathe very well. Many of us go days without even thinking about our breath, yet it is what helps to keeps us alive. Your breath has been existing since the beginning, fitting to each moment exactly as it needs to fit. The breath never asks you questions, and it also does not judge you. It simply does what is it needs to do.

Now, notice your nose and feel the air passing through, as you breathe. Notice your mouth. And take the awareness down your neck. If you notice any tension, just ask it to be released. Feel the sensations in your body, as they are making you relaxed and comfortable. Become aware of your chest, lungs as they expand and contract with your breath. Feel your heart beating, pumping with love. Now take your focus down your arms, all the way to each fingertip.

Feel the sensations of touch at your fingertips. Move your focus to your abdomen and to all your vital organs. Notice how your belly feels and how it is digesting. Notice your pelvis and hips, and the sensations of your weight as it's pressing it down. This should take you into a deeper state of relaxation. Your awareness should go down on each leg, over your knees, move down all the way to your feet, and touch each toe.

CHAPTER TWO

THE HISTORY OF HYPNOSIS

There are many contradictions in the history of hypnosis. Its history is a bit like trying to find the history of breathing. Hypnosis is a universal trait that was built in at birth. It has been experienced and shared by every human since the beginning of time. It has just been in the past few decades that we are beginning to understand this. Hypnosis hasn't changed in a million years. The way we understand it and how we control it has changed a lot.

Hypnosis has always been surrounded by misconceptions and myths. Despite being used clinically and all the research that has been done, some continue to be scared by the assumption that hypnosis is mystical. Many people think that hypnosis is a modern-day innovation that spread through communities that believed in the metaphysical during the 70s and 80s. Since the mid-1800s, hypnosis was used in the United States. It has advanced with the help of psychologists such as Alfred Binet, Pierre Janet, and Sigmund Freud, and others. Hypnosis can be found in ancient times and has been investigated by modern researchers, physicians, and psychologists.

Hypnosis's origins can't be separated from psychology and western medicine. Most ancient cultures from Roman, Greek, Egyptian, Indian, Chinese, Persian, and Sumerian used hypnosis. In Greece and Egypt, people who were sick would go to the places that healed. These were known as dream temples or sleep temples where people could be cured with hypnosis. The Sanskrit book called "The Law of Manu" described levels of hypnosis such as sleep-walking, dream sleep, and ecstasy sleep in ancient India.

The earliest evidence of hypnosis was found in the Egyptian Ebers Papyrus that dated back to 1550 BC. Priest/physicians repeated suggestions while treating patients. They would have the patient gaze at metal discs and enter a trance. This is now called eye fixation.

During the Middle Ages, princes and kings thought they could heal with the Royal Touch. These healings can be attributed to divine powers. Before people began to understand hypnosis, the terms mesmerism or magnetism would be used to describe this type of healing.

Paracelsus, the Swiss physician, began using magnets to heal. He didn't use a holy relic or divine touch. This type of healing was still being used in the 1700s. A Jesuit priest, Maximillian Hell, was famous for healing using magnetic steel plates. Franz Mesmer, an Austrian physician, discovered he could send people into a trance without the use of magnets. He figured out the healing force came from inside himself or an invisible fluid that took up space. He thought that "animal magnetism" could be transferred from the patient to healer by a mysterious etheric fluid. This theory is so wrong. It was based on ideas that were current during the time, specifically Isaac Newton's theory of gravity.

Mesmer developed a method for hypnosis that was passed on to his followers. Mesmer would perform inductions by linking his patients together by a rope that the animal magnetism could pass over. He would also wear a cloak and play music on a glass harmonica while all this was happening. The image that a hypnotist was a mystical figure goes back to this.

These practices led to his downfall, and for time hypnotism was considered dangerous for anyone to have as a career. The fact remains that hypnosis works. The 19th century was full of people who were looking to understand and apply it.

Marquis de Puysegur, a student of Mesmer, was a successful magnetist who first used hypnosis called somnambulism or sleepwalking. Puysegur's followers called themselves experimentalists. Their work recognized that cures didn't come from magnets but an invisible source.

Abbe Faria, an Indo-Portuguese priest, did hypnosis research in India during 1813. He went to Paris and studied hypnosis with Puysegur. He thought that hypnosis or magnetism wasn't what healed but the power that was generated from inside the mind.

His approach was what helped open the psychotherapy hypnosis centered school called Nancy School. The Nancy School said that hypnosis was a phenomenon brought on by the power of suggestion and not from magnetism. This school was founded by a French country doctor, Ambroise-Auguste Liebeault. He was called the father of modern hypnotherapy. He thought hypnosis was psychological and had nothing to do with magnetism. He studied the similar qualities of trance and sleep and noticed that hypnosis was a state that could be brought on my suggestion.

His book Sleep and Its Analogous States, was printed in 1866. The stories and writings about his cures attracted Hippolyte Bernheim to visit him. Bernheim was a famous neurologist who was skeptical of Liebeault, but once he observed Liebault, he was so intrigued that he gave up internal medicine and became a hypnotherapist. Bernheim brought Liebeault's ideas to the medical world with **Suggestive Therapeutics** that showed hypnosis as a science. Bernheim and Liebeault were the innovators of psychotherapy. Even today, hypnosis is still viewed as a phenomenon.

The pioneers of psychology studied hypnosis in Paris and Nancy Schools. Pierre Janey developed theories of traumatic memory, dissociation, and unconscious processes studied hypnosis with Bernheim in Charcot in

Paris and Nancy. Sigmund Freud studied hypnosis with Charcot and observed both Liebeault and Bernheim. Freud started practicing hypnosis in 1887. Hypnosis was critical in him invented psychoanalysis.

During the time that hypnosis was being invented, several physicians began using hypnosis for anesthesia. Recamier, in 1821 operated while using hypnosis as anesthesia. John Elliotson, a British surgeon in 1834, introduced the stethoscope in England. He reported doing several painless operations by using hypnosis. A Scottish surgeon, James Esdaile, did over 345 major and 2,000 minor operations by using hypnosis during the 1840s and 1850s.

James Braid, a Scottish ophthalmologist, invented modern hypnotism. Braid first used the term nervous sleep or neuro-hypnotism that became hypnosis or hypnotism. Braid went to a demonstration of La Fontaine, the French magnetism in 1841. He ridiculed the Mesmerists' ideas and suggested that hypnosis was psychological. He was the first to practice psychosomatic medicine. He tried to say that hypnosis was just focusing on one idea. Hypnosis was advanced by the Nancy School and is still a term we use today.

The center of hypnosis moved out of Europe and into America. Here it had many breakthroughs in the 20th century. Hypnosis was a popular phenomenon that because more available to normal people who were not doctors. Hypnosis's style changed, too. It was no longer direct instructions from an authority figure; instead, it became more of a permissive and indirect style of trance that was based on subtle language patterns. This was brought about by Milton H. Erickson. Using hypnosis for quick treatment of trauma and injuries during WWI, WWII, and Korea led to a new interest in hypnosis in psychiatry and dentistry.

Hypnosis started becoming more practical and was thought of as a tool for helping psychological distress. Advances in brain imaging and neurological science, along with Ivan Tyrrell and Joe Griffin's work, have helped resolve some debates. These British psychologists linked hypnosis to Rapid Eye Movement and brought hypnosis into the realm of daily experiences. The nature of normal consciousness can be understood better as just trance states that we constantly go in and out of.

There are still people who think that hypnosis is a type of power held by the occult even today. The people that believe hypnosis can control minds or perform miracles are sharing the views that have been around for hundreds of years. The history that has been recorded is rich with glimpses of practices and ancient rituals that look like modern hypnosis. The Hindu Vedas have healing passes. Ancient Egypt has its magical texts. These practices were used for religious ceremonies, like communicating with spirits and gods. We need to remember that what people view as the occult was science at its finest in that time frame. It was doing the same thing as modern science was doing now trying to cure human ailments by increasing our knowledge.

Finding the history of hypnosis is like searching for something that is right in our view. We can begin to see it for what it actually is – a phenomenon that is a complicated part of human existence. Hypnosis's future is to completely realize our natural hypnotic abilities and the potential we all hold inside us.

For so many years now, individuals have been contemplating and contending about this topic. All hypnosis scientists are yet to explain how it really works. With hypnosis, you'll be able to see an individual under a trance, but you won't understand what is going on. This trance is a little piece of how human personality works. It is safe to say that hypnosis will continue to remain a mystery to us. We all know the general aspects of hypnosis, but we can't truly understand how it works. Hypnosis is a condition of series portrayed by serious suggestive expanded and unwinding dreams. It is not sleeping, because when you are under hypnosis, you are still under alert. But you are simply wondering into fantasyland, and you feel yourself going into another dimension that is different from this physical dimension.

You are completely mindful, but you are not mindful of the environment around you. You are only mindful of that thing that is being portrayed in your mind and that dreamland that you are going into. In your normal

48

day of life, you can feel the universe and the universe effect on your feelings. Research has shown that hypnosis can be used to cure several conditions. It is effective in elevating conditions like rheumatism joint pains. It helps to elevate labor pains and childbearing pains. It has also been used to reduce diamante side effects. It also helps in ADHD side effects hypnotherapy. And it reduces the impact of sickness in the body. It also helps during torment. It can also help to improve dental pains and skin conditions like moles.

It also helps to cure disorder manifestation. Also, it can be used to ease the torment of agony brought about by childbirth and childbearing. It also helps to cure smoking, reduce weight, and stop bedwetting.

THE SUBCONSCIOUS MIND

Your subconscious mind is impartial, unrelenting, and faithful. It does most of the sifting through all of our thoughts and relates them with our senses then communicates with the conscious mind through emotions. The subconscious mind collects your thoughts and stimuli from your environment and works on forming reactions to it. For example, you may see a particular person, perhaps your neighbor and feel dislike; you may even form a scowl. Yet, you have never exchanged three words with your neighbor. Why do you feel like this towards him/ her? The information you fed your subconscious. The illusory truth effect is a phenomenon where something arbitrary becomes true because it was repeated over and over again when no one was paying any attention to it.

However, we do not know what the unconscious mind is working on because it does its works "behind the scenes." We cannot "sense" is hard at work, nor can we stop its processes. The good news then is that you can feed your mind with certain notions and ideals to elicit the emotions you have associated with them. Do not think, however, that the subconscious mind listens to reason; remember, it remains an impartial participant in your everyday life. Take an example and remember when you tried to reason with an irrational phobia- of heights or tight spaces- for example. The conscious mind knows for a fact that there is nothing to fear, but you cannot help reacting in a particular way to these fears like getting sick, for example, and feeling dizzy.

Therefore, because your subconscious mind goes in the direction you command it if you repeatedly affirm positive thoughts such as "I am beautiful," or "I can do this," you will automatically begin to develop a different attitude towards yourself.

You will develop an inner outlook of your life which will gingerly propel you toward recognizing and taking advantage of the opportunities that come knocking at your door. The conscious mind can willingly train the subconscious mind and test the outcome using your life experiences. An excellent example of this is the power of autosuggestion. Have you heard of a vision board? They are ideas or fantasies that you pin up on a board that is strategically placed near the eye line. The more you repeatedly see the board, the more information you are giving the subconscious mind. After a while, check to see if there are any notable improvements in your life. For most people, it takes roughly three months to see some progress, depending on how powerful your autosuggestions are.

What is involved during a hypnosis session?

During your first session, you will have to visit a specialist, and when you visit the specialist, that specialist will discuss the objective and the procedure that he's going to use with you. The specialist will assist you in being able to relax in a setting. And he will explain the entire procedure for you. When you are in the hypnosis state, your specialist will allow you to be able to move in the direction of the specific goals that you want to achieve, which will help you to be able to envision your future and guide you towards making beneficial decisions. Now doing one session might be beneficial to you, but you should do up to 4 to 5 sessions. Many specialists will educate you during the first session and what is required; thereby, both of you will discuss the number of sessions that you need and if you will need any additional support.

How does hypnosis work

Now hypnosis works by dominating the entrance of your mind. It helps you to get straight to your intuitive personality. You become mindful of what is directly before you. You also become mindful of the words that have been spoken to you, and you become mindful and intentional about where you left your keys.

The different procedures of hypnosis

There are different procedures that you will follow when doing hypnosis. The first one is analytical techniques. That technique is good for unwinding. There are various approaches to start an illogical treatment session. The first session will tend to put you in a comfortable chair and make you close your eyes, and then your specialist will utilize a smooth calming voice and move you down gradually intentionally. He might even put his hand on your chest at certain times. So when undergoing this hypothesis, try to keep the photos of the subject in a great way.

How to reprogram your mind using hypnosis

Your intuitive personality have an enormous impact on your background, and on the food, you eat and also and the exercise that you do each day and the income that you make and how you respond to unpleasant invent

How to lose weight with hypnosis

Now, as I am walking down the beach, I will come to an area with unpleasant bells written by me in the sand. Those labels have been given to me in the past. Those labels are the labels that have held me back in the past from reaching my true capacity and from reaching my true power. I see those labels in the sand, and I begin to use my leg to clean them and use my legs to wash it off and clean the area with sweeping. With my feet, I erase the words away with every stroke of my feet, and I watch as the water comes to the shore to clear them away and clear all this around me.

Those words mean nothing to me; they do not exist again because I was the only one that saw them. I turn them around, and I work a little way down the beach. I feel more confident and taller. I come to the middle of a large rock sitting in the middle of the sand, and on this rock, there is a little pick. I pick it up, and I begin to write all the things that I want about my life. I begin to write all the things that I want about my weight. I am writing all the things that describe me. I am writing that I am confident, I am talented, and I am accomplished. And that I am a good person. I write as many words as possible that describe me.

I write things like positive, attractive, and capable I look at all the words that I have written on this rock and I know that I am a great person. I begin to recall all the moments whereby I felt confident. I think of the time that I felt confident, and I recall those feelings again. I visualize those convenient moments in my life, and what it felt like, what it sounded like, and I then realize what it smells like. I believe this positive moment in my life. I think of the times where I felt confident in my life.

54

I feel those feelings. I picture those moments again, and I make the colors brighter and more vivid. I feel those feelings of confidence and pride, and I turn off the sounds and the smells. I get back into those moments where I was feeling so confident and powerful that I was feeling so confident in myself and all the things that I was doing. I am confident in the way I look. I am confident in the way I dress, and I'm confident in the way I act. I am confident in my relationship. I am confident in the relationship that I have with the members of the opposite sex. I am confident in the relationship that I have with my family with my friends and my coworkers.

Things come to me easily, with the way I talk to people. Conversations come out fluently from my mouth, and people respect what I have to say. I am strong and respected, and everyone around me sees me as confident and capable I take a look at myself, and I see that I am full of positive energy. I am the one that is radiating how everyone sees me. Everyone around me sees the positive energy in me, not only the people around me, but I also respect myself. I stand tall and strong. I stand proud of myself. I know that I can accomplish whatever I put my mind to accomplish. All I am seeing are positive things in my life.

I have practical and creative ideas, and I fill my mind with positive energy. I drop the future and go forward with confidence. I imagine myself one year from now, and I imagine the person that I will grow up

55

to be. When I imagine this image, I will not be able to recognize the person that I once was. I have accomplished great things in the past year, great things that will help me to reach my capabilities.

My confidence has enabled others to look at me with great confidence and respect. I enjoy talking with people, and they're interested in what I have to say. My career is going great, and I can voice my ideas and opinions to other people because they value them. The relationship with my friends and families are great. Most of my friends and families come to seek advice from me because they hold me in high esteem. I look at myself, and I see how positive I am. I can point others in the right direction that they should go. I have faith in myself. I have great ideas, and I know that my family and friends respect my ideas, and they know my values too. I hold my head high, and I know that nothing can bring me down. I stand tall and strong because I know that I am an accomplished, beautiful, capable, and confident person.

DIFFERENT TECHNIQUES OF HYPNOSIS

Count Your Breath

For people who are not particularly attracted to the physical, verbal, or visual practices to help them enter a hypnotic state, there are many types of mindfulness practices that you can engage in to begin your self-hypnosis. Many of these involve you using your breath to enter a hypnotic state. You can do this by using the following steps for counting your breath to enter your deep trance.

The idea of this practice is to be able to count as many breaths as you can before you lose focus on your breathing. Know that if you are brand new to meditation and hypnosis that you likely will not be able to count very high in the beginning. Instead, you may only count to a count of 2 or 3. This is completely fine and can still be valuable, so do not refrain from using this practice just because you don't make it to a particularly high number.

When you are ready, you want to get yourself into a comfortable position. With self-hypnosis, you should either be sitting or lying down. Then, go ahead and close your eyes and get relaxed. If you cannot keep your eyes closed, it is perfectly okay to keep them open. Simply keep them relaxed and focus on one area in front of you that does not steal your attention or focus easily, such as a blank spot on the wall or ceiling.

Now, begin breathing at a relaxed and comfortable pace. Do not try and control your breath. Rather, relax and pay attention to it as it comes naturally. Then, as it comes, begin counting your breath. Count as many as you can without rushing them, or otherwise influencing them to change. If you notice your awareness is being drawn away or that you are not able to stay focused, you can simply allow your thoughts to come and then let them leave on their own, too. Then, draw your awareness back to your breath.

You want to practice this as many times as you comfortably can. If you find that it is getting harder and harder to focus, that you are beginning to feel frustrated, or that you are otherwise working **against** hypnosis, then you can stop. As you continue to practice this, you will find that you can count your breath longer and that you stay in your hypnotic state longer, too.

This practice is very similar to what you are taught to practice in meditation, as it essentially is a form of meditation. Like meditation, entering a hypnotic state requires you to get into a deep state of relaxation. Therefore, using the same techniques you do to meditate can be a great way to enter your hypnotic state and begin practicing self-hypnosis.

Detailed Breathing

Detailed breathing is a form of breathing whereby you pass through any need to count, and instead, you will focus on details or sensations within your body. While you can typically do this in any way that you prefer, there is also a pattern you can follow to help you stay focused and present with your breathing practice. It is as follows.

Begin by finding a comfortable place to sit or lie down so that you can begin your self-hypnosis. You can choose anywhere that is going to allow you to stay focused without interruption for as long as possible.

When you are ready, draw your awareness to your breath. Do not attempt to control it in any way, rather notice how it is in its natural state.

Then, take a nice relaxing, deep breath in. As you do, notice any sensations you may feel on, in, or around your nose. Notice these sensations as you breathe out, too. When you are ready, do it again. Then, again. You want to complete this detailed breathing practice through three breaths, with all of your body parts. You can follow this list if you need to recall what parts you should focus on:

Your cheeks

Your eyes and forehead

Your scalp

Your neck

Your shoulder blades

Your middle back

Your lower back

Your hips

Your glutes

The backs of your thighs

Behind your knees

Your calves

The heels of your feet

The balls of your feet

Your toes

The tops of your feet

Your ankle

Your shins

Your knees

The front of your thighs

Your pelvis

Your lower abdomen

Your solar plexus

Your rib cage

Your chest

Your throat

Your chin

Your mouth

Your nose

Once you have completed your entire body, you should be in a completely relaxed state so that you can begin directing your self-hypnosis on whatever your intention is.

In the beginning, you may find it difficult for you to complete this entire detailed breathing practice. Instead, you may wish to focus on larger areas such as your face, head, torso, arms, hands, legs, and feet. Then, you can become more detailed the more you practice.

Pyramid Breathing

Pyramid breathing is another breathing practice you can use to enter your hypnotic state and begin self-hypnosis. This practice includes something that is known as mindful movement, which is an intentional movement that you will practice within your body to locate physical stress or resistance and bring your awareness to gently releasing this feeling. For example, pressing against a wall, curling your toes, stretching your shoulders, or otherwise physically moving your body and noticing any resistance you may feel. The idea is that you want to actually experience the resistance and then let it gradually eliminate itself through mindful intention. You can complete this practice using the following steps.

Begin by taking a deep breath and focusing on your breath. Relax for a few moments using the breathing techniques from the previous practice. You do not need to count as high as you can, rather, but simply relax into three or four counted breaths.

When you are ready, gently move part of your body. This is a mindful movement you can practice. You may choose which movement you want to make based on where you can physically feel resistance in your body. For example, if you feel physical resistance in your chest, you can gently raise your arms above your head and feel that resistance and the many ways that it is physically affecting you.

Notice all of the pressures in your body and any sensations you may experience as a result of these movements.

When you are ready, go ahead and take another breath and then perform another mindful movement. Once again, take your time to notice any physical resistances, pains, or other sensations you may notice in this area of your body. Feel into them, and try and take the time to become aware of why they are there and what you may be able to do to consciously and subconsciously release them completely.

You want to continue practicing this over and over again through any resistance you may have. You may even repeat this practice with persistent sensations if you want to so that you can completely release them and let them go.

Doing this all the way through is a great way to allow you to enter a calmer state of mind. Once you have acknowledged all of these physical sensations and how they are affecting your body, you will likely notice how much more relaxed your mind is. Then, you can go ahead and begin directing your self-hypnosis practice.

Body Scan

The body scan practice is somewhat like detailed breathing in that you will focus on sensations all over your body. However, this practice does allow you to use mindful movements, and it is also a little quicker than the detailed breathing. Whereas detailed breathing lets you focus on any sensations in your body no matter what they are, a body scan allows you to quickly scan your body and notice any areas that may need attention. These are areas where you might feel resistance, tension, or simply a buildup of emotions. You can do this practice using the following steps.

Begin by laying down or sitting with your legs outstretched, such as in a reclining chair. You want to have your feet up off of the ground and be completely comfortable.

Gently close your eyes and draw your focus to your body. If you want, you can use the handy energy exercise that we discussed earlier in the chapter, whereby you rub your palms together to generate friction and warmth. This may help you begin entering your trance-like state right away.

When you are ready, draw your dominant hand up above your head and let your other hand rest on your side, palm facing up.

You want your dominant hand to be facing toward the floor, about 4-5 inches above your body, and slightly above your head so that your palm is focused on the space above your scalp.

Gently and slowly draw your hand in a line from above your head down to your pelvis in one sweeping motion. Take time to rest over various areas of your body where you may be feeling any tension or resistance within.

Anywhere that you may notice tension, take some time to breathe into this space. Imagine your breath swirling into this space as a white light and filling it out, as though it is intentionally drawing a state of relaxation into this part of your body. You can also imagine that your exhale is drawing the tension away from you.

As the tension begins to eliminate, go ahead and move down your body. Again, if you notice anywhere that may be experiencing tension, let it go through your intentional breath.

By the end of your body scan, you should notice that any areas that were experiencing tension or resistance before will now be experiencing relaxation. You should also notice that you are in a deeper state of relaxation now that will allow you to facilitate the rest of your self-hypnosis practice.

Handy Energy

Creating handy energy is a practice whereby you use your physical hands to explore the energy around you and enter a deep trance-like state. This practice requires physical movement, which, for some, is a powerful way to experience your trance. If sitting still is not your preferred mode of relaxation, this is a great opportunity to use mindful movements to help you relax. It works like this:

Rub your hands together so that you begin to feel a warm sensation brewing between the palms of your hands.

Once the heat begins to feel recognizable, separate your hands slowly until there are several inches between them. They should be about level with your shoulders.

Gently move your hands together and apart, feeling how they naturally feel drawn together almost as though you have magnets between them pulling them together.

Continue playing around with this energy, focusing on it as it grows stronger. As the strength grows, let this draw you into a trance.

As your trance develops, do not worry about the placement of your hands or anything. Simply let the space between your hands, no matter how small or large, to intensify your experience and relax even deeper.

67

Visual Exploration

For some people, creating a static visualization can be difficult and can result in them not being able to visualize anything. In this case, it may be beneficial to engage in visual exploration. This is essentially a form of visualization whereby you visualize a place that you are familiar with and add an explorative measure to it. For example, exploring the home in which you live. To do so, use the following steps to get started.

Start by sitting somewhere relaxing and closing your eyes. The entire visualization will be done with your eyes closed, to ensure that you are comfortable enough that you can stay still and keep your eyes closed for this entire practice.

Start by creating a basic visual of a room that you are familiar with within your mind, now. Then, begin exploring this room. As you are adding the details, visualize yourself walking around and touching them or interacting with them. For example, sit on a couch, run your hand over the wall, or pick up and object and begin exploring it with your hands.

After you have completely designed the first room in your mind and have interacted with various elements of the room, you want to begin exploring other elements. Go ahead and leave that room and build the next room. Whether it's a hallway, another room, or even outside, go ahead and begin following the same practices. Enter the room and begin exploring that one. As you are decorating it in your mind, interact with the decorations that are there.

Continue doing this with several rooms until you notice that you are in a hypnotic state and that you are ready to begin using the driven intention behind your self-hypnosis to achieve your results.

A Pantomimed Mentalization

This is a visual-meets-physical practice that can help those who are aided by visuals but who also like to be in motion. You can use this to begin visually seeing things in your mind but also cementing them in using physical movements.

For this practice, you are again going to begin visualizing a room that you are familiar with. You want to pick one where you will know as many details about the room as possible. Then, you will mentally describe them to yourself as you pantomime the actions associated with that room. For example, if you are explaining that the room is large, you might spread your arms wide to physically symbolize the largeness of the room. If you are talking about the window in the room, you might consider opening the window and then physically act out the process of opening the window.

For some people, incorporating as many sensations into their visualization as possible can strengthen your visualization practice. Eventually, you should be able to eliminate the pantomiming and verbal descriptions so that you can begin visualizing even deeper and more effectively, thus strengthening your ability to enter a self-hypnotic state.

Using a Power Pendulum

One of the most common tools we consider when we consider hypnosis is a pendulum. In stage hypnotherapy, many hypnotists are known to use a pendulum to get their volunteers to enter a hypnotic state and begin listening to them on a deep, subconscious level. Any pendulum will work, such as those with a gemstone suspended from the bottom, or one that you have made on your own. Then, once you have one, begin using the following steps to get the most out of your pendulum.

Begin by holding your power pendulum comfortably between your thumb and index finger in your dominant hand. It should be held loosely, but not so loose that the pendulum slips from between your fingers.

Rest your elbow in a free-floating manner, not against any form of surfaces such as your chair or the table. It should not be locked in place, either. It should simply be relaxed and floating with the pendulum out in front of your face.

You can then instruct your pendulum to begin moving. Simply place your attention on the pendulum and begin mentally asking it to move. Soon, it will begin moving before you.

Stay focused on your pendulum and watch it move. Do not let your awareness or attention break, instead simply continue watching your pendulum. Keep it moving, and keep your awareness, attention, and intention of this movement.

Soon, after watching your pendulum swing for a while, you will begin to feel yourself enter a hypnotic trance-like state. Once you have, you can begin directing yourself for any intention you desire.

The Betty Erickson Technique

Betty Erickson was an accomplished hypnotherapist who was the wife of famous hypnotherapist Milton Erickson. Throughout her life, Betty was known to use self-hypnosis as a means to accomplish many goals.

One, in particular, was known as her 3-2-1 technique, which you can use to enter a hypnotic state in your own life. It works like this:

Begin by keeping your eyes open and looking for three different objects or things that you can see. This can be anything from the ceiling to something outside of your window, or any object nearby.

Then, you want to focus on hearing three different things that are around you. They can be any three things that you hear, from your own breathing to a noise somewhere else in the room, in your house, or outside.

Then, focus on three things you can feel. This may be the pressure of the surface you are sitting on, the breeze on your skin, or anything else that you can feel physically.

Now, you want to go through everything that you can see, hear, and feel, only this time you are only going to look for two things each.

Then, go through again but only look for one thing that you can see, one thing you can hear, and one thing you can feel.

Now, you want to close your eyes. Then, you will go through all three cycles again, starting with three things you can see, hear, and feel, then two things, then one thing.

Once you have completed all six cycles of the 3-2-1 practice, you will be in a deep hypnotic state whereby you can direct yourself to accomplish anything you have intended to upon entering this state.

Arm Levitation

Arm levitation is another form of meditative or hypnotic exercise you can do that works with the "magnetic" feeling we get in our bodies when we perform certain movements. Using the arm levitation method to enter a hypnotic state is a great way to use physical movement to take advantage of your trance-like state and begin self-hypnosis. You can do it by using the following guidance.

Take your right arm and begin lifting it so that it is at a 90-degree angle from your body, then drop it back into your lap. Repeat this a few times so that your body becomes used to the sensation of your arm moving in this way.

As you are gently moving your arm up and down, pay attention to the sensations you feel throughout it. What part of your muscles is being awakened by this movement? Where are you feeling it outside of your arm?

After a few times, go ahead and say this to yourself: "Subconscious mind, lift my right arm. Lift it. Lift it more. I can feel my arm getting light and lifting on its own, now."

Your arm will begin to slowly lift as you say this and may even twitch slightly as it lifts. If it does not, continue the practice from the start and try again. For some beginners, it may take a few tries for this to happen as sometimes the unconscious mind will be in disbelief and "hold" the arm down against the subconscious mind's will.

Continue doing this until your arm raises to the point that it touches your face. You will want to stay focused on all of those small movements that you feel like your arm lifts and all of the gentle movements you experience along the way.

Pay attention to the state you enter as you stay focused on this movement. Keep your attention into this state as this is where the self-hypnosis lies. Once you are completely in this trance and entirely focused on your arm and its movements, you can begin practicing your self-hypnosis direction and intention.

Can I be hypnotized?

To find a person who cannot be hypnotized or effect, self-hypnosis is unusual. People who did not want to be hypnotized and resisted, those with extremely low IQ's and patients with mental illness are the only documented failure Cases to reach the hypnotic state.

Hypnotic trance

Hypnotherapy is the giving of suggestions to the subconscious mind to create or promote positive change. It is carried out when a client is in a trance state. A trance state is not sleeping and not awake; it is a brainwave frequency between the Beta wave of full consciousness and the Delta wave of sleep. A light trance is thought to be in the Alpha frequency of brainwaves, and a deep trance is in the Theta frequency of brain waves.

IS IT DANGEROUS?

Hypnosis is thought to be safe if it is performed by an experienced and qualified practitioner. Some risks have been associated with hypnosis. These could arise from being treated by someone who hasn't been properly trained. In certain cases, a patient could have some side effects, such as:

False memories

Upset stomach

Anxiety

Headache

Dizziness

Feeling low

Vomiting

Nausea

Hallucinations

Psychosis

Guilt

Delusional thinking

A danger of being hypnotized by an amateur is not in their ability to hypnotize a person but by their carelessness and by using the wrong words to give them a bad post-hypnotic suggestion.

Most people think hypnosis should be used as a last resort to help cure an ailment, but by this time, they are so used to the pain, they don't think they can be cured. This makes the hypnotherapist's job harder.

Anybody who has mental problems might have these problems amplified by a hypnotist that is an amateur. An untrained hypnotist could create new symptoms. There have been cases where one addiction has been replaced by another one.

Just because someone can put a person into a trance doesn't make them a good hypnotherapist.

A bad hypnotherapist could be dangerous since hypnosis is a powerful tool.

There have been cases of people driving home who weren't dehypnotized correctly. They felt dizzy, confused, and were involved in crashes.

Finding a good hypnotist shouldn't be taken lightly. You should try to find one that comes highly recommended and who has many letters after their name.

CHAPTER THREE

USING HYPNOSIS TO TRANSFORM YOUR MIND

The idea of hypnotherapy brings out reactions ranging from "cross-arm and wary in dismay" to "shocked in unadulterated amazement and surprise." There is no denying the supernatural quality encompassing spellbinding; it stays to puzzle individuals' psyches around the world.

As a result, we tend to live our lives amid a society in which the day to day rush of events doesn't leave us much time for thought and contemplation. This means that we are faced with making difficult choices in terms of dealing with our happiness and wellbeing.

Fortunately, this idea is a long way from a reality of true to life when you grasp spellbinding. In this way, we have a greatly improved idea. What about utilizing the incredible intensity of hypnotherapy rather than manufacturing a universe of a completely perfect world?

Since there is a persuading reason for hypnotherapy behind the cloak of wizardry and visual impairment, to fix our brains, bodies, and in the long run our universe.

As a general rule, trance has been utilized worldwide as an instrument for mending for in any event 4,000 years; however, science has just begun to exhume this entrancing riddle in most recent years. Their outcomes hugely affect our ability to change our thoughts and convictions, conduct, and practices, just as our recognition and reality to improve things.

In any case, most importantly, science has discovered a solid reality: entrancing is valid. What's more, on the off chance that you accept you've never had mesmerizing, accept again.

Hypnosis' characterizing practices are:

Increased suggestibility. Making musings progressively open and responsive.

It improved creative thinking—creation in the eye of our psyches of striking, frequently illusory symbolism.

Without thinking, discernment. Quieting the cognizant systems that create thoughts while improving passionate mindfulness.

These three characterizing highlights make spellbinding a particular and effective instrument for private transformation.

A large portion of the issues that unleash destruction on the globe today happens because we have significant mental wounds to which there has been no inclination.

We download information from the globe around us at lightning speed until we're around nine years of age. During this minute, our subliminal feelings and practices are normally shaped — before we built up our balanced reasoning (got when our mind frames the prefrontal cortex).

In our childhood, for instance, someone can let us know, "you're ugly." At the time, our brains can't defend the likelihood that any individual who reveals to us this will have a poor day or experience the ill effects of their psychological wounds. Rather, our energetic, honest personalities accept, "goodness, I'm frightful." That works for "you're stunning" on a kinder note, just as some other great attestation. We are importance making machines in this incredibly porous minute in our life.

We quickly credit importance to them when certain events happen in our youthfulness. What produces our subliminal convictions is that allotted significance.

This is the place hypnotherapy comes in. Nothing fixes these significantly established enthusiastic wounds more rapidly than the hypnotherapy prescription. We have discovered that, in the condition of mesmerizing, we can get to and interface legitimately with these intuitive zones of our psyche— without our normal cognizant reasoning.

During trance, a trance inducer controls their patients back to their youth's zenith occasions. The patient can reassign centrality to them once recollections of the case are gotten to.

Reprogramming your Mind through Hypnosis

Your intuitive personality has an enormous impact on dealing with your background— from the sorts of sustenance you eat to the exercises you take each day, the income level you get, and even how you react to unpleasant conditions.

Your intuitive feelings and understandings manage all of it. In a nutshell, your subliminal personality resembles an airplane's auto-pilot work. Following a particular way has been pre-modified, and you cannot go astray from that course except if you initially change the customized guidelines.

The "intuitive" is your mind's part that works underneath your customary arousing cognizance level. At this moment, you are primarily utilizing your cognizant personality to peruse these expressions and retain their centrality. However, your subliminal personality works hectically in the background, engrossing, or dismissing information dependent on a present perspective on the globe around you. When you were a tyke, this present observation began to shape. Your intuitive personality drenches like wipe data with each experience.

While you were youthful, your consciousness rejected nothing since you had no prior perspectives that would negate what it saw. It simply recognized that it was genuine every one of the information you acquired during your initial puberty. You can almost certainly observe why this sometime down the road turns into an issue. Each time you were called by somebody stupid, useless, slow, apathetic, or more terrible, your subliminal personality put away the information for reference.

You may likewise have messages about your life potential or requirements relying upon your physical aptitudes, the shade of the skin, sex, or money related status. By the minute you were 7 or 8 years of age, you had a solid premise of religion on all the programming you viewed from people in your lives, network shows, and other natural impacts. S

ince you are developed, you may figure you can simply dispose of the destructive or false messages you've consumed in your initial life. However, it isn't so basic. Keep in mind this information is put away underneath your cognizant awareness level. The main minute you understand this is the point at which it constrains your advancement in building up an actual existence that is adjusted, prosperous, and gainful.

Have you, at any point, endeavored to arrive at a target and consistently undermined yourself? Goading, right? It is fundamental to comprehend that regardless of what you do, you are not flawed or destined to come up short. You are bound to have some old, customized messages that contention with the new conditions that you need to make. This is incredible news since it suggests that on the off chance that you first set aside the effort to reconstruct your intuitive personality, you can achieve pretty much anything! Before we discover how to reconstruct your psyche, it's fundamental to comprehend that the programming proceeds right up 'til today. You draw certain discoveries with each experience you have and store the messages that will direct your future conduct.

Practical Hypnosis Exercises

Exercise not only will make you feel healthier, but it will also improve your mental health and make you feel more in control of your body. The trick to exercise is to do something you like instead of feeling that you are exercising to compensate for binge eating.

Exercise should feel like fun, not torture. Do not do anything you hate. If you hate running, walking or hiking, look for a new activity, such as salsa dancing, Pilates or volleyball. You will have fun doing something you like, and you will get more health in the process. Find a gym or exercise with a friend. Having a friend who works with you will make your training more fun and make you feel more motivated.

TIPS

Do not diet. Most likely, dieting will make you feel restricted and consumed by your cravings. Instead, focus on maintaining a healthy lifestyle.

First, consume healthier foods. If you are at a party, start with some healthy entrees, which will slow your appetite and make you less likely to enjoy less healthy foods later. Never eat standing up. Take your time to sit down to eat and focus on food.

Control the portions. Never eat anything from inside a bag or box, or you will not know how much you are eating.

EATING

There are multiple types of diets or nutritional options, such as Paleolithic diet, autoimmune diet, GAPS diet, Okinawa diet, food guide according to the study of China, Mediterranean diet, intermittent fasting, ketogenic diet, detox diet, Montignac diet, diet Dunkan, Atkins diet, macrobiotic diet, vegetarian diet, vegan diet, and so on.

Some of the diets are supported by the official scientific community, and others are not. However, from my point of view and experience, all are valid depending on each person, moment, and circumstance. Besides, we all have much to discover, including the official scientific community.

All diets or eating guides have something in common, which is to restrict food to improve digestion. And by improving digestion, more nutrients are obtained with less effort. The function of our digestive system is optimized, and health is improved. On the planet, energy is neither created nor destroyed; it simply transforms. And our digestive system transforms the energy of food into useful energy for our body. Consuming less quantity, as long as it allows us to reach the energy we need, means being more sustainable with the environment and with our body. Our body becomes more efficient in all its functions and stays healthier and younger. And the same goes for the planet.

But how do you get to eat a small amount, feel satiated, be nourished and have energy?

Success is based on the perfect combination and processing of food. That is, balanced macronutrients and boost micronutrients. The components of the food and drink we consume interact with each other. Knowing how to process and combine them correctly, we improve digestion and maximize their bioavailability. This will bring us enormous benefits for our health (better nutrition) and the planet (better use of resources). An example is as follows:

Kale, strawberries, corn, eggs, black garlic, and olive oil Balance the macronutrients of each meal. For example, according to the healthy dish of the example, for an adult: 2 boiled eggs (animal protein has greater bioavailability), 200 gr. Sweet corn (carbohydrates: starch and sugar), 100 gr. Of kale (curly cabbage) massaged with olive oil (healthy fats) and strawberries (vitamins, minerals, and fiber).

Combine micronutrients to improve digestion and enhance its nutritional value. For example, green leafy vegetables with healthy fats. Green leafy vegetables help digest fats, and fats help absorb vitamins from vegetables. Save work for the intestine, eating predigested food. As for example: crushed, marinated, massaged, fermented vegetables; yogurt; extricated bread; hot proteins; natural sweet food. Distinguish between physiological and emotional hunger. And eat only in the presence of the first.

ELIMINATE CRAVINGS

Imagine a scenario in which you could disconnect from your desires. Seclude them and send them away? Some weight reduction hypnotic systems assist you with doing this. For instance, you may be approached to imagine sending your yearnings – state on a ship ceaselessly out to the ocean. Recommendations can likewise help you reframe your yearnings, and figure out how to oversee them all the more adequately.

WEIGHT LOSS

The initial step of utilizing entrancing for weight reduction: Identifying why you aren't accomplishing your objectives. How does this work? Regularly, a subliminal specialist will ask you inquiries identified with your weight reduction, for example, inquiries concerning your eating and exercise habits.

This information gathering recognizes what you may require help chipping away at. You'll, at that point, be guided through acceptance, a procedure to loosen up the brain and body, and go into a condition of entrancing. While in entrancing, your psyche is exceptionally suggestible. You've shed your basic, conscious personality – and the subliminal specialist can talk straightforwardly to your unconscious thoughts.

In hypnosis, the hypnotherapist will furnish you with positive proposals, insistences and may request that you envision changes. You can attempt it right now with our many weight loss entrancing chronicles! Positive recommendations for weight loss entrancing may include:

Improving Confidence. Positive proposals will engage your sentiments of certainty through empowering language.

You are picturing Success. During hypnosis, you might be approached to picture meeting your weight loss goals and to envision how it causes you to feel.

You are reframing Your Inner Voice. Entrancing can assist you with restraining an inward voice who "wouldn't like" to surrender unfortunate nourishments, and transform it into a partner in your weight reduction venture who's fast with positive recommendations and is progressively balanced.

You are tapping the Unconscious. In the hypnotic state, you can start to distinguish the oblivious examples that lead to undesirable eating. You can turn out to be progressively mindful of why we are settling on undesirable nourishment decisions and bit control and build up increasingly careful procedures for settling on nourishment decisions.

They are fighting Off Fear. Hypnotic recommendations can assist you with subduing your dread of not making weight reduction progress. Fear is a No. 1 reason individuals may never begin in any case.

Distinguishing and Reframing Habit Patterns. Once in hypnosis, you can inspect and investigate ways you use eating and "turn off" these automatic reactions. Through rehashed positive insistences, we can start to slow and eventually totally evacuate programmed, oblivious idea.

You are growing New Coping Mechanisms. Through entrancing, you can build up increasingly solid approaches to adapt to pressure, feelings, and connections. For instance, you may be approached to picture an upsetting circumstance and afterward envision yourself reacting with a solid bite.

You are practicing Healthy Eating. During entrancing, you might be approached to practice settling on good dieting decisions, for example, approving of taking nourishment home at a restaurant. It enables these sound decisions to turn out to be progressively programmed. The practice is additionally useful for controlling yearnings.

You are settling on Better Food Choices. You may want and love undesirable nourishments. Hypnosis can assist you with beginning to build up a taste or inclination for more beneficial choices, just as impact the bit sizes you pick.

You are expanding Unconscious Indicators. Through reiteration, you may have figured out how to muffle the signs your body sends when you feel full. Hypnotherapy encourages you to become increasingly mindful of these pointers.

Changing eating habits

There are certain ways that we tend to consume our food. Some of these ways are not beneficial to us at all, and they create more harm to our bodies. Most times, we tend to ignore the time factor that eating requires. We barely look at the decisions that we make regarding food. All we do is to make decisions. Having an eating routine is important. Nutritionists have advised us of the correct ways to consume our food.

One of them is that it is wrong to drink water immediately after a meal. First, you have to allow the food to settle, and after that, you should only drink water for some minutes. On the other hand, they advise that fruits should be consumed before meals for them to benefit your body rightfully. When you consume them together with your meals, they will not have the impact they would have if you had eaten them before your meal.

Most of these healthy facts are simple and easy to follow. It's just that we just choose not to follow them. Additionally, you tend to consume your foods in those moments that you should not be consuming it. For instance, you tend to eat a lot of food at night, and the only activity that you will do is to sleep. You will find out that much of the food that you eat is not well utilized in the body, and they tend to waste away. The result is that you just end up gaining more weight due to the poor eating habits that you're making.

So meditation will allow you to realize the impact of the decisions that you're making concerning food and help you to change how you make those decisions. You will realize that you have some poor eating habits and you will decide to change them for the sake of your health and so that you will be in the right shape and weight.

What are good eating habits to weight loss

Do you struggle to eat well nourishment?

Do you attempt to imagine you appreciate eating soundly, however following two or three days, you truly miss your ordinary nourishments?

Do you think that it's hard to eat well nourishment reliably?

If you truly need to create smart dieting propensities, at that point, this straightforward, normal hypnosis audio can support you.

Also, to our "stop comfort eating" title, this will change your whole demeanor towards nourishment. Dissimilar to the stop comfort eating collection where a ton of the attention is likewise on creating mental quality and self-discipline to oppose urges, this collection truly centers around this side of things more - to assist you with developing good dieting propensities by re-wiring how you consider nourishment on a more profound subconscious level.

You will think about the negatives of eating an unfortunate eating routine. As opposed to seeing desserts, cheap food, or simply your preferred greasy nourishments as alluring, you will think about the negatives - the weight you will pick up, the negative wellbeing suggestions, and how low and self-basic you will feel after you have completed solace eating.

You will likewise normally think about the positives of good dieting - how it will assist you with losing weight, improve your wellbeing, and how awesome and positive you will feel about yourself that you figured out how to defeat your solace eating inclinations! This straightforward change from negative to positive reasoning will profoundly affect your dietary patterns, and you will think that its a lot simpler and considerably more characteristic to eat strongly.

You will turn out to be progressively predictable in your dietary patterns. You will stop "yo-yo-ing" between eating soundly, not all that strongly and pigging out. You will normally eat a significantly more adjusted, and sound eating routine, substantially more reliably.

At last, smart dieting will quit being a struggle for you as you build up the sort of attitude shared by the individuals who normally eat steadily without contemplating it. It is this last change in mentality and convictions which will transform you, decrease your waistline, and change how you consider nourishment until the end of time.

What to expect

If you are new to hypnosis, at that point, you will locate this a wonderful encounter. You will turn out to be increasingly looser as you proceed to tune in, and relying upon your learning style, you could conceivably recollect all aspects of the experience; you will anyway consistently stir feeling revived and positive. Short term

Over the short term, you will encounter genuine, substantial outcomes practically straight away. You will get yourself less powerless to enticements, and simply settling on better nourishment decisions normally. You will feel significantly more positive about yourself and your capacity to remain "on track" and create enduring, positive, smart dieting propensities.

Long term

After some time, the hypnotic recommendations will construct and make perpetual, enduring changes to your examples of reasoning and conviction sets related to yourself, abstaining from excessive food intake, and nourishment. You will steadily get one of those individuals who eat strongly normally. You won't fight or need to "be acceptable," you will normally eat a reasonable, sound eating regimen, and in light of this, you will wind up shedding pounds, getting more advantageous and more advantageous and capitalizing on life!

SELF-HYPNOSIS

Self-hypnosis has a powerful ability to help you accomplish virtually anything you desire to achieve. Whether you want to reduce or manage stress, motivate yourself to achieve something, relax from stress or other upsetting emotions, concentrate more efficiently or effectively on a task at hand, or direct yourself to do or accomplish something, self-hypnosis can help you drastically.

How Do You Enter a Hypnotic State?

When it comes to effectively making use of self-hypnosis, it is generally important that a person has first experienced hypnosis in some other form. This can include attending a professional hypnotherapist and being hypnotized, or it may include regular practice through guided hypnosis sessions that may be retrieved through audio files. An individual first must learn to become familiar with the hypnotic state and what it feels like before embarking on self-hypnosis, as this will ensure that they are clear on what to look for and what to expect. While you can certainly engage in self-hypnosis without prior experience or practice, this may reduce results and benefits as you may not be clear on what to expect or how the experience or process should be facilitated.

Once you have already experienced some form of hypnosis, you should have a fairly good idea of what to expect and what will be experienced during the process. You will be familiar with how the hypnotic state is achieved, what it feels like, and what happens once you have entered a hypnotic state. From there, you can follow these same practices to achieve the hypnotic state in your self-hypnosis practice.

The hypnotic state is not guided by an external influence when it comes to self-hypnosis. Instead, it achieved through facilitating deep relaxation within yourself and your body. You do this through a series of breathing practices and intentions, whereby you clear your mind and focus solely on your body and breath. This is very similar to meditation practice, so people who are already fluent in achieving a relaxed state through meditation will have a general idea of how self-hypnosis can be achieved. If you have not practiced meditation in the past, it may be ideal to begin your practice now so that you can practice entering a deep state of relaxation that allows your mind to be influenced by hypnosis.

How Are You Guided?

When it comes to self-hypnosis, you are guided by yourself. This comes through self-suggestion, as well as self-exploration. The best way to guide yourself through an intentional hypnosis practice is to set the expectation of what you want to be guided through or toward before you enter the hypnotic state. For example, say that you want to hypnotize yourself and practice self-hypnosis as a means to help you quit something, such as smoking. Before entering the state of deep relaxation that is required for hypnosis, you would set this intention and repeat it to yourself and over and over. Then, you would begin working on setting yourself into the hypnotic state of deep relaxation. Once you are in that state, you can begin repeating the intention over and over once again. This will set the intention into your mind and allow the message to sink even deeper into your subconscious, allowing it to help rewrite and reprogram your subconscious just as any other form or state of hypnosis would.

Being in a state of both physical and mental deep relaxation such as that which is experienced when you are undergoing hypnosis means that the intention you set and the message you repeat goes far beyond your conscious mind. Your conscious mind is the "first step" of your mind that is used to process information. This part of your mind will easily attest or contest anything that you feed your mind with. The idea is that you allow yourself to enter a deep state of relaxation and then begin directing your mind through intention, which results in these intentions bypassing your conscious mind and entering your subconscious or unconscious mind, which is the one that is responsible for all that you do. This results in information that may no longer be serving you being redesigned by your intention, making it easier for you to facilitate complete changes.

How is Anything Achieved Through This?

The ability to achieve results through self-hypnosis works the same as your ability to achieve results through any form of hypnosis. Whether we realize it or not, our subconscious or unconscious mind is directly responsible for virtually everything that we do. This is where our "survival" information is stored. Anything that urges us to jump into action or produce certain results are all stored within this part of our mind and is responsible for virtually everything that we do. From breathing and digesting food that we eat to telling us who to trust and who not to, and even helping us make an opinion about things and form judgments on various topics, our subconscious mind is directly responsible for these actions.

The conscious mind can recognize and become aware of things, but it is not directly responsible for what we ultimately choose to do. So, by consciously choosing to make a change, we must then relay that change into our subconscious so that it happens. Just as with any other form of hypnosis, performing self-hypnosis allows you to take a conscious desire to change and relay it back into your subconscious mind so that it takes effect, and true changes are seen and experienced in our lives. For example, if you want to stop biting your nails, you may tell you're conscious mind that you want to do so. Then, later, you begin biting your nails without realizing it because it is a practice that has become a part of your subconscious psyche. Therefore, if you want to instill real change, you have to bypass your conscious mind and directly tell your subconscious mind to change this behavior. This is achieved through self-hypnosis and intention, and the results can be just as powerful as any other form of hypnosis.

What Is The Big Difference?

There truly is no major difference between regular hypnosis and self-hypnosis, aside from who is facilitating the hypnotic state and directing the subconscious mind in that state. As we have already discussed, hypnosis is something that is facilitated by a third-party to direct the relationship between your conscious and unconscious mind. Self-hypnosis, however, is done directly between your conscious and unconscious mind and allows you to perform the practice at any given time, in any given place, for any particular reason.

Choosing between self-hypnosis and hypnosis is personal, and both have their unique benefits that outweigh the benefits given by the other. For example, if you are inexperienced and are looking to be hypnotized by a professional to achieve something big, such as to motivate yourself to lose weight or become healthier, professional hypnosis can help you facilitate this change. Professional hypnosis will be able to facilitate quicker results than an inexperienced self-hypnosis practitioner, and they will also be able to use a broader range of words and intentions because they are not in the hypnotic state, but rather you are, and they are simply directing it. By this understanding, a hypnotherapist can take you through a broader range of intentions and experiences when it comes to hypnosis.

However, professional hypnotherapists can become rather costly and may not always be able to provide you the level of help that you need for various intentions. For example, they may not entirely understand what change you want to make, they may not be within your budget, or they may simply not be available at the exact times that you need hypnosis to help you. In these cases, self-hypnosis is a great option. You can enter a hypnotic state and then focus on your intention and, as a result, facilitate change directly at the moment that change is needed. This can increase the benefits and results you experience from your hypnosis, and it can make hypnotherapy more effective for you.

If you are wondering which to choose: hypnosis with a professional hypnotherapist or self-hypnosis, the best answer is likely to choose both. Seeking help from a professional hypnotherapist can help you learn about hypnosis and begin navigating the world of hypnotherapy and facilitate major changes in a shorter amount of time. Then, coupling this practice with a self-hypnosis practice can help you get the most out of your experience and see greater results. You can engage in shorter, more direct self-hypnotherapy sessions as needed to supplement your professional hypnotherapist's results and ultimately facilitate a total change.

As you become more practiced with self-hypnosis, you may begin to discover that you no longer need as much help from professional hypnotherapists. While seeking professional help in the face of major, difficult, or stubborn changes may be desirable, you will likely find that you can facilitate major changes in a shorter time, the more you practice. For that reason, you become your change-maker and influencer. This can make the idea of increasing your skills around self-hypnosis more desirable and can prove why it is important to begin practicing and taking advantage of this incredible practice as soon as possible.

CHAPTER FOUR

WHAT IS DEEP SLEEP MEDITATION

One of the best ways to really become relaxed and find the peace needed for better sleep is through the use of a visualization technique. For this, you will want to ensure that you are in a completely relaxing and comfortable place. This reading will help you be more centered on the moment, alleviate anxiety, and wind down before bed.

Listen to it as you are falling asleep, whether it's at night or if you are simply taking a nap. Ensure the lighting is right and remove all other distractions that will keep you from becoming completely relaxed.

Meditation for a Full Night's Sleep

You are lying in a completely comfortable position right now. Your body is well-rested, and you are prepared to drift deeply into sleep. The deeper you sleep, the healthier you feel when you wake up.

Your eyes are closed, and the only thing that you are responsible for now is falling asleep. There isn't anything you should be worried about other than becoming well-rested. You are going to be able to do this through this guided meditation into another world.

It will be the transition between your waking life and a place where you are going to fall into a deep and heavy sleep. You are becoming more and more relaxed, ready to fall into a trance-like state where you can drift into healthy sleep.

Start by counting down slowly. Use your breathing in fives in order to help you become more and more asleep.

Breathe in for ten, nine, eight, seven, six, and out for five, four, three, two, and one. Repeat this once more. Breathe in for ten, nine, eight, seven, six, and out for five, four, three, two, and one.

You are now more and more relaxed, more and more prepared for a night of deep and heavy sleep. You are drifting away, faster and faster, deeper and deeper, closer and closer to a heavy sleep. You see nothing as you let your mind wander.

You are not fantasizing about anything. You are not worried about what has happened today, or even farther back in your past. You are not afraid of what might be there going forward. You are not fearful of anything in the future that is causing you panic.

You are highly aware of this moment that everything will be OK. Nothing matters but your breathing and your relaxation. Everything in front of you is peaceful. You are filled with serenity, and you exude calmness.

You only think about what is happening in the present moment where you are becoming more and more at peace.

Your mind is blank. You see nothing but black. You are fading faster and faster, deeper and deeper, further and further. You are getting close to being completely relaxed, but right now, you are OK with sitting here peacefully.

You aren't rushing to sleep because you need to wind down before bed. You don't want to go to bed with anxious thoughts and have nightmares all night about the things that you are fearing. The only thing that you concern yourself with at this moment is getting nice and relaxed before it's time to start to sleep.

You see nothing in front of you other than a small white light. That light becomes a bit bigger and bigger. As it grows, you start to see that you are inside a vehicle. You are lying on your bed; everything around you is still there. Only, when you look up, you see that there is a large open window, with several computers and wheels out in front of you.

You realize that you are in a spaceship floating peacefully through the sky. It is on auto-pilot, and there is nothing that you have to worry about as you are floating up in this spaceship. You look out above you and see that the night sky is gorgeous than you ever could have imagined.

All that surrounds you is nothing but beauty. Bright stars are twinkling against a black backdrop. You can make out some of the planets. They are all different than you would ever have imagined. Some are bright purple, and others are blue. There are detailed swirls and stripes that you didn't know were there.

You relax and feel yourself floating up in this space. When you are here, everything seems so small. You still have problems back home on Earth, but they are so distant that they are almost not real. Some issues make you feel as though the world is ending, but you see now that the entire universe is still doing fine, no matter what might be happening in your life. You are not concerned with any issues right now.

You are soaking up all that is around you. You are so far separated from Earth, and it's crazy to think about just how much space is out there for you to explore. You are relaxed, looking around. There are shooting stars all in the distance. There are floating rocks passing by your ship. You are floating around, feeling dreamier and dreamier.

You are passing over Earth again, getting close to going back home. You are going to be sent right back into your room, falling more heavily with each breath you take back into sleep. You are getting closer and closer to drifting away.

You pass over the earth and look down to see all of the beauty that exists. The green and blue swirl together, white clouds above that make such an interesting pattern. Everything below looks like a painting. It does not look real.

You get closer and closer, floating so delicately in your small space ship. The ride is not bumpy. It is not bothering you.

You are floating over the city now. You see, random lights flicker on. It doesn't look like a map anymore like when you are so high above.

You are looking down and seeing that gentle lights still flash here and there, but for the most part, the city is winding down. Everyone is drifting faster and faster to sleep. You are getting closer and closer to your home.

You see that everything is peaceful below you. The sun will rise again, and tomorrow will start. For now, the only thing that you can do is prepare and rest for what might be to come.

You are more and more relaxed now, drifting further and further into sleep.

You are still focused on your breathing; it is becoming slower and slower. You are close to drifting away to sleep now.

When we reach one, you will drift off deep into sleep.

HOW MEDITATION HELPS WEIGHT LOSS

Meditation is known to be an effective tool for weight loss. It aligns the unconscious mind with the conscious mind in order to facilitate changes that we want to make in our behaviors. Such changes may include avoiding unhealthy foods by altering them with healthier foods. Your unconscious mind must become engaged in the change process because it is where the weight-gaining, poor habits such as emotional eating are cultivated. Through meditation, you will be able to become more aware of your surroundings and will be able to overcome your unhealthy habits.

But there is even a more immediate effect of mediation. It can reduce the level of stress hormones in the body. Hormones like cortisol give the body signal to store more calories. If you have high levels of cortisol moving through your system, it is going to be difficult to cut down weight even if you are eating healthy foods. Most of us are stressed in most cases, but it takes only 25 minutes of meditation three times in arrow to reduce the effects of stress.

In 2016, a study that was conducted by Texas Tech University found that increased relaxation, attention, body-mind awareness, calmness, and brain activity result from just a few sessions of meditation. The study also suggested that your self-control could increase with daily meditation. The researchers found that the brain is most affected by meditation, which means that with a few minutes of meditation, you will be able to pass by that ice cream when feeling stressed.

How to Start Meditating for Weight Loss

Even without training, anyone who has a body and mind can practice meditation. For most of us, the most challenging aspect of meditation is getting time. You can start with as little as 8 to 10 minutes a day.

Ensure that you can access a quiet place for meditation. If you have children or other people around you, you may need to squeeze time when they are not awake or after they have left the house to avoid distractions. You may even practice your mediation while in the shower.

Once you are in a place of silence, take a comfortable position. You can either lie down or sit in a position that makes you feel at ease.

Start meditating by putting your focus on your breath. Watch the way your stomach or chest rises and falls. Feel the air that you breathe in and out of your mouth. Listen keenly to the sounds around you. This should be done for 2 or 3 minutes until you begin feeling relaxed.

Next, do the following steps:

Take in a deep breath, and hold for a few seconds

Slowly breath out, and repeat the process

Breathe in a natural manner

Observe the way your breath enters your nostrils, influence the movement of your chest, and moves your stomach.

Continue focusing on the way you breathe in and out for about 8 to 10 minutes

Your mind may begin to wonder, which is a normal occurrence. Just acknowledge this and return your attention back to the process

As you wrap up, reflect on your thoughts, and acknowledge how you can easily bring your mind together

Practical Methods To Sleep Meditations

Although you might be tired, you may still struggle to actually fall asleep because you aren't able to become fully relaxed. Going to bed doesn't mean just jumping under the covers and closing your eyes. You will also want to ensure that you are keeping up with incorporating relaxation techniques into your bedtime routine so you can stay better focused on getting a complete rest, not one that is constantly disturbed by anxious thoughts.

The following meditation is good for anyone who is about to go to bed. You will want to include this for getting a night of deep sleep, or one that will last for several hours. Keep your eyes closed, and ensure the lighting is right so that there is nothing that will distract you from falling asleep. No lighting is best, but if you do prefer to have some sort of light on, ensure that it is soft yellow or purple/pink. Always choose small lights and nightlights instead of overhead lighting.

OTHER BENEFITS OF DEEP MEDITATION

Meditation reduces stress

With meditation, you will feel calmer as well as have a stress-reducing impact on your body. With endless roles in life, including work, children, and home activities, it is not surprising that you may be overwhelmed, which may contribute to increased stress. Unfortunately, these stressors affect your body by producing more cortisol, a stress hormone that affects the levels of sugar and insulin in the body. As a result, the hormone causes weight gain. Studies have revealed that meditation activates a relaxation response, regulating the nervous system and, in turn, lowering the cortisol levels.

With a few minutes of deep breathing and conscious relaxation, you will be able to obtain the cortisol-lowering benefits as well as your overall stress levels.

Meditation promotes a focus on intention

Often, meditation techniques involve focusing on specific goals or concepts. Meditating on cutting down weight streams your energy, thoughts, and intentions to a particular goal. In this case, you submit to the intentions by revealing your goals to the world, which makes both your conscious and subconscious mind to be aware of the goal that you want to lose some weight. The outspoken intention will stay with you for a long while, enabling you to achieve your weight loss goal both consciously and subconsciously, and dodging all possible distractions.

With meditation, you will learn conscious eating

With daily meditation, you will be able to boost your levels of mindfulness and awareness. This can allow you to live in the moment and always focus on what you are doing in the present. The process of meditation can help you gain an increased sense of awareness of actions and thoughts, thus helping you to think twice before you have taken action. Rather than enabling your cravings to take over you, you will develop the power of controlling your mind, thus handling your cravings with greater intention and awareness. When you are ready to eat, your awareness will make it easier to recognize the textures and flavors of the food you are eating, instead of taking them for granted.

Meditation stabilizes mood hormones

Common daily stressors and activities can affect the way your system operates normally and may throw your hormones out of normal functioning. Apart from keeping your cortisol and adrenaline levels regulated, meditation goes further than this. The technique for relaxation releases both oxytocin and serotonin hormones, which boost your moods and ensure your hormones remain stable.

Meditation regulates sleep

Lack of sleep may hinder your weight loss progress. You see, by having a deep sleep, your cortisol levels will rise, which in turn will sabotage your progress in losing weight. Also, when you lack sleep, ghrelin, a hunger signal hormone, is also produced in plenty, thereby increasing your chances of eating more for weight gain. With meditation, you will be able to balance the circadian rhythms that promote quality sleep. Meditation increases the levels of melatonin, a hormone that also determines and controls when you sleep.

CHAPTER FIVE

WHAT ARE AFFIRMATIONS

Affirmations are necessary when you want to focus on another thought pattern. During affirmations, you phrase your statements positively, attach personal meaning to them, and repeat them to yourself multiple times throughout the day. Corresponding emotion helps the subconscious to understand the statements and believe them as the new status quo. At first, getting your conscious mind on board with affirmations that may seem far-fetched can be difficult. As time goes on, however, the power of these affirmations has taken root into your subconscious, and you start to believe them to be true even with your rational mind.

You should change your lifestyle if you want to have experience permanent weight loss or control. Powerful affirmations are important in helping to change your lifestyle slowly.

Thus, you should practice regular affirmations for weight loss to be able to realize your dream of losing weight. Notably, weight control is a direct function of your lifestyle because you are solely responsible for your own behavior. In other words, your weight is determined by your mental attitude, rest and sleep, physical exertion, your manner, and frequency of eating.

You can use effective weight loss affirmations to be able to initiate these measures from your mind. Thus, you should change your thinking; otherwise, no form of dieting will ever help. Weight loss affirmations are significant in your mind, as they help you to become a comfort in your desired weight.

You should also consider the words of your affirmations to ensure that you focus on the solution and not the problem. For instance, you shouldn't say "I am not that fat" because that is the problem that you're saying. Instead, you should focus on the solution and say words such as "I am getting slimmer" or "I am losing weight every day."

Try to write down some healthy weight affirmations or take a cue from the samples in this book. Repeating these words over and over, which will help to show that you are determined to take the bold step of living and fitter life.

So here are the words:

I weigh _____ pounds: this affirmation states the desired weight in your mind instantly, and as you repeat the words, you are reminding yourself about your destiny and all measures that you should take.

I will achieve my ideal weight so that I can enhance my physical fitness: you are embracing a lighter weight and improving your physical activity.

I love eating healthy food because they help me to be able to attain my ideal weight: This statement promotes healthy eating and cravings for healthy food.

I ease digestion by chewing all my food to reach my ideal weight: This affirmation is perfect to say before every meal because it guides the rate and amount of food that you consume.

I am controlling my weight by combining healthy eating, and it helps me to be able to control my appetite and my portion sizes: It is great to repeat this particular affirmation with others in front of a mirror to keep reminding your subconscious mind about your goals. Also, these affirmations work best when you're meditating or in a trance state. The combination will help to do wonders in your weight loss endeavor.

Positive Affirmations

Beliefs are formed by repetitive thought that has been nourished over and over for an extended period. Affirmations are positively charged proclamations or pronouncements repeated several through the day, every day. These words are often terse, straightforward, memorable, and repetitive. Affirmations are phrased in the present tense, and they lead to belief. The most crucial element of any self-improvement process is to set an intention. Muhammud Ali once said that "It is the repetition of affirmations that cause belief, and when the beliefs become deep convictions, that is when things start to happen."

Let's say you intend to shed some weight. That being the sole goal, it is paramount that all your efforts are focused on achieving it. Therefore, affirmative statements should be in the lines of, "Shedding pounds is as easy as packing them on," "I am what I eat," "A healthy mind is a healthy body," "I feel beautiful on the outside as I do on the inside," and so on. Keep in mind that not all the words you utter will yield results. For affirmations to work, they have to be coupled with visualization and a feeling of conviction. Therefore, it is advisable to focus more on positive thoughts than negative thoughts and for a prolonged period.

Remember to use words that resonate with you. The affirmations need not be empty for you. They ought to have a close relation and meaning attached to them. The proper statements for the appropriate situation goes a long way in achieving success.

You can try repeating your affirmations before you go to bed. As the brain gets ready to go on "autopilot" mode, the subconscious mind becomes more active, thereby absorbing the last bits of information for the day. Repeating affirmations before you sleep not only makes you slip into dreamland in a more confident and relaxed state but also helps to convince the mind.

You might begin to wonder why, if affirmations work, they are not used to get out of "tricky" situations. For example, if you are feeling sick, would you proceed to state, "I am cured. Am I well"? Affirmations work best with an aligned state of mind. If you believe to be well, it is more likely that you will begin to notice a decline in symptoms. If you do not believe in your affirmations, you will continue to battle through the temperature and other physical discomforts.

Finding the right words to use can be a stroll in the park; however, remembering to repeat these words, severally could present itself as a challenge. The other obstacle you might face is having two conflicting thoughts. One of them is the carefully considered affirmation, while the other is a counterproductive negation. Try the best you can to disprove the negative thoughts but do not feed them time nor energy. It will be quite challenging to believe affirmations too at the beginning. However, as time goes on, it will become easier to convince yourself. Practice makes perfect.

HOW AFFIRMATIONS AFFECT THE MIND

The act of repeating positive statements anchors your thoughts and energy, driving you toward their fulfillment

Affirmations program the subconscious mind, which in turn processes your reactions to circumstances.

The more frequently you repeat the affirmations, you become more attuned with your environment. You start seeing new opportunities, and your mind opens up to new ways of fulfilling your goals

Somewhere down in our unconscious minds, we've created solid thoughts regarding unfortunate practices. Actually, after some time, we may have prepared the psyche to accept that these unfortunate practices are basic — that they are important for keeping up our prosperity. Also, if the mind accepts these practices are fundamental, long term change is troublesome.

Stress or passionate eating is only one model. There are numerous affiliations that we build up that contrarily sway our relationship to nourishment. Some regular affiliations that forestall weight reduction include:

Nourishment is a solace cover; we use it to comfort ourselves amid stress, or trouble Eating occupies us from sentiments of trouble, uneasiness or anger

Indulging greasy, sugary, or unfortunate nourishments is related to festivities and other great occasions.

Unfortunate or sugary nourishments are a prize.

Indulging encourages you to pack the dread that you won't have the option to get in shape.

Nourishment is a wellspring of amusement when exhausted.

At last, accomplishing long term weight loss requires these main drivers to be surveyed, comprehended, and reframed. What's more, that is actually what hypnosis can enable us to accomplish.

100+ Affirmations For Weight Loss

1. I am fit, attractive, energetic, and healthy.

2. I am getting healthier, more energetic, and fitter every day.

3. I am stunning, inside out.

4. I care for myself by eating right, sleeping properly, and exercising.

5. I take longer, deeper, calm, and relaxed breaths.

6. I love, care for, and nurture my body, and it cares back for me.

7. I am very beautiful, fit, and attractive.

8. I am completely relaxed and filled with serenity and peace of mind.

9. I am in a relaxed state of mind.

10. My body heals, replenishes, and repairs itself quickly.

11. I am beautiful in my body, mind, and spirit.

12. I go to bed early, sleep deeply, and am an early riser.

13. I create healing energy throughout my life.

14. I am healthy, relaxed, and happy.

15. I am healthy and confident and physically and emotionally strong and happy.

16. I am totally in control of my health, healing, and wellness.

17. I have abundant and inexhaustible energy.

18. I am capable of maintaining my perfect weight.

19. I am healthy in every aspect of existence.

20. I am an effective, healthy, fit, and energetic individual who is capable of handling anything that arises.

21. I will dedicate 15-20 minutes a day for exercise.

22. I feel vibrant, enthusiastic, and energetic every moment.

23. I enjoy eating nutritious, balanced, and healthy meals.

24. I have the complete power to control my fitness and health.

25. I love to eat healthy food and exercise.

26. I am the recipient of glowing health and a vibrant mind, body, and spirit.

27. I am completely enjoying my daily exercise routine now.

28. I am fit, healthy, and active, and practice regular exercises.

29. My body is fit and healthy, and all my organs function perfectly well.

30. Each day, I get closer and closer to my perfect weight.

31. I eat to fuel and nourish my body when required.

32. I have a strong heart and a formidable steel body. I am healthy, vigorous, energetic, and filled with vitality.

33. My body is a temple. It is holy, clean, and filled with a sense of goodness.

34. I am completely free from diabetes, high blood pressure, and any life-threatening disease.

35. I express my gratitude to God and everyone in my life.

36. I am healthy, wealthy, and wise. My body is healthy, my mind is wise, while I am always wealthy.

37. I eat healthy food that benefits my body.

38. I drink large quantities of water, which cleanses my body.

39. I feel good, my body feels good, and I radiate good feelings.

40. I am in possession of a healthy mind and a healthy body.

41. I have a strong heart and healthy body. I am energetic and vigorous.

42. I treat my body as a temple. My body is clean, holy, and full of goodness.

43. My body is healthy, I am wealthy, and my mind is wise.

44. I surround myself with people who encourage me to be healthy.

45. I honor my body.

46. I am looking forward to a healthy old age because I take care of my body now.

47. I am grateful for my healthy body.

48. I enjoy living life.

49. I am worthy of good health.

50. I focus on positive progression.

51. I am a friend to my body.

52. I look after my body with unconditional compassion.

53. I am doing everything possible to keep my body well.

54. I am willing to participate in my wellness plan.

55. I have a strong immune system. I am able to deal with germs, bacteria, and viruses.

56. My body is full of energy.

57. My body is free from pain.

58. My body heals itself, and I feel better every day.

59. I send lots of love and healing to all my organs.

60. I pay attention to my body. I listen to what my body needs.

61. I am a good sleeper. I sleep soundly and wake up feeling rested.

62. I surround myself with people who support my healthy choices.

63. I speak, think, and act in perfect health.

64. I choose to make all my thoughts healthy ones.

65. I enjoy taking care of my body.

66. I breathe deeply to lift my mood and bring energy to my body.

67. I allow all the cells in my body to repair and replenish it.

68. I nourish my body with lots of water.

69. I have fun when exercising my body.

70. I listen to my body, which communicates what it likes to me.

71. I am full of energy and full of life.

72. I control my state at all times.

73. I am happy and always in control of how I feel.

74. I decide to feel gratitude and joy right now.

75. I am more than I seem to be, and all the powers of the Universe are within me.

76. My reason for eating is to fuel my body.

77. Being healthy is better than any taste in the world.

78. My healthy thoughts create a healthy body.

79. My body is my temple.

80. I am worthy of being healthy.

81. My daily habits are leading me to become healthier and healthier.

82. I choose to eat healthy because the food I eat is construction material for my body.

83. I get plenty of energizing sleep.

84. I make healthy choices and respect the body I've been given.

85. The water I drink cleanse my body and give me clarity of mind.

86. I love being healthy, and it feels wonderful.

87. I take deep breaths every day and remind myself that air is a gift.

88. I am in control of my own health.

89. Every cell in my body embodies the spirit of health.

90. I love myself and the body I've been given.

91. Every day and in every way, I am becoming more and more healthy.

92. I feel great, and I radiate joy and gratitude.

93. I am vigorous and full of vitality.

94. I now demand my body to release all ill feelings about events or people.

95. I now forgive myself as well as other people.

96. I am a creator; I create my future and decide my own health.

97. I deserve to live a life filled with energy and joy.

98. I honor my body, and I am surrounded by people who want me to be healthy.

99. I trust the signals my body sends me.

100. I am so grateful to be alive and to feel good.

101. My thoughts are supporting my body to become healthier and healthier.

102. I give my body what it needs.

103. I love every cell of this body that I have.

104. I am always healing rapidly, and I constantly feel wonderful.

105. I fill my mind with positive thoughts.

106. I use my body in a way that creates positive emotions.

107. I often smile and stand up straight.

108. I release the past and relish the present moment.

109. The Universe is conspiring to keep me healthy.

110. I relax my jaw and keep my teeth separated slightly.

111. I relax my body often and let my body rest when it needs to.

112. I do things that are good for my body.

113. I feel incredibly healthy, and I love it.

114. I am strong and feel good about myself.

115. I am at peace with my health.

116. My mind is brilliant, and my soul is tranquil.

117. I always sleep in peace and wake up with incredible joy.

CHAPTER SIX

HOW TO PRACTICE EVERY DAY

For your quick workout routine, walk up through the stairs at the office. Park your car at the farthest spot and trek all the way distance. Take your dog on a long walk. Participate in every way you can. That is the goal of exercising. If you miss any workout or you couldn't get going one day, don't just hang up on it, just get back on track the next day.

Set a routine for everyday hypnosis meditation and affirmation for weight loss

If you are stuck in the same old aerobics classes, then you could mix things up and try to take a new class at your gym. Some of the hottest gym classes that you could take include indoor cycling, boxing based programs, yoga classes acrobatics, and martial art. This will help you to be able to combat boredom, which is the number one reason why you participate in emotional eating and quit exercising. Try always to drink a lot of water while exercising. Warm-up before exercising. If you haven't warmed up, then you have to get into the habit of warming up before every exercise. Make it a habit to warm up. It isn't necessary to warm up before any strenuous exercise, but by doing so, you'll be able to get your blood flowing, and you be able to prepare yourself for any activity ahead.

Standing Reach Stretch

One of the stretching exercises that you can do is the standing reach stretch. This stretch involves the upper body's movement. So start with your arms, keep your arms straight down, besides your body's with your palms facing backward. Use one arm, raise it forward, and raise it up as high as possible. Now tighten your abs and use the opposite arm to touch your shoulders and stretch across your chest slightly. Now hold the stretch for 10 to 30 seconds.

Repeat the same stretch with your arms reaching in the opposite direction. The neck stretches the chest and backstretch. Use your hands to grab the ends of a small towel in both hands. Now bring your arms to the chest level and slightly tuck on the ends of the towel and hold it for about 10 to 30 seconds.

Neck Stretch

Neck stretch is the upper-body stretch. This stretch is very good for golfers. Grab the end of a small towel with your end and slightly tuck them to the end of the wall.

The chest and Shoulders stretch

Now the next stretch is the chest and shoulder stretch. This stretch is great after swimming. So take your hands behind you, and hold the end of a towel at your hip. Now raise your chest high and raise your arms forward now hold the stretch for about 30 seconds.

Quadriceps Stretch

The next stretch is the quadriceps stretch. This stretch is good for runners, high-cut cyclists, and walkers. Sit behind the chair and hold onto the chair for balance and support. Now take one hand and grab your other ankle. Gently push your foot forward towards your gluts. Do not tuck or lean forward but keep your chest lifted high. Now do this stretch for about 10 to 30 seconds. Now repeat the same thing using the other leg.

Standing outer thigh stretch

Stand behind the chair, and hold onto the back of the chair for balance. Place one of your feet behind the chair and diagonally press your heels to the floor. Hold the stretch for about 30 seconds and put it doing using your other leg.

Tendon Stretch Arms Lenght

The next stretch is the tendon stretch stand. Keep your arm's length behind the chair and hold onto the back of the chair to support and balance yourself. Now keep your feet a few inches apart from your toes why you point your heels to the ground. Slowly push your pelvis while bending your elbows and leaning forward. Support yourself with your hands to the back of the chair. Now do this for about 30 seconds.

Standing thin stretch stand

The next stretch the standing shin stretch. Stand at the back of a chair and hold the back of the chair for support and balance. Bend your nails slightly and raise the toes of your feet off the ground while resting on your heels. Do this stretch for about 30 seconds.

Hip Stretch

The next one is the hip stretch. Stand at the back of a chair for support and balance while bending your nails across and cross one ankle over the opposite leg. Now sit back watch and hold it straight for about 30 seconds. Repeat the stretch, crossing the other ankle over the opposite knee.

Upper back Stretch and shoulder stretch

The next one is upper backstretch and shoulder stretch. This stretch is perfect for activities that require the upper body and bending movements. So to begin the stretch, stand behind the chair and hold onto the back of the chair for support. Then take one step away from the chair until your arms are fully stretched. Now move and bend forward from your waist and stretch your shoulders forward, then hold onto the knee for about 30 seconds.

Try to stretch as many ways as you can; the more stretches that you do, the more likely, you will be to avoid tight muscles, prevent injuries, and feel better if your muscles are tight, patient with it. It will take some time for your muscles to go back to their normal length. Stretching throughout your life will help to reduce the effect of aging and will help me to lose weight and reduce the wear and tear of your joints and tissue.

Studies have shown that it is possible to maintain your flexibility through a wide-stretching program that you can follow. You should remember that stretching is not a contest, you shouldn't compare yourself with other people because everybody is different. Some days you might be feeling bar where are some days you might feel tighter. Stay comfortably within your limits and allow the flow of your energy to come through you.

Now let us look talk about some simple exercises that will help you during your hypothesis session.

Abs

The first one is the abs. So grab a bubble chair or a dumbbell and then lay your back on it while pointing your feet straight. Take the weight and extend your arms over it, and then contract your abdominal muscles while lifting the weight up towards the ceiling. Exhale while moving up and inhale while moving downward. Now you should remember not to bounce on the ball. Moves slowly so that your muscles will be tight throughout the entire set also try to bring your weight at an angle and try to push the weight straight all perfectly vertical. Now the equipment that you need for this exercise are dumbbells and exercise balls, whereas the muscles that you are working out are the upper abdominal and the core muscles.

CHAPTER SEVEN

YOUR THINNER AND HAPPIER LIFE

Benefits Of Eating Healthy And Detoxifying

Most times, we don't eat because we are hungry, we eat because food is available. The same way you make random decisions to purchase items you don't actually need in a supermarket in the same way that you purchase food. Most times, when you get a job that offers you some financial freedom, you begin to go to that expensive restaurant you have always dreamt of going because you can now afford it.

Now that you can afford the food there, you start to visit the restaurant frequently and purchase food that you do not really need. You are just buying the food because you have the money to do so, and the food is readily available. Many of the bad decisions that make us eat food that we do not need to eat can be avoided if we start to focus our thoughts on getting what is necessary.

The process of getting that what is necessary requires you as an individual to be able to acquire some personal discipline. Before you purchase any food, you need to ask yourself if buying the food is really necessary. Ask yourself if the food that you are eating will add any value to your overall health. After asking yourself that question, you will know

135

the right thing to do based on the response to the questions. It is an easy process to do, and it will help to save you from eating those carbs that only add unnecessary weight to your body.

Maintain a healthy body

Once we consume food, our bodies respond to what we have consumed. The response could be negative or positive. Different foods generate different feelings. You may not believe what some of these feelings are, except you focus your minds on realizing them. The power of meditation is that it allows you to be able to focus, concentrate on a certain thing that requires your attention. This is an easy task to accomplish, and you only should evaluate how your body reacts to the foods that you are consuming. Once you eat some foods, you will notice that you feel energized, while some foods will make you feel tired.

Once you overeat, you will experience some sudden feelings of tiredness. You will begin to feel as if your body is too heavy, and so all you want to do is take a nap or a rest. Now when this happens, you should realize that it is a sign that whatever you ate was unnecessary, and hence the body will not use the food. As a result, most of what you ate will become something that your body needs to eliminate. Thus, you will start to add extra weight, because the excess food in your body becomes excess fat in your body. On the other hand, if once you eat, it immediately makes you feel energized; it means your body was receptive to the food that you eat.

It means that your body was able to convert much of the food into energy, and each of that component present in the food will be well utilized by your body. This is beneficial for the wellbeing of your body, and it can help you when losing weight and prevent you from adding unnecessary weight.

Maintain the bodyweight

Your eyes are shut. Envision coasting your desires ceaselessly. Envision what's pleasant for you to eat a day. Envision spellbinding helping you get in shape as the news seems to be. Psychotherapist Jean Fain from the Harvard Medical School gives ten trancelike recommendations to endeavor.

When I tell people how I make a lot of my life — as a psychotherapist who entrances thin individuals — they ask: Does that work? Typically, my reaction lights up their eyes with something among energy and unbelief.

A great many people don't comprehend that adding daze to your weight reduction endeavors can enable you to lose more weight and look after it. Spellbinding originates before the tallying of carb and calories by a few decades. However, this well-established technique for centering consideration presently can't seem to be completely held onto as an effective methodology for weight reduction.

As of not long ago, the real claims of prestigious trance inducers have been bolstered by insufficient logical proof, and an excess of pie-in-the-sky responsibilities from their issue kin, stage trance specialists, have not made a difference.

Indeed, even after a powerful reanalysis of 18 sleep-inducing studies in the mid-1990s demonstrated that psychotherapy clients who appropriately self-trance lost twice as much weight as compared to the individuals who didn't (and held it off in one research two years after the part of the bargain) unless if you or somebody you know has joyfully been constrained by entrancing to buy a crisp, littler closet, it might be hard to believe that this psyche over-body procedure can enable you to take a few to get back some composure on eating.

Seeing is thinking absolutely. So, investigate yourself. To gain proficiency with a portion of the priceless exercises that trance must instruct about weight reduction, you don't need to be spellbound. The ten smaller than expected ideas that pursue contain a portion of the eating regimen modifying recommendations that my gathering and individual hypnotherapy weight the executive's clients get.

138

The power is inside. Trance specialists believe that you have all you should be effective. You truly needn't bother with an alternate accident diet or the ongoing suppressant of hunger. Thinning, as you do when you ride a bike, is tied in with confiding in your innate abilities. You may not recall how terrifying it was the point at which you previously endeavored to ride a bike. However, you kept on rehearsing until you had the option to ride, consequently, with no idea or exertion. Getting more fit may appear past you moreover. However, it's just about finding your balance.

You see your conviction. Individuals will, in general, do what they accept they can achieve. That is even valid for mesmerizing. Those fooled into deduction they could be entranced (for example, as the trance inducer proposed they would see red, he turned the switch on a disguised red bulb) demonstrated improved mesmerizing reaction. It is essential to hope to be made a difference. Give me a chance to propose you anticipate that your arrangement should work on weight reduction. Highlight the positive. Recommendations, for example, "Doughnuts will sicken you," negative or aversive, work for some time, however on the off chance that you need lasting change, you need to think emphatically. Specialists Herbert Spiegel and David Spiegel, a dad child hypnotherapy group, considered the most well-known valuable trancelike proposition. "I need my body to live in. I owe regard and security to my body." I

139

elevate clients to create their very own energetic mantras. A 50-year-old mother who shed 50 pounds more rehashes day by day: "Superfluous nourishment is a weight on my body. I will shed what I needn't bother with."

It's going to come if you envision it. Like competitors who are getting ready for the challenge, you are set up for a successful truth by picturing triumph. Envisioning a smart dieting day will enable you to envision the means expected to turn into a decent eater. Is it too difficult to even think about photographing? Locate a comfortable old photograph of yourself and recall what you did another way. Envision these schedules reviving. Or, on the other hand, picture acquiring direction from an older, more astute self later on in the wake of contacting her required weight.

Get rid of cravings. Subliminal specialists utilize the intensity of emblematic symbolism on a standard premise, welcoming subjects to put sustenance desires on fleecy white mists or inflatables in sight-seeing and send them up, up, and away. On the off chance that you can direct off your eating routine from McDonald's brilliant curves, trance inducers comprehend that a counter-image can control you back. Welcome your psyche to flip through its picture Rolodex until you develop as an indication of yearnings throwing out. Push.

There are two preferred procedures over one. A triumphant mix is entrancing and Cognitive Behavioral Treatment (CBT) with regards to getting more fit and holding it off, which patches up counterproductive thoughts and practices. Clients learning both lose twice as much weight without falling into the lose-a few, recuperate more trap of the health food nut. On the off chance that you've at any point kept up a sustenance journal, you've officially endeavored CBT. They monitor everything that experiences their lips for possibly 14 days before my clients learn mesmerizing. Each great trance inducer comprehends that raising cognizance is a principle move for the tyke towards suffering change.

Modify and then change. The late pioneer of spellbinding, Milton Erickson, MD, focused on u's essentialness. To change the lose-recuperation, the lose-recuperation example of one customer, Erickson recommended that she put on weight first before losing it — an intense sell today, except if you're Charlize Theron. Simpler to swallow: Modify your craving for high calories. Shouldn't something be said about some solidified yogurt rather than 16 ounces of dessert?

Like it or not, it is the fittest for survival. No proposal is sufficiently able to supersede the nature of survival. Similarly, as we like to believe, it's the fittest survival, despite everything we're modified for survival in case of starvation. A valid example: a private dietary mentor needed a proposal for her dependence on a sticky bear. The advisor attempted to clarify that her body felt that her life relied upon the chewy desserts and wouldn't surrender them until she got enough calories from progressively nutritious food. No, she demanded, all that she required was a proposition when she dropped out.

Practice makes perfect. There are no washboard abs delivered by one Pilates class, and one spellbinding session can't shape your eating routine. Be that as it may, discreetly rehashing a useful suggestion 15 to 20 minutes daily can change your eating, especially when combined with moderate, regular breaths, the foundation of any program of social change.

Improved mental functioning

This practice is extremely similar to the previous practice, only instead of simply visualizing the room you want to describe it to yourself. Imagine as though you are mentally chatting with yourself or someone else, and describe what the room looks like as you go about doing it. Say, for example, "The room has white walls, a white door, and white framing around the door. It has a green chair in the corner, a white desk on the north-facing wall, and a window that faces the East."

You want to describe this room down to the most minute detail you can possibly recall for that room. Do not skip on details, describe everything you can recall. The idea is that you want to complete this exercise while also improving your attention and mental awareness. As you do this, you will be engaging in both visualization and verbalization, which can be helpful to those who are not entirely visually-oriented. You can also describe the details out loud if you feel that you need even more of a verbal to your practice.

If you are not someone who prefers to use movement to enter your trance-like state but would rather do so by remaining still and calm within yourself, then you can try taking advantage of visualization. Visualization is a great practice that allows you to take control of your mind's eye and "leave" your physical body by entering your mind, instead. The following visualization practice is a great way to get your mind in control and enter a trance-like state so that you can begin your self-hypnosis practice.

Get into a comfortable position and then let your eyes fall closed. Once they have, consider a room that you are used to entering. It can be any room that you know well, and that helps you feel comfortable.

Once you have considered the room, begin to visualize it. You want to place as many details into that room as possible. Consider the colors of the walls, the door frame, the door itself, and any windows that might be in that room. Consider the view you get on the outside of the window, and then visualize all of the contents of the room. All of the furniture, decorations, and other objects that fill the room should be "built" into your visualized version of this room.

Once you have done this, consider a room that you are less familiar with. Practice putting it together in the same way you did the room that you knew well.

Now, consider the differences between the two experiences. Notice how well you were able to mentally design the first room and your discrepancies in the second room. As you do, also notice how deep of a relaxation you have entered, and use that to help you relax further. Then, you can begin practicing your self-hypnosis practices.

CHAPTER EIGHT

WHAT IS EMOTIONAL EATING?

Emotional eating is described as the "propensity to consume in response to negative and positive emotions. While the expression of emotional eating frequently describes eating as a way of coping with negative emotions, in addition, it includes ingestion for positive emotions like eating meals when observing an occasion or eating to improve an already very good disposition. In such circumstances, emotions continue forcing the ingestion but not in an adverse manner.

Emotional eating includes ingestion in Response to some emotion, if that's negative or positive. Most often, people consult with emotional eating as"eating to deal with negative emotions" In such scenarios, emotional eating can be thought of as a kind of disordered eating that's defined as"an increase in food consumption in response to negative emotions" and may be thought of a maladaptive strategy. More especially, emotional eating so as to ease negative emotions would be eligible as a kind of emotion-focused coping, which tries to minimize, modulate, and protect against emotional distress.

A study found that emotional eating Occasionally doesn't decrease emotional distress but rather enhances emotional distress by triggering feelings of extreme guilt following an emotional eating session. The ones that consume as a coping plan are at a particularly large risk of creating binge-eating disease, and people with eating disorders are at a greater risk of taking part in emotional eating as a way to cope. In a clinical setting, emotional eating can be evaluated from the Dutch Eating Behavior Questionnaire that includes a scale for controlled, emotional, and external eating. Other studies like the Palatable Eating Motives Scale can ascertain reasons why an individual eats yummy foods when they're not hungry; sub-scales contain eating for benefit augmentation, coping, social, and conformity.

Emotional eating usually happens when one is trying to meet her or his hedonic drive, or the drive to consume palatable food to acquire pleasure from the lack of an energy shortage but can also happen when one is looking for food as a reward, ingestion for societal reasons (for instance, eating in a party), or even ingesting to adapt (which entails eating as friends or family needs the person to). If one is participating in emotional eating, they are typically looking for palatable foods (like sweets) rather than simply food generally. Sometimes, emotional eating may result in something called"mindless eating" through which the person is eating without being mindful of how much they're consuming; this may happen during both negative and positive settings.

Emotional hunger Doesn't arise From the gut, such as a rumbling or growling gut, but will begin when an individual believes about a desire or desires something special to consume. Emotional responses will also be distinct. Giving in to a craving or eating due to stress can lead to feelings of sorrow, shame, or remorse, and such reactions are normally related to emotional appetite. On the flip side, satisfying a physical appetite is providing the body the nutrients or calories it needs to function and isn't associated with negative emotions.

Emotional eating implies that you consume For reasons aside from hunger. You will eat since you are depressed, depressed, stressed, or lonely. Or perhaps you use food as a reward. Food could be soothing and divert you from what is really bothering you.

If You're an emotional eater, then you May not hear your body's natural hunger and fullness signals. You will eat more than you want or desire.

Emotional eating can hinder Making healthful food choices. And it can prevent you from getting to a healthy weight and staying there.

We do not always eat Simply to meet Physical appetite. A lot of us also turn to food to relaxation, stress relief, or to benefit ourselves. And once we do, we are apt to reach for junk foods, candy, and other soothing but foods that are unhealthy. You may reach for a spoonful of ice cream when you are feeling down, order a pizza if you are tired or alone, or swing from the drive-through following a stressful day at work. Emotional eating is using food to make yourself feel better to fulfill emotional needs instead of your gut. Regrettably, emotional eating does not mend emotional problems. In reality, it usually makes you feel much worse. Then not only does the initial emotional issue stay, but you also feel guilty for overeating.

Emotional hunger cannot be filled with meals. Eating might feel good at the moment; however, the feelings which triggered the ingestion continue to be there. And you frequently feel worse than you did earlier due to the unnecessary calories you have just swallowed. You conquer yourself for messing up rather than having additional willpower.

Regardless of the problem, you cease learning healthy ways to manage your emotions, you've got a more difficult and Harder time controlling your weight, and you also truly feel powerless over Both meals and your own feelings. But no matter how powerless you are feeling over food and Your feelings, it's likely to generate a positive shift. You can find out

Healthier ways to manage your emotions, avoid triggers, conquer cravings, And eventually put a halt to emotional eating.

THE DIFFERENCE BETWEEN EMOTIONAL HUNGER
AND PHYSICAL HUNGER

Before you can break loose from the Cycle of emotional eating, first you must understand to differentiate between emotional and physical hunger. This may be trickier than it seems, particularly if you frequently use food to take care of your feelings.

Emotional hunger could be powerful; therefore, It is easy to confuse it for bodily hunger. However, there are clues you can search for to assist you in informing bodily and emotional hunger apart.

Emotional hunger is derived from suddenly. It strikes you in a minute and feels overwhelming and barbarous. Physical hunger, on the other hand, is determined by more slowly. The impulse to eat does not feel too dire or need prompt satisfaction (unless you have not eaten for a lengthy period).

Emotional hunger wants specific Comfort foods. When you are physically hungry, virtually anything seems great --such as healthy things like vegetables. But emotional hunger Requires junk food or sugary snacks, which offer an instantaneous rush. You truly feel as though you want cheesecake or pizza, and nothing else will do.

Emotional hunger frequently leads to mindless eating. Before you know it, you have eaten an entire bag of fries or a whole pint of ice cream without actually paying attention or completely enjoying it. When you are eating in response to physical hunger, you are typically more conscious of everything you are doing.

Emotional hunger is not satisfied as soon as you're complete. You keep wanting more and more, frequently eating till you are uncomfortably stuffed. Physical hunger, on the other hand, does not have to get stuffed. You feel fulfilled when your belly is full.

Emotional hunger is not found in The gut. As opposed to a growling stomach or a pang in your stomach, you feel that your hunger for an urge you can not escape from your mind. You are focused on particular textures, tastes, and smells.

Emotional hunger frequently leads to Sorrow, guilt, or shame. If you eat to satisfy physical hunger, you are not likely to feel guilty or embarrassed as you are just giving your body exactly what it requires. Should you are feeling guilty after you consume, it is probably because you understand deep down that you are not eating for nutritional factors.

Emotional Eating (Comfort ingestion)

Both are phrases that have become common and might have you wondering exactly what they mean and if they apply to you personally. Emotional eating (along with also the more particular 'comfort eating' (meaning to relaxation by eating) is your tendency of using food instead of, or in reaction to, emotional triggers.

Many People Today imagine It Is a Response to negative emotions, and while this may be true, there are various men and women who turn into emotional eating in reaction to positive emotions. Examples include things like going out for foods to celebrate decent information and treating yourself to a dessert once you are feeling joyful. Frequent cases for negative emotions such as the stereotypical ingestion of Pot after being chucked, ordering takeaway after a stressful day at work, and ingesting substantial bags of potato chips when feeling exhausted.

The fact is, we're emotional Eaters occasionally. Most of us react to emotions on events by ingesting - if it's cooking a high-calorie meal to our loved ones when they're encouraged on the job or purchasing an unhealthy lunch following a traumatic assembly.

Food is so entwined with our Emotions the occasional instance of relaxation eater can't be prevented, so people who fall into this trap aren't ordinarily classed as authentic emotional eaters.

The expression refers more to the folks who habitually react to emotional triggers using meals. These people today see good and bad news, negative and positive emotions as causes to consume the feed. These individuals may also go through the relevant emotional reaction but occasionally can use food instead of these emotions.

If you're an emotional eater, it's Probably (although not necessarily true) which you'll be obese and will have tried unsuccessfully to shed weight previously. You might have experienced temporary weight losses however have always recovered the burden in the long term

Food is a safety blanket for many And also to be limited may make us feel exposed and vulnerable, even when we are not entirely conscious of it (that we are not due to the time we've become fair, after a fantastic old binge, we're too numb to feel anything).

Emotional eating Method to consume to meet emotional hunger. You consume food for relaxation, or a means that will assist you to cope in your life. You eat for reasons, apart from nutritional supplements.

Most of us do this. Emotional eating is Part of our civilization. We use food to observe, to take care of upset, to take care of a challenging day on the job and even boredom (actually sit in the front of the TV eating mindlessly?) It's part of our culture. The problem with this is it is not really regarded as a problem in society; however, it's just one.

We invest so much time numbing ourselves; when we don't have a chance to accomplish this, we do not understand how to take care of the emotions that come up in us. Food also has addictive properties inside it, which can influence our mood too, so that can be extremely overwhelming. As soon as we do not reside at the present moment and permit emotions to flow, but rather numb ourselves, we take a good deal of baggage around liberally. Occasionally this may surface in a bout of aggression or another kind. The thing is, even if we do not confront it, do not learn to manage our emotions, then we simply continue to live a lifetime of numbing, bingeing, or urge. You lose out on the capacity of lifestyle, of adopting emotions.

Individuals suffering from this Method of Eating are compelled to eat so that they do not need to confront what's bothering them. They become addicted to the way that they handle life. That is the reason why dieting and calorie restriction does not do the job. And because most diets don't teach you about emotional eating, we never become completely conscious of it and think that it is something wrong with us.

Unless you Learn How to stop emotional Eating and handle your emotions at the current moment, you'll find it impossible to eliminate weight and keep it off. And of course, you'll find it pretty difficult to enjoy life completely if you're always fighting this problem with your weight reduction. If it resonates with you, then you aren't alone, and you're able to defeat it.

In Today's world, There's an extreme Concentrate on what we consume and about the significance of exercise. If a person eats the ideal foods and arranges them in the perfect time, alongside the ideal quantity of exercise, then you are very likely to wind up in the bodily form. But for some, this will operate, and for many others, this won't be adequate.

However, the emotions which drive one To eat such large quantities of food, to eat when a person is not hungry or to consume foods which aren't that healthy, are seldom mentioned or considered. This might be from the mainstream press or in a more private setting.

Perhaps emotions Aren't spoken of From the mainstream media on account of the quantity of money that's created of such high Ingestion, and there are no doubt lots of different theories and thoughts as to why this is. However, in order for this scenario to exist in the first place, the requirement has To exist in the user.

Conscious Eating

If one is really a conscious person or Is fairly aware, then it would not matter what foods that this individual was exposed to or aesthetically pleasing to the eye that they had been. Though this might be snacks or cakes; this may also have any sort of food and meals that you might have a specific craving for.

For a mindful eater means that One has a choice as to if they'll eat or not, rather than eating on impulse or whenever they're emotionally affected. And when one participates in emotional eating, they are typically doing so without becoming aware and conscious of what's happening.

Emotional eating is when we consume in order to curb and escape out of a specific emotion or an emotional encounter, with meals altering the way we feel. And due to how quickly and natural that this procedure often is, it's not likely it will be detected or questioned - and - thus ceased or changed.

This Might Have Been a pattern that One has completed for so long; it is has come to be a custom. And exactly what the food is performing, is permitting one to emotionally modulate themselves.

A Closer Look

First off, emotional eating is Likely something that everyone does from time to time. We're all human after all; we all aren't perfect, and neither are we supposed to be. The purpose here isn't to label emotional eating as right or wrong or bad or good; this is a strategy that is only going to make matters worse and would likely result in more emotional eating.

It's only to have a closer look and To generate awareness around this field. To attract one's focus, what's causing them to behave in certain ways. Finally, emotional eating is not any different than anything else; in this, if it's done to the intense, it's the potential to result in dysfunctional consequences. With this being a place associated with our health, it's definitely an important area to check into.

A Unique Relationship

In Addition to the effect the food Is getting per se, there are institutions that might also be triggered via meals. At the very start of life, one comes to experience meals as nurturing through being breastfed. And

157

when one was not breastfed, then you are very likely to have fond memories of being handed food to cheer them up and particular varieties of meals which were produced by somebody near them.

The Standard of nurturing that you Obtained in those early years will frequently specify how much one is going to rely on meals to help in emotional regulation.

Emotional Legislation

During being given food from the Individuals around us as a youngster, our emotional state has been affected. And when food was not used, then our caregivers could have been there to mimic, Heal, and control our emotions. We'd also have been awarded the emotional nurturing that we had to grow. As a young kid, it's stated that our nervous system isn't developed enough to perform this job, and we want our caregivers to get this done for us.

And as a result of our Caregivers being there during times of emotional distress or perhaps if emotions arise, we'll then start to develop this skill ourselves. The practice is a good deal more complicated than that, but this really is a fundamental comprehension of it.

The Actual World

For a few, the above may be authentic, and These can be people that are familiar with their emotions and that feel emotionally complete. They are going to be able to just sit together to soothe themselves and to channel them to something more effective. Or they'll be comfy enough to discuss their emotions with other people. But for those who have not experienced these early experiences of being emotionally controlled and nurtured, emotions will probably be problematic, overpowering, and even something to be ashamed of.

As one's emotions were permitted to Build up and weren't acknowledged when they had been shaped, they are going to be a great deal more powerful than they'd normally be. And with this, I mean that; since they're being fuelled from the past which hasn't yet been processed, it's inevitable that they'll be more powerful.

When this internal capability Isn't There, food is the perfect alternative. On the side, it will enable one to control their emotions, and on the other hand, it enables one to temporarily possess the emotional nurturing, which you did not have as a kid. The problem with food is it is simply a short-term solution. And nearly all meals that are sought after nowadays are unhealthy. Foods such as chocolate, release endorphins to our brains, as does exercise. This is the joyful chemical and certainly will be welcome if you were to be experiencing 'negative'

159

emotions. Exercise, even if not taken to the extreme, is fitter than consuming plenty of food. Though this is so, it might also turn into another escape and dependence.

Self-evident

The best here is to have the ability to self Heal and to feel comfortable in reaching out to other people when this isn't feasible. This capacity is not likely to be developed during the night, and it'll require patience and dedication. And based on the individual wants and mental disposition, other choices may need to be thought about. So check out your truth and insights.

One thing a Fantastic therapist, healer, Or trainer can do is to enable you to express their own emotions in a secure atmosphere. From here, an individual can start to develop a relationship with their emotions. And begin to obtain the emotional nurturing that they did not get all the years back. Here one will start to view their emotions as opinions and as a tool that has to be heard and recognized; to not be stressed or runoff from.

Awareness is the key to herewith it; an individual can observe they are more than their emotions, and with no, emotions can Appear like there is. The center may also help in emotional regulation.

SIGNS YOU MAY BE EMOTIONALLY EATING

Everybody eats for motives other than Hunger once every so often. But if you discover that you often reach for meals from boredom or for relaxation, you might be eating for emotional reasons.

Frequent signs of emotional eating Are:

- Changing your eating habits once you have additional stress on your life.
- You are eating when you're not hungry or when you're full.
- Eating to prevent coping with a stressful position.
- You are eating to soothe your emotions.

There Are Several Different ways in That we emotionally consume. There is the clear cliché of sitting down with a spoonful of ice cream after a separation and polishing off it; however, there are several other, more subtle ways we consume more because of our own emotions. Essentially, in the event that you ever eat whenever you aren't hungry, there is a strong probability that you're eating because you're subconsciously attempting to take care of some sort of emotion. Boredom is a choice illustration of this: how often do you get snacky once you spend the day zoned out in front of this TV? Our brains crave stimulation, and tv is really a fairly bad stimulator since our bodies aren't involved at all. We bring our own bodies into the mixture by catching some popcorn or chips to bite on-but that packs on the pounds too.

Anxiety and stress are noteworthy Causes of emotional eating too. We frequently give ourselves excuses to cheat our healthful eating fashion once we're at a period of duress. If you end up turning more frequently than mac and cheese once the boss yelled at you daily or into a cookie or brownie as a"cure" for inhabiting a demanding assembly, you are likely letting your emotions dictate your own palate.

CHAPTER NINE

CAUSES OF EMOTIONAL EATING

Whether You're pleased with your body fat or not, it's what it is, Accept your present weight is a direct outcome of your lifestyle habits, namely the quantity and kind of food and beverage you like and your routine exercise habits and activity levels. A whole lot of bad eating habits are due to emotional eating; this is if our ingestion is ordered by how we're feeling, and we work with food to help us feel better. This is also referred to as relaxation eating, and generally entails excessive snacking or binging fatty foods that are fatty.

Emotional eating is a massive problem for a lot of men and women who struggle with their weight and typically highlight a poor men relationship with food. You may just break the custom of emotional eating should you determine what causes one to bite in this fashion; you need to discover the feelings and situations that cause you to lose control of your eating habits. Eating for comfort to cheer up yourself can develop into a vicious circle since you are able to become more miserable as you pile weight, forcing you to flip into food and make things worse (so it goes).

Here are a number of the usual triggers that could let you eat too much on a normal basis:

· Stress.

· Inadequate self-esteem.

· Depression.

· Boredom.

· Loneliness.

· Unhappy with your own body form.

· Marital or relationship problems.

· Financial worries.

· Deficiency of energy and inactivity.

· Greed.

People Rarely meet their emotional needs with a fresh green salad or even excessive quantities of fruit. Emotional eating normally involves consuming copious quantities of crap and convenience foods and candy snacks like chocolate and cake. Let's examine a few strategies that can help you manage your relationship with food and prevent you from binge eating

Stress

Ever see how stress causes you to be hungry? It is not only on your mind. If stress is chronic, as it so often is in our hectic, rapid universe, your body generates elevated levels of the stress hormone, cortisol. Cortisol causes cravings for sweet, salty, and fried foods--foods that provide you a burst of energy and pleasure. The more rampant stress in your lifetime, the more inclined you should turn into food for emotional relief.

Stuffing emotions

Eating is a method to temporarily Silence or"things down" uncomfortable emotions, such as anger, anxiety, despair, anxiety, loneliness, bitterness, and shame. As you're numbing yourself with meals, you can prevent the difficult emotions you would rather not believe.

Boredom or feelings of emptiness

Do you eat just to give Yourself something to do, to alleviate boredom, or as a means to fulfill a void in your life? You truly feel unfulfilled and empty, and meals are a way to occupy your mouth and your own time. At the present time, it fills you up and distracts you from inherent feelings of purposelessness and dissatisfaction with your life.

Childhood customs

Think back to your own youth Memories of meals. Can your parents reward good behavior with ice cream, just take you out for pizza once

166

you have a fantastic report card, or even function you candies if you're feeling unhappy? These customs may often carry over into adulthood. Or your ingestion might be driven by nostalgia--for precious memories of grilling hamburgers at the backyard with your father or drinking and baking snacks with your mother.

Childhood growth

For many people, emotional eating is A learned behavior. Throughout childhood, their parents provide them snacks to help them cope with a challenging day or scenario, or as a reward for something great. As time passes, the kid who reaches a cookie following a bad grade on evaluation might grow to be a grownup who catches a box of biscuits after a demanding day on the job. For instance, like this, the roots of emotional eating are heavy, which may cause breaking the habit incredibly challenging. Sometimes, people may eat so as to adapt; for instance, people could be told"you've got to complete your plate," and also, the person may eat beyond the point where they feel fulfilled.

Social influences

Getting along with other Men and Women To get a meal is a good way to alleviate stress, but it could also lead to overeating. It's easy to overindulge because the food is there or simply because everyone else is eating. You could also overeat in social situations from anxiety. Or maybe your family or circle of friends motivates you to overeat, and it is a lot easier to go together with the group.

Negative impact

Total, high levels of this negative Influence attribute are linked to emotional eating. Negative affectivity is a character trait involving negative emotions and inadequate self-concept. Negative emotions experienced in negative effects contain anger, guilt, and anxiety. It's been discovered that certain adverse impact regulation scales called emotional eating. An inability to pronounce and recognize the emotions made the person feel inadequate at controlling negative impact and thus more inclined to participate in emotional eating as a way for coping with these negative emotions. Further scientific research concerning the relationship between negative affect and ingestion uncover that, after undergoing a stressful event, food intake is associated with decreased feelings of adverse effect (i.e., Feeling awful) for individuals enduring high levels of chronic stress. This relationship between feeling and eating better indicates a self-reinforcing hierarchical pattern involving elevated levels of chronic stress and the consumption of highly palatable foods as a working mechanism. Contrarily, a research conducted by Spoor et al. Discovered that negative affect isn't significantly linked to emotional eating, but both are associated through emotion-focused coping and avoidance-distraction behaviors. Though the scientific consequences differed somewhat, they suggest that adverse influence does play a part in emotional eating. However, it might be accounted for by other factors.

Connected Ailments

Emotional eating as a Way to deal Might be a precursor to developing eating disorders like binge eating or bulimia nervosa. The relationship between emotional eating as well as other ailments is large because of how emotional eating and those ailments share key attributes. More specifically, they're equally associated with emotion-focused coping, maladaptive coping strategies, along with a powerful aversion to negative emotions and stimulation. It's very important to say that the causal management hasn't been established, meaning that although emotional eating is thought to be a precursor to those eating disorders, in addition, it might be the result of those ailments. The latter theory in which emotional eating happens in reaction to some other eating disease is supported by research, which has revealed emotional eating to be common among people already suffering from bulimia nervosa.

Biological And environmental variables

Stress impacts food tastes. Quite a few research -- given, many of these in creatures -- have demonstrated that physical or emotional distress raises the consumption of food high in sugar, fat, or even in the absence of metabolic shortages. Once ingested, fat- and - sugar-filled foods appear to get a feedback effect that combats stress associated reactions and emotions since these foods activate dopamine and opioid releases, which protect from the unwanted effects of stress. These foods actually are"comfort" foods because they appear to counteract stress, but rat studies reveal that occasional access to consumption of those highly palatable foods generates symptoms which resemble opioid withdrawal, implying that high fat and high-sugar foods may get neurologically addictive a couple of examples in the American diet could include: burgers, pizza, French fries, sausages, and salty pastries. The most typical food tastes are in decreasing order from candies energy-dense meals, non-sweet energy-dense food afterward, vegetables, and fruits. This may bring about people's stress-induced craving for all those foods.

The stress reaction is a Highly-individualized response, and individual differences in physiological reactivity can also result in the evolution of emotional eating customs. Girls are somewhat more prone than men to resort to eating as a coping mechanism for stress, as are overweight people and people with histories of dietary restraint. In 1 study, girls were subjected to an hour-long social stressor activity or even a neutral control condition. The women were subjected to every condition on various days. Following the actions, the girls were invited to a buffet with healthy and unhealthy snacks. People who had elevated chronic stress rates and very low cortisol reactivity to the intense stress task consumed more calories out of chocolate cake compared to women with reduced chronic stress levels following both control and stress conditions. High cortisol levels, together with higher sugar levels, might be accountable for stress-induced ingestion, as research suggests high cortisol reactivity is associated with hyperphagia, an abnormally enhanced desire for meals, during stress. Additionally, because glucocorticoids trigger hunger and especially increase one's desire for high fat and high-sugar foods, those whose adrenal glands normally exude larger amounts of glucocorticoids in reaction to a stressor are somewhat more likely toward hyperphagia. Furthermore, people whose bodies need more time to clean the blood of excess glucocorticoids are likewise predisposed.

These biological variables can Interact with environmental components to additionally activate hyperphagia. Regular intermittent stressors activate recurrent, irregular releases of glucocorticoids in periods too short to permit a comprehensive return to baseline levels, resulting in elevated and sustained levels of desire. Thus, those whose lifestyles or professions involve regular intermittent stressors over extended intervals thus have higher biological incentive to come up with routines of emotional eating, which places them at risk for long-term undesirable health effects like weight reduction or cardiovascular disease.

The rationale is supporting stressful Ingestion: (1) emotional charge of food selection, (2) emotional reduction of food consumption, (3) impairment of cognitive consumption controllers, (4) ingestion to modulate emotions, and (5) emotion-congruent modulation of ingestion. These split into subgroups of Dealing, reward improvement, societal, and conformity purpose. Therefore, providing a person with is a stronger comprehension of personal emotional eating.

Favorable Effect

Both negative and positive emotions Were assessed When folks were undergoing favorable emotional states or scenarios, the underweight group reporting ingesting over the other two groups. For example, the normal character of underweight people is to consume less and through times of stress to consume much less. But when positive emotional states or situations appear, folks are more inclined to indulge themselves with food.

Like many emotional symptoms, Emotional eating is regarded as the end result of lots of variables as opposed to just one cause. Some study is consistent with women and girls being at greater risk for eating disorders, demonstrating they're at greater risk for emotional eating. However, other research suggests that in certain inhabitants, men are more inclined to consume in response to sense anger or depression, and girls were more likely to consume too in response to neglecting a diet program.

It Is Believed That the increase in The hormone cortisol that's only one of the human body's reactions to stress is like the drug prednisone in its own consequences. Especially, both often activate the body's stress (fight or flight) response, such as increased breathing and heart rate, blood flow to nerves, and visual acuity. Part of the stress response frequently includes increased desire to provide the body with the fuel it must fight or flee, leading to cravings for so-called comfort meals. Individuals who've been exposed to chronic instead of momentary stress (such as occupation, college, or family stress, vulnerability to abuse, or crime) are at risk for getting disproportionately substantial levels of cortisol in their own bodies, contributing to growing chronic emotional-eating patterns.

Psychologically, people who are inclined to Join meals with comfort, power, positive emotions, or for any other motives than supplying fuel for your own body may be more prone to emotional eating. They might consume to fill an emotional void, when physically complete, and take part in mindless eating. Some individuals whose emotions lead them to consume might have been increased to link food with feelings rather than sustenance, especially when food has been scarce or frequently utilized a reward or punishment, or as a substitute for emotional intimacy.

Emotional eating is the trend of Its victims to react to stressful, hard feelings by eating, even if not experiencing bodily hunger. Emotional eating or emotional hunger is frequently craving for high-calorie or calcium-rich foods that have minimal nutritional value. The foods which emotional eaters crave are usually known as comfort foods, such as ice cream, biscuits, chocolate, fries, French fries, and pizza. Approximately 40 percent of individuals are inclined to consume more when stressed, while roughly 40 percent consume less, and 20% experience no change in the total amount of food they consume when subjected to stress. Thus, stress could be correlated with weight gain and weight reduction.

While emotional eating could be a Symptom of what mental health professionals predict intermittent depression, many individuals who

174

don't have clinical depression or another mental health problem Participate in this behavior in reaction to momentary feelings of chronic stress. This behavior is highly frequent and is important since it can hinder Keeping a nutritious diet program and contribute to obesity.

MATCHED TREATMENT FOR OBESITY

The role of emotion regulation in Youth obesity and its consequences for treatment and prevention of obesity has just been evaluated by Aparicio et al. It was reasoned that instructing emotion regulation abilities might be an effective strategy for treating obesity in kids. For obese adults, in which a new systematic review found no evidence for an overall shortage in emotion processing, so I'd instead propose a coordinated treatment strategy, an approach in which the treatment is matched to the particular qualities of the person.

One Reason that many weight Reduction programs don't lead to permanent weight loss for the majority of people could possibly be a lack of match between individuals and treatment. Overeating has different motives for various persons. As previously indicated, one individual may overeat following a period of reducing as soon as the cognitive function to consume less than desirable is left-handed (as an instance, because of stress or negative emotions) (controlled eating), another might have the propensity to overeat when viewing or smelling yummy food (outside eating), though a third eats a lot when experiencing negative emotions (emotional eating). Every kind of eating behavior has its etiology, and each type requires its own kind of therapy.

When remedies are associated with a single kind of eating behavior, it may be anticipated that the acquired weight reduction is longer lasting.

Feeling sad is normally Related to loss of appetite and subsequent weight loss. There is, however, a subtype of melancholy that's distinguished by the a-typical characteristics of greater appetite and subsequent weight gain. Emotional eating was regarded as a marker of the melancholy subtype since it shares this subtype that the a-typical characteristic of greater desire in reaction to the distress, for example, feelings of melancholy. Depression was found to be related to subsequent weight gain and obesity, and the issue arose whether emotional eating is that the missing link between depression and obesity or weight reduction.

In various cross-sectional studies, Emotional eating was really found to work as a mediator between obesity and depression. In further potential research on the parents of the teens from the Van Strien et al., Emotional eating acted as a mediator between maternal depression and weight reduction after five decades. Depressive symptoms were associated with high emotional eating; emotional eating also forecasts higher gains in BMI independently of melancholy. No causal sequence between melancholy, emotional eating, and weight reduction was found from the dads, maybe because both a-typical melancholy and emotional eating are somewhat less widespread in men.

It Needs to Be noted that many studies That discovered mediation consequences for emotional eating have been completed in countries which can be found in northern latitudes, in which a-typical depression is much more prevalent. Exceptions would be the analysis in females that were conducted following stressful life events. The analysis by Clum et al. Was conducted one year after the hurricane Katrina, at the Greater New Orleans region (30°00' northern latitude), whereas enormous unemployment following the 2008 banking crisis was an ego-threatening stressor at Spain (26°00'--44°00' northern latitude).

Depression and obesity are equally Frequent conditions with acute medical implications and high prices for society. The finding that emotional eating is a mediator between the two indicates a Reduction of emotional eating might be an important remedy goal for both Obesity and obesity (a-typical) depression.

CHAPTER TEN

CREATING A MIND RELATIONSHIP WITH FOOD

Occasionally we can feel out of control In regards to eating. We feel pressured to go on fad diets, or even work out extra hard in the gym. Even though it's extremely important to exercise and watch what you eat, it is equally critical that you build a great relationship with meals. This will determine the level of your life--both at the office and at home.

A healthy relationship with Food requires effort, but working towards feeling more at peace with ingesting is worth it. Here is what you could do so as to avoid unhealthy habits from ongoing.

Be flexible.

"Our minds like to Consider in Vintage stipulations," states Susan Albers, author of 50 Ways to Soothe Yourself Without Food. "Right vs. Wrong. Fat versus lean. Perfect versus destroyed." If you slide on a diet, do not let yourself mentally spiral. While this occurs, you'll end up overthinking, overeating, as well as thinking all kinds of negative thoughts and decisions on your own. Think about being strict with what you consume. Albers advises to occasionally split your diet even only a little bit--as being elastic can alleviate a lot of the stress you might feel.

And, as she notes, "When you notice that nothing awful happens, flexibility will not be intimidating. Perhaps you will like it."

Be attentive.

When would you overeat or eat food that is bad? Can a particular event or feeling activate your unhealthy eating habits? Occasionally, by way of instance, we crave particular foods if we are tired at work, and we visit the vending machine to solve the craving. Be mindful of your hunger triggers and cues when you eventually notice and focus on some unhealthy eating patterns, you're able to effectively purge them.

Be relaxed.

Maintain a comfortable approach when it Comes to meals --not only does that aid with weight care. However, in addition, it enables you to make progress with your health all around. Relaxed eating makes it possible to eat till you are nutritionally pleased and helps facilitate emotional eating, therefore look at slowing down through all foods -- lunch at your own desk. Inspect different textures, tastes, and elements of your meals, and overall--love.

1. Stop punishing yourself for everything you ate.

It is not serving you personally or your physique! In reality, your entire body reacts to the negative jumble, which generates undesirable stress in the body! Stress is the number one health killer.

2. Practice mindful eating: Really look at it. Taste it. Smell it. Use your perceptions! Enjoy what's on the plate. This way, your brain will indicate"satiety," and you will be less inclined to overeat.

3. Have gratitude for your meals!

Hate to seem like another Airy-fairy wellness preacher, yet this term gratitude may change your own life. Stop and consider how this food obtained to a plate and just how blessed you are to get access to it. It's a present: intending to nourish your body with this much goodness. Your heart hormones, brain, and tissues require the nutrients to work for you.

4. Relish your food.

Don't cloud your consumption experience With negative ideas such as, "I shouldn't be eating this" or even"I am a loser that I couldn't control what I ate." Your own body will manifest those ideas into physiological stress! Hi, cortisol!!! Goodbye to optimum digestion! Please, be in peace with your plate.

5. Stop the vicious cycle of all-or-nothing.

Should you make a poor food choice, attempt To let it all go! Your entire body reacts to everything you do the majority of the time, maybe not occasionally! The majority of us think, "well, I ate which donut so that I may as well keep moving" this turns into what's called a 'food binge.' Now see that is where the problem appears. That your body doesn't mind the donut so much, but it is going to begin to mind all of the rest, which you simply fill it with. It just does not understand exactly what to do with it all at one time.

6. Practice positive affirmations.

Affirmations are a powerful instrument to Reverse negative ideas and reprogram your beliefs, actions, and behavior. They could alter how you find the planet and most certainly helped me improve my relationship with my physique. Someones I enjoy

This plate of food is really great for me.

My body knows how to utilize this food.

My cells are all going to be not nourished with this much goodness.

7. Give up the need to eat and be absolute.

Nobody eats perfectly. Perfect does not exist! Try out a release that wants and remember you're good enough.

8. Quit comparing!

Your body and nutrient demands are Different from those of your friends, your sister, and your mom! Their relationship with food doesn't have anything to do with you. They have an entirely different and elaborate body mechanics. You can't take their relationship with their meals, my love!

9. Do not be difficult with meals.

It is important not to allow your Healthful lifestyle to get in the way of your life. (I try really hard for this one!) If you are outside with family and friends, do not be concerned about the food choices. It is not important. Just select the finest available for you. Otherwise, you may just complicate your relationship with meals.

10. If you are reaching for food when you are not hungry afterward, something emotional is happening.

Why are you reaching that Relaxation? Just spot it. If you understand you are not really hungry, I urge you to do something else that is pleasurable!

Go for a walk, massage, spa, Paint your nails, be romantic with your spouse, watch your favorite TV series with a cuppa, have a talk for your bestie or move stalk some wellness sites and write off your fave recipes! Anything!

11. Remember: that is it. One life. One body! Treasure it. Look after it. Feed It since it requires the nutrients. Your own body is determined by you for your love And care so as to operate and proceed with its biochemical activities! It Works so damn difficult!! I believe that it deserves our admiration. I see my body since my infant.

STRATEGIES FOR MAINTAINING A HEALTHY RELATIONSHIP WITH FOOD

Some People Today eat emotionally to Insulate themselves from their feelings, and this can be detrimental to keeping a healthy lifestyle and shedding unwanted pounds. Folks occasionally eat since they're stressed, unhappy, tired, or lonely. Individuals who consume emotionally normally reach for unhealthy"comfort food," like ice cream or french fries, which may result in obesity, diabetes, and cardiovascular disease.

Then there are people hooked on Food, frequently unhealthy items like chocolate, pizza, and snack chips. Some individuals [are compulsive] about meals, the exact same way some are all about gambling or alcohol. You will find parallels.

However, a food compulsion Differs From different ailments. You will find rehabilitation centers and 12-step applications for alcoholism and gambling, but everybody should eat. Experts offer these tips to achieve and maintain Wholesome eating habits and prevent having food turned into an adversary or even a too-close buddy:

1. Do not tag Certain foods as Bad or good. A cup of broccoli doesn't have angelic wellbeing powers, along with a piece of pizza that isn't demonic. Some foods are better for well-being than many others, but no food is evil or benevolent.

Ascribing moral attributes to foods Provides them unwarranted power. If you deviate in the daily diet and eat crap food, which does not make you a terrible man, and you should not beat yourself upon it, which might result in a feeling of overeating and defeat. Keep a wholesome outlook on meals by recognizing that certain foods are better for the health than others, but no single kind of food or part will guarantee or mess up your well-being.

2. Reduce your chances of making poor decisions. If you are on a low-sugar diet, then it is OK to have a few special cake events, including your birthday or any time you are out having dinner with friends.

Restrict your cake intake to unusual events. Do not keep the cake at the house -- maintaining particular foods near can encourage a tradition of eating them. In case you've got a birthday party at your house and have left cake, give it away or toss it out.

3. Do not get overly restrictive. Instead Of cutting out certain foods altogether, let yourself one day per week to have a small part of your favorite treat. By way of instance, rather than attempting to banish donuts permanently from your daily diet, allow yourself every seven days.

Attempting to never consume a certain Food for the remainder of your life may be unrealistic. As opposed to feeling like a failure if you've got that food -- that may lead to more binge eating -- integrate that meals in your eating regimen.

4. Keep a food diary. Write down. Not just what you consume, but what you are feeling at the moment. Assessing your eating habits and emotions can allow you to find patterns.

You may see that you backslide From the eating habits by ingesting carbs, biscuits, or other junk foods if you feel depressed, depressed, or anxious. Instead of reaching for the unhealthy snack, consider doing some deep breathing or moving for a brief walk. Should you try that rather, plenty of instances that the craving will pass.

5. Try cooking. Rather than heating Your meal up in a microwave or selecting your food from a deli or even fast-food combined on the way

home, take some opportunity to cook. Create a list of yummy and healthful ingredients that you want in the shop and revel in selecting them.

You should not become a master chef. Cooking Can be really straightforward. "You can purchase a steamer and toss your veggies inside. You will find a great indoor grill. It makes you love your meals more when you went into the shop to select your ingredients and prepared them. It gets you mindful."

6. Set yourself up for success at The supermarket. The struggle to keep a balanced relationship with food starts at the grocery store, in which what you purchase will greatly determine if you'll maintain wholesome eating habits.

You can strategize your purchasing Excursions to steer clear of aisles packed with unhealthy products. "The last thing that you wish to do is load up your cart with biscuits, snack chips, chips, and other Processed or processed foods which are high in carbs. "They're the Single main reason we're facing an obesity epidemic." Attempt Shopping in the outside of the supermarket, where fresh produce, lean meats, Dairy products, and baked things are sold and prevent within aisles, where bite Things and sugary desserts are often marketed, Russo says. When

188

You're in the Bakery section, select up whole bread and steer clear of the cakes, muffins, and Biscuits.

CHAPTER ELEVEN

MINDFULNESS EXERCISE TECHNIQUES AND ACTIVITIES

To be clear, mindful eating isn't a diet plan. No radical clogs, no removing specific foods, no emptying out your cabinets, no fads, and no quick fixes. Mindful eating may be utilized as a means to help direct more mindful food decisions which may result in weight reduction, even though it's well worth noting that any moment we choose foods based on a specific outcome, we're not eating mindfully -- we're eating with a way to an end, which can be possibly self-defeating.

Mindful eating only invites us to Be present while eating or cooking, permitting us to really savor our meals with no judgment, guilt, anxiety, or internal commentary. This method is all about spending time focused on your weight along with the storylines on your weight. In adopting mindful eating, individuals learn to naturally discover the weight that is ideal for them.

Traditional diet culture causes Much of our stress about eating, bringing a pile of stress, strength, and false expectations. Consequently, a lot of people tend to see food as a reward or punishment. It's the reason why we believe we"deserve" a specific snack or bite or spoonful of something and respect it as"a cure" like we had been a well-behaved puppy or kid. People obsessed with being thin may undereat and suppress feelings of hunger, whereas individuals who overeat may dismiss feelings of fullness.

Moreover, when Folks internalize Ideas constructed around dieting-- buying into the advertising that indicates the losing weight is as simple as 1-2-3--the stresses and emotions are improved. Mindful eating attempts to reverse this thinking, encouraging us to forego the conventional all-or-nothing mindset, and rather eat based on our normal body weight, not the human body weight prescribed by magazine graphics and media-fueled stress. There's not any approach or calorie-counting involved. We're just attempting to become aware.

When we're more conscious, the mind is Calmer; if your mind is calmer, we are less likely to become agitated or stressed or to consume in an emotional manner. In addition, we have improved clarity, so we are better able to determine that our routines of eating, which clarity frees us to make better decisions. After we're calmer and better, we feel much more content about how we consume. After we're calmer, better, and articles, we are more compassionate toward ourselves, and thus, on these days we slide or consume emotionally, we're less self-judgmental.

Bringing mindfulness into the dining table Signifies a kinder, gentler way of eating. The focus is not automatically on Altering the food that we eat (although it could be); it is on altering our thinking around food.

Mindfulness Interventions, Techniques, And Worksheets For Adults

There Are Lots of ways to Participate in Mindfulness on a single level, such as modalities, techniques, and unique exercises.

If the Concept of engaging in Group mindfulness exercises is anxiety-provoking or stressful on your own or your customers, then diving into mindfulness exercise alone could be the very best method to move.

Listed below are six exercises that can help to construct mindfulness in various ways.

1. It's a Perfect worksheet for many Who struggle to reveal themselves empathy, even though they could be fast to extend compassion to other people. It's also a wonderful way to practice mindfulness by bringing consciousness to emotions and remaining at the moment together. Begin with taking a little time to stop actions and thoughts, using a concentrated sense that being mindful will help;

Next, the worksheet teaches you to maneuver a hand in your chest, give yourself a hug, or make physical contact with your self in another manner, and take some deep breaths;

Following this really is an important step in recognizing suffering. This measure is a place to practice mindfulness and promotes mindfulness, consequently. The aim isn't to become overwhelmed with the pain or emotion, but instead to admit it as genuine and hurtful when offering yourself permission to feel it.

The final step Might Be the maximum Difficult, but it's extremely important. It entails vocalizing three announcements:

"That is enduring" (or something comparable);

"Suffering is a part of being human" (admit that all people suffer and battle);

A term that you feel provides empathy, like"May I love and accept myself as I'm."

2. The Observer Meditation appears at why

Adopting an Observer standpoint can Help us place some space between who we are and problematic domain names in life, which we are overidentifying with.

To start the practice, follow these Measures:

Have a comfortable seated posture and listen to this script.

Permit yourself to settle into your own body and mind.

Attempt to give up ideas and clean the mind of its customary considerations.

Focus your attention initially to the area you are sitting in. Picture yourself on the outside as you sit exactly as an outsider could. Then shift your focus inwards to your skin. Attempt to feel that your skin as you're sitting at the seat.

Attempt to picture the shape your skin is creating as you sit directly in touch with the seat, shifting your consciousness toward any bodily sensations you're having. As you are feeling everyone, acknowledge its presence before allowing your awareness to let go of it and proceed naturally.

Recognize them and make the distance for them. Then bring your focus back to your own celebrating self--your own feelings and ideas are there; however, you're different from them, discovering them. Here is actually the"Observer that you."

This exercise could be continued for As long as wanted, and there are numerous phrases you're able to work through that can allow you to practice having an observer of yourself. It's not a simple exercise initially since we're often habitually inclined to respond to and over-identify together with our feelings.

If You're having trouble stepping Outside your mind and body, consider practicing the Self-Compassion Pause, to begin with, to make the adventure more comfortable. The objective of bettering the Observing Self would be to input another mode, which lets you step back from your own experiences. Simultaneously, however, you're linking with a stronger continuous self that's untouched by lively emotions.

3. This exercise is known as "five Sensations," and provides tips on practicing mindfulness fast in virtually any circumstance. All that's required is to detect something you're experiencing each of those five senses.

Follow this arrangement

Look around you and also deliver your Focus on five things which you are able to see. Pick something which you don't typically notice, like a shadow or a little crack in the cement.

Bring awareness of four things that You're presently feeling, such as the texture of your trousers, the feeling of the wind in the skin, or the

196

smooth face of a desk you're resting your hands on—three things which you hear from the background.

Bring your consciousness of smells that You normally filter out, if they are pleasant or disagreeable. Maybe the breeze is taking out a whiff of pine trees in case you are outdoors, or the odor of a quick food restaurant throughout the street.

Notice something you may taste.
Concentrate on one thing Which You Can Taste at this time, now.

This is a Fast and relatively Simple Exercise to make you a mindful state immediately. If you just have a moment or 2, or do not have the time or resources to try out a body scan or complete a worksheet, the five senses exercise can assist you or your customers deliver consciousness of the present instant in a brief quantity of time.

4. You can locate another Fantastic exercise In this practice; you will find just three steps:

Measure 1: step from"auto-pilot."
Attempt to pause and choose a comfy but dignified posture. Notice the ideas that appear and admit your emotions, but let's pass.

Measure 2: bring consciousness into the Breathing for six breaths or even a moment.

The objective is to concentrate attention on something: the breath. Know about the motion of your entire body with every breath, of the way your chest rises and drops, how your stomach pushes out and in, and the way your lungs expand and contract.

Measure 3: expand consciousness outward, First into the body to the surroundings.

Permit the consciousness to extend out to your physique. Notice the sensations you're having, such as tightness, aches, or possibly a lightness on your shoulders or face. Keep in mind that your own body as a whole, as a comprehensive vessel for your internal self;

If you want, you may then expand your consciousness even further into the surroundings around you. Bring your focus to what's facing you. Be present in this instant, on your consciousness of your environment.

When You're ready to complete the

5. Strategy

One core process that could be This consciousness creates space for a decision involving runners, and activity which may help develop working skills and positive behavioral modification.

At step one of the intervention, the facilitator assists the client to envision a situation in which they're walking down a familiar street when they appear and see someone they know on the opposite side of the road. The tide, but another person does not respond and proceeds to walk past.

1. As you're imagining, did you really Notice some of your ideas?

2. As you're imagining, how did you observe any one of your emotions?

At the next and last thing, the facilitator asks the customer to reflect on the collection of emotions and ideas that came up, the way this impacts their behavior, whether the practice was useful, and also for any last comments.

6. Contrary to meditations or even a body scan, This exercise is quick to execute and helpful in receiving a mindfulness practice began.

With meditations along with the entire body scan, Ideas frequently pop up, and maintaining a quiet and very clear mind can be challenging. This last practice of 3-Minute Breathing Space may be the ideal technique for people who have busy lifestyles and minds.

The next minute is spent keeping awareness of the breath.

The final minute is used to get a growth of focus outward in the breath, feeling the methods by which your breathing impacts the remainder of the human body.

Maintaining a calm mind could be quite Challenging, and ideas will frequently pop up. The idea isn't to block them but instead to allow them to come in your mind and then vanish again. Attempt to simply observe them.

Each of the exercises Mentioned Previously May be utilized for the sake of your self, individual customers, and even in class settings. They're beneficial to all customer groups, but some are going to be more satisfied than others; therefore, a procedure of open-minded trial and error may frequently be necessary.

The most Significant Part mindfulness Is to realize it is a practice of the mind, and such as every exercise will take a while to find the positive aspects.

Becoming aware of our ideas and Emotions is one thing, but being conscious of what is occurring in our stomachs attracts a whole additional layer to our consciousness.

When we've burnt All of the food in The problem, many scientists agree, is the fact that it requires a good 20 minutes prior to that message is obtained. Therefore, a lot of our overeating occurs throughout that 20-minute window.

Understanding exactly what your body needs

This means not simply being present but also inquisitive and curious, having a willingness to research how and why we feel and think how we do -- with no ruling. This is no longer apropos than when it has to do with our eating habits.
Consider the questions most People do not inquire: How hungry am I really? Can I scarf down my meals or appreciating it? Can I deny myself food that I enjoy because I think that it's"poor"?

Individuals who implemented mindful Eating in their lives ate smaller parts, which can be great for those attempting to eliminate weight, follow a fitness regime, or keep up a nutritional balance (although this does not imply mindful eating requires small parts -- as always, eat anything dimensions meal is ideal for your body).

Bring into the supermarket along with the kitchen. It helps us understand not to make decisions that are mechanically influenced by outside ideas, emotions, or instincts but rather by our very own inner understanding of exactly what our bodies want.

Untrained, it is sometimes vulnerable to both emotion and dependence. We meditate to train your mind -- to get the room to make better decisions in the interests of our general wellbeing, not our own body shape or weight. And also, the starting point for this change in perspective is just one simple question: What is your relationship to food?

Why we eat how we consume
Different in precisely the identical way, everybody's bodies are different. There's nobody perfect way to consume in precisely the exact same manner that there's nobody ideal body.

A number of people gorge; a number of us graze. Some bite; some relaxation consumes. Some are health club bunnies obsessing about piling on the pounds while some others are diet junkies, obsessing about shedding the pounds.

Bringing consciousness to the table
We all have our own perspectives and Patterns of behavior around meals, whether this can be due to genetics, conditions, or family conditioning.

Us be conscious of our very own decision-making. It is almost like we had been slowing down a listing to determine that our process phase by stage: the clues, the emotions which kick, and the whole sensory effect of eating. Just if we cease to observe this series of events, can we begin to modify our behavior or thinking about meals?

With this particular observational awareness, We are more inclined to observe how reactive or spontaneous we're sometimes. This really is the ability mindfulness affords, meaning we could consider our food choices ahead of time. In bringing additional preparation to our supermarket, restaurant, or kitchen, we're somewhat less inclined to feel some shame or guilt about our balanced options.

Food is only food. In detecting the mind in this manner, we could free ourselves out of emotions that fuel our customs. We do not need to consume our feelings, and on the events that we do understand that we do not need to beat ourselves up to doing this.

Imagine what it'd be like to no longer be directed by our internal conversation around meals. Imagine instead using a more As We measure away from all of the unhealthy thinking about meals we cultivate a Sustainable and balanced approach to how we consume and how we look. Basically, we get to ourselves.

Practicing Mindful Eating

Eating as mindfully as We All Perform on Retreat or within a mindfulness class isn't realistic for a lot of us, particularly with families, occupations, and also the myriad distractions around us. This isn't to mention our friends, family, and coworkers may not have the patience to consume us as we take five minutes with every snack. Have some self-compassion, also think about formal mindful ingestion on holiday and exceptional events, in addition to casual mindful eating in your ordinary life.

1) Allow your body to catch up to your brain

Eating quickly past complete and Dismissing your body's signs vs. Slowing eating and down and quitting when your system says it's complete.

Slowing down is among the best ways. We could get our mind and body to convey what we really want for nourishment. The body sends its satiation sign about 20 minutes following the brain, and that's the reason why we often automatically overeat. However, if we slow down, then you may give your body an opportunity to catch up to a brain and listen to the signs to consume the ideal quantity. Easy approaches to slow down may just include following a lot of your grandma's ways, such as sitting down to eat chewing every bite 25 days (or longer), placing down your fork between bites, and also those in previous ways which are perhaps not as useless as they appeared. Here are a few ways you can slow down eating and listen deeply to your body's signs

2) Know that your body's Individual hunger signs
Are you reacting to an emotional Desire or reacting to your body's requirements?
Frequently we listen to our minds; however, like most mindfulness clinics, we may detect more wisdom by tuning to our own bodies. Instead of simply eating when we undergo emotional signs, which might differ for each of us, be they stress, depression, frustration, depression,

or perhaps merely boredom, we could listen to our own bodies. Is your stomach growling, energy low, or feeling a bit lightheaded? Too frequently, we consume when our mind tells us rather than our bodies. True mindful eating is really listening deeply to our own body's signals for hunger. Ask yourself: Which are the body's hunger signals, and also what exactly are your emotional hunger triggers?

3) Develop Wholesome eating surroundings
Eating independently and randomly vs. Eating With others in set times and areas.

Another way we eat mindlessly Is by drifting around searching through cupboards, eating at arbitrary times and areas, as opposed to simply thinking ill about our snacks and meals. This frees us down for a single thing but prevents us from growing healthful environmental cues regarding what and how much to consume and wires our brains for fresh cues for eating, which not necessarily perfect. (would you really need to produce a custom to consume every single time you get in the vehicle or other scenarios?) Sure, all of us bite from time to time, but it can enhance your mind and body's wellbeing, and of course, greatly helping your mood and sleep program to consume at constant times and areas. Yes, that means sitting down (in a desk!), placing food onto a plate or bowl, not eating it from the container, and using utensils, not our palms. Additionally, it helps to eat with other people, not just are you currently discussing and receiving some healthy relationship, but additionally, you slow down and may take pleasure in the food and dialogue longer, and we take our cues from our supper spouse, not over or undereating from emotion.

When we place away from our food in Cabinets and the refrigerator, we are more inclined to eat healthful amounts of healthful meals, so consider what is about, where it is, and if it is insight. If we restrict eating to kitchen and dining space, we're less inclined to consume mindlessly or consume while multitasking. When food is about, we consume it. And meals, maybe not necessarily the safest, is frequently around in the holidays.

There Are Lots of reasons that the Raisin is eating it's such a powerful workout; however, one is when we slow down and consume healthful foods such as raisins, we frequently enjoy them over the story we tell ourselves about healthful foods.

You do not need to plan your own meals Down to every snack, and its essential to be flexible, particularly on particular occasions, but only know of the simple fact that you may be altering your eating habits at various times of the year or for various events. When you do plan ahead, you're even more inclined to consume the amount that your body requires in that instant than undereating and indulging after, or overeating and regretting it afterward.

Traditional advice is to not store When hungry; however, the center course applies here too. A psychological impact called"moral licensing" has proven that shoppers who purchase kale are more inclined to then head into the alcohol or ice cream department compared to people who don't. We seem to believe that our karma will balance out and we could"invest" it on crap food, or other less than perfect behaviors.

4) Know your motives

Eating meals Which Are emotionally Reassuring Calorie eating foods which are nutritionally healthful.

This is just another tricky balance, and We could discover nourishing foods that are additionally satisfying and reassuring. But return to this very first mindful raisin. Did that look attractive before you attempted? There are numerous reasons that the raisin is eating it's such a powerful workout; however, one is when we slow down and consume healthful foods such as raisins, we frequently enjoy them over the story we tell ourselves about healthful foods. As we exercise eating a healthier and also larger variety of food, we're less likely to binge on the comfort foods, and much more likely to enjoy healthful foods, finally discovering many foods mentally and aesthetically pleasing compared to only a couple.

5) Join more deeply with your own food

Contemplating where food comes out of Vs. Thinking of food as a result of the product.

Unless you're a hunter-gatherer or Sustenance farmer, we've got each become more disconnected from our food in the past couple of decades. A lot of folks don't even contemplate in which a meal comes from outside the supermarket packing. This is a reduction because eating provides an unbelievable chance to connect people more deeply to the organic world, the components, and to every other.

When we pause to Take into Account All the People involved with the meal which has arrived on your own plate, by the loved ones (and yourself) who prepared it, to people who transported the shelves, to people who planted and picked the raw components, to people who encouraged them, it's really hard to not feel equally thankful and interconnected. Be more mindful of the water, dirt, and other components that were a part of its own creation as you sit down to eat anything you're eating. It is possible to reflect on the cultural customs that attracted you this food, the recipes liberally shared by friends, or brought in a distant location and time for given down in the family.

Since you consider everything which went To the meal, it will become simple to experience and express gratitude to each the men and women who gave their time and effort, the portions of this world that led their talk, our pals or ancestors that shared recipes as well as the beings who might have contributed their lives into part of producing this meal. With only a bit more mindfulness similar to this, we might start to make wiser decisions about sustainability and wellness in our meals, not only for us but for the entire planet.

6) Attend to a plate

Distracted eating vs. Just Ingesting

Multitasking and ingestion is a recipe For being unable to listen deeply to our body's needs and wants. We have all had the experience of going to the movies using our luggage filled with popcorn, and prior to the coming attractions are all over, we're inquiring who ate all our popcorn. If we are diverted, it becomes more difficult to hear our body's signs regarding food and other demands. Together with your next meal, then attempt single-tasking and only eating, without the distractions of screens besides enjoying the organization you're sharing a meal and talk with.

So while proper mindful eating Practices may be exactly what we think of if we return on a mindfulness program or escape we appreciated, the truth is that people do live and consume, in the actual world, that's a hectic location. But we could take the insights obtained from our proper clinic - slowing down, listening to our own bodies, doing something at one time, making even tiny rituals, and believing all of that went right into our meal to a regular basis and deliver more casual mindfulness to our everyday foods.

7. Eat A Plant-Based Diet

Researchers at the University of Chicago estimates the normal Americans could reduce global warming by becoming vegetarian. It's definitely more helpful than purchasing a Camry or even Prius.

When eating beef products, especially red meat, there's a larger prospect of colon cancer and cardiovascular disease. Switch red milk and meat to eggs and poultry one day per week as a start tool. This is very good for both you and our surroundings.

8. Do Not Skip Meals

Cutting meals makes it tougher to make mindful choices. When hunger pangs strike, you're vulnerable to catch whatever is nearest to your own hand. This may indicate quitting in a fast-food restaurant or purchasing something sterile from a vending machine.

Plan regular foods to help provide a Constant eating rhythm into your system. Don't eat quickly, but consume slowly! This permits the entire body to process all that's moving within you.

9. Chew Thoroughly

Chew each bite until it's liquified. This may be around 20 to 40 times, but it's well worth it. Chewing helps the palate and tongue taste the food better and lowers the potential for choking.

10. Avoid Overeating

There's a Massive difference between Eating adequate and eating as if you can not include the contents of the food you ate. Mindful eaters clinic the prior, so they don't overtax their own bodies.

11. Eat Slowly

Eat slowly so That You understand when you can Stop until you consume a lot of. You'll be amazed to discover in Oriental medicine; one would be to eat till he or she's just 80% complete so as to keep the digestive system working effectively.

12. Concentrate on the Meal

Opting to Concentrate on the food or Meal permits you to genuinely appreciate the eating experience.

13. Drink Water Before Eating

If you drink a glass of water, until you eat, you consume less water and do not wear as many calories. Besides, you stay far out of dried, and your entire body becomes sufficient hydration to keep you awake and filled with energy.

14. Engage All Six Senses

As you eat and serve your meals, Observe the noises, colors, scents, and textures included in your meals. Don't just depend on the taste. When you set your first bite in your mouth, behave like this was the very first time you tasted the specific food.

15. Honor The Food

Begin the meal with five Contemplations or whichever conventional prayer or kind of gratitude you opt to prefer. The five contemplations:

- This Food is the gift of the entire world: the earth, the skies, many living beings, and even hard, adoring work.

213

- May We consume with mindfulness and mindfulness in order to be worthy to receive it.

- May We understand and alter our unwholesome mental tendencies, particularly our greed, and also learn how to eat with moderation.

- May We maintain our empathy living by eating in this way that we decrease the anguish of living beings, conserve our planet, and undo the process of global warming.

- We Take this food so that we can nurture our sisterhood and brotherhood, fortify our neighborhood, and nourish our ideal of serving all living beings.

16. Rate Your Hunger

Know-how hungry you're. Afterward, speed yourself. Eat based on how hungry you're. If you aren't full, eat a bite later on in a couple of hours. This helps you control your weight.

Conquering Emotional Eating

Food May also be a way by which you subconsciously self-sabotage. It's your brain's job to safeguard your identity and your belief systems. When reality doesn't match your senses, your brain will do whatever it can to fix the inconsistency. If you find yourself as useless and fat, when you start losing several pounds and gaining any momentum with your daily diet plan, guess what? You may encounter self-sabotage and overeat. Your subconscious mind is"assisting" you bring realism and your self-image into alignment. To describe it another way, consider your brain as though it had been a thermostat. When you decide on a thermostat, then the heater or A/C kicks in to correct the temperature accordingly, and that temperature is preserved forever. In the same way, if your mental "thermostat" is put for you weighing 170 lbs when you fall to 135 lbs, your brain's thermostat will revert into self-sabotage to bring you back to the weight you imagine/expect of yourself.

Food may be a coping mechanism for trauma. Your additional fat may be a physical representation of this emotional shield that you built on your own. When you get started losing it, it may cause one to feel unprotected and excessively vulnerable. Therefore, you build up to it.

The power of the subconscious is Exploited continuously from the food sector in their advertising. They perfect the flavor, odor, and texture of their food so as to keep us hooked. Eating becomes about dealing rather than nutrition. "You aren't you once you're hungry," based on Snickers. "Come hungry, leave happy," claims IHOP. "Every dinner ought to feel so good," says Stouffer's. Who would not wish to"Cheer up your lunch" with Oreos? The list continues on and on. It is laborious. (The best selling book Salt Sugar Fat is a superb study on U.S. food firms harnessing our emotional eating.)

Whether You're emotionally eating To feel better or because you lack the confidence to take a healthy you, keep reading for 12 ideas, which can allow you to master your emotions, and overcome emotional eating.

1. Change the story you're telling yourself.

You're talking to yourself daily long. Not out loud, but inside your mind. That tiny voice never shuts up! It incessantly overanalyzes, self-criticizes, disempowers and misinterprets. If the incorrect story you tell yourself is"I feel deprived when I prevent eating snacks," then change it to something more empowering just like"I am proud of myself for taking good care of my body and saying no to those unhealthy snacks!" Making a conscious decision to modify the story you tell yourself will alter your brain's interpretation of this situation and cause positive emotions. It sure beats the flood of negative emotions which the old narrative could have triggered. This requires practice, and thus don't quit once you slide back to the unwanted self-talk! Just jump back to the mat. For those of you in psychology, you might already be knowledgeable about the re-framing method as cognitive behavioral therapy or CBT.

And in the Event That You still hear your internal Critic calling you"fat" or ridiculing you on your physical appearance, then try this exercise: First, inform your internal critic, "Thanks for sharing," then shut your eyes and envision a pleasant-sounding internal voice saying something positive and empowering. Repeat as necessary until you do not hear that adverse self-talk. Basically, you're wrestling hands from the disagreeable inner critic who is not you.

2. Change your benefits system.

Disconnect food out of your benefit System, and begin rewarding yourself with additional satisfying activities. For instance: go for a walk, purchase something in your wish list or treat yourself to a massage or bubble bath.

3. Transforming your mind is Essential to Changing up your entire body.

Neuro-Linguistic Programming (NLP) Is a powerful system for bettering your mind. Try this out NLP workout for breaking up the gratifying associations you have with your favorite snacks: First, shut your eyes. Consider a favorite food that you're attempting to avoid. Maybe you can't stop bingeing on pizza, for instance? Now, consider something which disgusts you. Let us say you're grossed out by spiders and cockroaches. Now imagine that yummy pizza, which you love a lot, with lions and roaches crawling from this steamy melted cheese. The real, large, and vibrant you create this"movie" on your mind's eye, the harder it'll be to want that fattening pizza, which you used to crave a lot better.

4. Treat yourself as you would a Loved small kid.

We would not dream of fixing a Stranger, let alone a loved child, as harshly as we cure ourselves occasionally. Perhaps you have berated yourself over something absurd? Said cruel things to yourself that

218

caused you to feel unworthy? For the love of all things sacred, please treat yourself with love, kindness, and admiration! Make it your mission to guard your emotional being. Feeling secure, powerful, and protected dissolves emotional eating.

5. Create small success customs.

Create new empowering customs such As exercising in a standard period or writing down your little successes as you reach them. This may cause your brain to release endorphins, which will, in turn, get you hooked to exercising and staying healthy.

6. Maintain your commitment to yourself

You're preparing yourself to follow Through, to keep your promises to yourself, to achieve the goals which will result in a fitter you. When you get accustomed to keeping your promises to your self, you become self-motivated, driven in the interior.

7. Do not keep junk around

Life is simpler, with fewer temptations around. Were you aware that willpower is a finite resource, which it depletes over the course of the day? Maintaining a jar of biscuits around wastes precious willpower, which may be utilized instead to operate on important life objectives. Do not just place the snacks from perspective, as your brain understands they're still within easy reach. Instead, eliminate the cookies altogether - as in throw them in the garbage! You will save as much willpower. Instead of depriving yourself of snacks completely, you can stock your refrigerator and pantry with healthy choices (miniature carrots, anybody?).

8. Create a new individuality

Make an alter ego or an avatar, a Brand new 2.0 version of your self together with the characteristics of the individual who you need to become. Visualize that fresh, powerful, joyful, and secure variant of yourself readily handling a variety of emotions without running into the refrigerator. Adopting a new, fitter, more empowered identity can change any range of annoying behaviors, not merely overeating.

9. Reduce stress

Being on a diet is stressful. So is Attempting to be like somebody else, while it's a star on TV or a buddy who published a bikini picture of herself Facebook. Trying to be somebody else may drive you mad. There's a good deal of stress these days for us to appear a specific way, particularly for ladies. If you're the sort of person who adheres to the pressure and emotionally overeats, then you ought to de-stress. Try some relaxation methods, such as mindfulness meditation, meditation, or perhaps just chilling by the pool. Watch a funny movie; laughter is really the best medication. Stress triggers crap food cravings and releases the hormone cortisol, which stores fat in the human body! Aim to remain relaxed and happy.

10. Breathe

Breathing not just disturbs you, it Can clear your mind of those negative emotions which drive one to overeat. Here's a very simple breathing exercise that you can do anytime you are feeling overwhelmed with your eyes shut in a comfortable position with your spine straight. Put your hands on your tummy and take deep breaths through your nose, then exhale slowly through your mouth area. Continue reading for at least 3 to 5 minutes. In this relaxed state, your junk food cravings will dissipate.

11. Ensure it is a conscious Option

For many people, It's Only a thing Of creating a conscious decision and sticking with it. Create a listing of all of the advantages and disadvantages of emotional eating. Focusing on your goals will reinforce your resolve to make enduring changes in your lifetime.

12. Change your value system

Create a decision to appreciate Your Wellbeing Over instant gratification, to appreciate the long term within the brief term. Residing in a body that's healthy, slim, and agile is much more satisfying than the immediate gratification you get from binge eating.

Unhealthy Overeating may stem from emotions that don't serve you. The Fantastic news is that you Are in charge of your emotions. Ascertain your emotional triggers, seem out For all those triggers and take control over your mind and body. Achieving mastery Over your emotions will be a learned skill; together with exercise, you'll get better and better in it.

7 Mind Tricks That Really Work

With emotional eating, the Actual Problem isn't in our kitchens, but in our own minds. Here is the way to equip yourself with plans to conquer temptation.

Compose a 5 x 5 listing

Distraction gets a bad rap in our Civilization: it is connected with mindless behavior like texting while driving (or walking, for that matter) or using too little focus. But distraction--as it pertains diverting our focus in a focused, purposeful manner --may be among the greatest weapons against emotional eating. It"can shake loose ideas of ingestion and put a stop to the loop of meals chatter which causes you to mindlessly munch," By providing yourself something to do or concentrate on, you give time to the idea about meals or the emotion forcing you to consume to cool down and dissipate." Attempting this exercise: Take out a sheet of newspaper, and write down five fast lists of five things each: 5 people you can call if you are feeling down, angry, or mad; five strategies to unwind (ex: choose a hot shower); five locations to visit calm down (ex: your porch); five items you'll be able to say yourself under stress (ex: "This too will pass"); and five actions to divert yourself (ex: watch a series on Netflix). Display this list in your fridge or a kitchen cupboard. The next time you are driven to bite to soothe your self, examine the list and select among those 25. Do it five minutes, and make sure you give it your whole focus.

Learn the Emotional land before you

Sometime over the weekend, then sit down, grab a sheet of paper and a pen or pencil, and sketch out your path for another week (successful individuals do so, also!). Not roads and highways: Simply make a rough map that includes all of your intended stops (work, college for a parent-teacher convention, doctor's appointment, film theater together with all the family) in addition to potential detours (a grocery trip, a mall operate). After that, choose an icon that signifies emotional eating and place one in the areas (a meeting to ask your boss to get a raise, brunch along with your in-laws), which may trigger emotional eating. "Using a map set out to your week, which clearly defines problematic events, can help you become aware of these," writes Dr. Albers. Then, plan beforehand. If you understand, you're very likely to stress-eat in brunch, for example, examine the restaurant's menu online ahead and pick a tasty yet healthy alternative so that you don't binge on Eggs Benedict. Below are a few items geniuses do daily; you might choose to grow your to-do listing, also.

Squeegee Your insides

Most of Us know it is a Fantastic idea to take A deep breath once we're stressed; however, doing it is another issue. Inhale deeply, and envision a squeegee (yes, like the type that you use to clean a windshield or a window) someplace near your mind. Slowly exhale as you envision it draining clean your insides--finish with your worries--from the head down to your feet. Repeat three times. Here are a few more rapid strategies to ease stress and stress.

Talk to yourself like royalty

Emotional eating is frequently Accompanied by self-criticism, together with your internal voice saying poisonous comments like"I am a loser," "I never do anything right," or"When will I ever know how to deal with disappointment?" --which directs you directly to the closest drive-through. Though they're fleeting, these opinions are like acid rain on your own well-being, slowly eroding it. Next time you capture statements such as those going through your mind, give yourself space by changing into the next person. "I needed to do what is ideal for getting LeBron James and also to perform exactly what makes LeBron James happy." When you believe, "I actually messed up," change that rather to"[your first name] actually brightens up" It could appear to be an insignificant change but try it, and you will see it might help prevent the negative idea loop playing on the mind and give you a bit of perspective. These are different recommendations to enhance confidence (if you are feeling anything but).

Ground that your mind

Grounding techniques are a Powerful Way to encourage yourself through significant emotional occasions. They help bring one back to the current minute, preventing you from being swept away from their own feelings and fretting to mindlessly eating" This is just one great grounding strategy for your brain espoused. Get a magazine or book, flip through it, and decide on a passage. Read it backward on your own start with the previous word from the passage and continue till you get to the very first term. Do this with two passages.

Ground that your Body

There Are Several Different ways in which You're able to jolt your body to the here and now and from your mind. Hold a sheet of ice and texture it melts between your palms; bite to a bit of carrot, lemon, or grapefruit; put your hands under hot or cold water; dig among your heels to the ground; sit in a seat, grab the arms or seat snugly, and discharge.

Leave your Worries about the doorstep

Many People have developed the not-so-good custom of getting a house, placing our Things, and instantly going into the kitchen to bury

226

our emotions in java Cake or leftover pizza. Make a new homecoming habit. Whenever you enter Your own house, discard your shoes and possessions and say out loud, "I abandon my Issues here." Then substitute the usual trip to your kitchen using a non-food Action that brings you joy, like placing on music, showcasing your puppy or Kitty, or admiring the view in a window. Do this daily for a Couple Weeks, and You are on your way to creating a brand new ritual. Here are additional non-food-related Techniques to enhance your mood.

PRACTICAL STEPS TO STOP EMOTIONAL EATING DISORDER

Keep a food diary and write down. The times if you are feeling, such as emotional eating, you should begin to find a pattern that can help you identify your triggers. You want to locate an action which may replace the action of eating in your most vulnerable instances. Exercise is a good way to burn off calories, get fit, lower your stress levels, and feel great about yourself. Exercise doesn't need to be around lifting weights or spending hours at the gym, find something interesting you will like, such as a dance course or a sport of badminton. Also, learn how to relax a whole lot longer as stress often contributes to a bad diet. Take long walks along with a herbal tub and also make some very time each day just for one. It's possible to break the cycle of emotional eating with favorable actions.

Emotional hunger is not easily quelled by ingesting

While filling up might work in the Moment, eating due to negative emotions often leaves people feeling much madder than before. This cycle typically does not finish until somebody addresses emotional needs head-on.

Find other ways to cope with stress

Finding another way to Manage Negative emotions is frequently the initial step in overcoming emotional eating. This may mean writing in a diary, reading a novel, or even finding a couple of minutes to unwind and decompress in the day.

It takes some time to change your mindset From reaching for meals to participating in different kinds of stress relief, so experimentation with an assortment of actions to discover what works for you.

Transfer your body

Many People Today find relief in becoming Normal exercise. A jog or walk around the block or even a quickie yoga regimen might assist in especially emotional minutes.

In 1 study, participants had been asked to participate in eight months of yoga. They were then evaluated in their mindfulness and educational comprehension -- essentially their comprehension of themselves and of course scenarios surrounding them. The results demonstrated that regular yoga might be a useful preventative measure to help diffuse emotional states like anxiety and depression.

Try meditation

Others are calmed by turning inward To practices such as meditation.

There are a number of studies that Encourage mindfulness meditation as a treatment for binge eating disorder and emotional eating.

Straightforward deep breathing is meditation. You can do it almost everywhere. Sit in a quiet area and pay attention to your breath -- gradually flowing in and out of your uterus.

You can browse sites like youtube for free guided meditations. By way of instance, Jason Stephenson's"Guided Meditation for Anxiety & Stress" has more than 4 million viewpoints and undergoes a set of breathing and visualization exercises for over half an hour.

Start a food journal

Maintaining a log of everything you consume and When you consume it could help you identify causes that result in emotional eating. You may jot notes down in a laptop or switch to technology using a program like myfitnesspal.

While it can be hard, attempt to add All you consume -- however large or little -- and capture the emotions you are feeling in that instant.

Furthermore, If You Decide to seek medical Help on your eating habits, your food journal may be a helpful tool to talk with your physician.

Eat a Nutritious Diet

Making Certain That You Get enough nourishment To fuel your body can also be crucial. It can be tricky to differentiate between authentic and emotional hunger. Should you eat well during the day, it could be much easier to see when you are eating from anxiety or despair or stress.

Still, having difficulty? Consider attaining For healthful snacks, like fruit or veggies, plain popcorn, along with another low carb, low-carb meals.

Take common offenders from your pantry

Consider devoting or devoting foods On your cabinets that you frequently reach for in minutes of strife. Think of high quality, candy, or calorie-laden items, such as fries, chocolate, and ice cream. Additionally, postpone trips to the supermarket when you are feeling angry.

Maintaining the foods you crave from Reach when you are feeling emotional may help break the cycle by providing you time to consider before noshing.

Focus on volume

Fight to grab an entire bag of chips Or other foods to bite. Measuring out parts and picking small plates to assist with portion control are mindful eating habits to work on growing.

As Soon as You've completed one serving, Devote time before heading back for a moment. You might even need to try out a different stress-relieving technique, such as deep breathing, in the meantime.

Seek assistance

Fight isolation in minutes of Anxiety or anxiety. Even a fast telephone call to your friend or family member can work wonders for your disposition. Additionally, there are formal service groups that can help. Overeaters Anonymous is a Firm that addresses overeating against emotional eating, compulsive overeating, and other eating disorders.

Your Physician may Provide you a referral To your counselor or trainer who will help you determine the emotions in the path of your hunger. Locate different classes in your area by looking for social networking sites such as Meetup.

Banish distractions

You may End up eating in front of the tv, personal computer, or another diversion. Try switching off the tube, putting down your phone next time you end up in this routine.

By focusing on your meals, the snacks You choose, and your degree of hunger, you might find that you are eating emotionally. Some find it beneficial to concentrate on chewing gum 10 to 30 days before swallowing a bite of food. Doing these items gives your mind time to grab up to your gut.

Work on optimistic self-talk

Feelings of guilt and shame are Related to emotional eating. It is very important to operate on the self-talk you encounter after an event -- or it might result in a cycle of emotional eating behavior.

Rather than coming down hard, try studying Out of your drawback. Use it as a chance to plan for the long term. And make sure you reward yourself with self-care steps -- taking a bath, going for a leisurely stroll, etc. -- when you create strides.

Remedy For Emotional Eating

Overcoming emotional eating is different to Involve teaching the victim healthier ways to see food and create better-eating habits, comprehend their causes for participating in this behavior, and develop suitable approaches to prevent and relieve stress.

An important step in managing stress Is exercise, because routine physical activity tends to soften the creation of stress compounds, even resulting in a drop in melancholy, anxiety, and sleeplessness as well as reducing the propensity to participate in emotional eating.

Participate in meditation and other Relaxation methods is also a powerful means to handle stress and so reduce emotional eating. Thus, engaging in a couple of meditation sessions per day may have lasting beneficial effects on health, even diminishing elevated blood pressure and heart rate.

Refraining from medication use and Consuming no more than moderate levels of alcohol are several other important ways to successfully handle stress since a number of these substances heighten the body's reaction to stress. Additionally, indulging using these chemicals frequently prevents the individual from confronting their problems directly, so they aren't able to create effective techniques to deal with or remove the stress.

Other lifestyle changes that can reduce stress contain taking breaks in your home and on the job. Refrain from over-scheduling yourself. Learn how to recognize and react to your stress causes. Take normal days off at periods that are ideal for you. Structure your own life to accomplish a cozy method to react to the sudden.

For People Who may need help coping With stress, stress-management counseling in the shape of individual or group treatment can be extremely helpful. Stress counseling and group treatment have shown to decrease stress symptoms and enhance general wellness.

Cognitive-behavioral treatment (CBT) Has been proven to be successful as part of therapy for combating emotional eating. This strategy will help to relieve stress by assisting the person change her or his way of considering particular problems. In CBT, the therapist uses three methods to accomplish these aims:

Didactic part: This stage can help to set up favorable expectations for treatment and market the individual's alliance with the treatment procedure.

Cognitive component: This will help to recognize the ideas and assumptions which influence the person's behaviors, especially the ones that may predispose the victim to emotional eating. A version of this cognitive part of treatment is teaching mindfulness, paying nonjudgmental focus on the current moment. Mindfulness involves believing more reflectively, raising one's emotional consciousness, also will result in a heightened capacity to distinguish one's emotions out of hunger.

Behavioral component: This applies behavior-modification methods to teach the individual how to stop emotional eating and utilize more efficient strategies for managing problems.

If stress generates a full-scale Psychiatric problem, such as posttraumatic stress disorder (PTSD), clinical depression, or anxiety ailments, then psychotropic drugs, especially the selective serotonin reuptake inhibitors (SSRIs), can be exceedingly helpful. Examples of SSRIs include sertraline (Zoloft), paroxetine (Paxil), fluoxetine (Prozac), citalopram (Celexa), or escitalopram (Lexapro).

Overeaters' Anonymous is a Longstanding self-help team that may be a significant source for creating healthy ways to see meals and recognizing and dealing with causes for participating in emotional eating. Nutritionists, therapists, as well as other support classes, maybe other valuable resources.

Treatment

There Are Many ways in which People can decrease emotional distress without participating in emotional eating as a way to cope. The very salient choice would be to minimize maladaptive coping strategies and to optimize flexible plans. Research conducted by Corstorphine et al. In

2007 researched the relationship between distress tolerance and disordered eating. These researchers especially focused on just how different coping plans impact distress tolerance and disordered eating. They found that people who participate in disordered eating frequently employ emotional avoidance plans. When someone is confronted with powerful negative emotions, they might opt to prevent the problem by deflecting themselves. Discouraging emotional prevention is, consequently, an important aspect of emotional eating therapy. The clearest approach to restrict emotional avoidance would be to face the matter via techniques such as problem-solving. Corstorphine et al. Revealed that people who participated in problem-solving approaches enhance one's capacity to endure emotional distress. Since emotional distress is connected to emotional eating, the capacity to manage one's negative impact should make it possible for someone to deal with a situation without resorting to overeating.

One way to fight emotional eating Is to use mindfulness methods. By way of instance, coming cravings using a nonjudgmental inquisitiveness will help distinguish between hunger and emotionally-driven cravings. Someone could inquire or herself if the craving grew quickly, as emotional eating has been triggered. Someone may also spend some opportunity to notice their bodily senses, such as hunger pangs, and coinciding emotions, such as shame or guilt, to be able to be conscious decisions to prevent emotional eating.

Emotional eating is also Enhanced by assessing physical facets, for example, hormone balance. Female hormones, particularly, can change cravings as well as self-perception of somebody's body. Furthermore, emotional eating can be exacerbated by societal pressure to be slim. The focus on thinness and dieting within our civilization can make young women, particularly vulnerable to falling into food limitation and subsequent emotional consumption behavior.

Emotional eating disorder Predisposes people to more severe eating disorders and bodily complications. Thus, combatting disordered eating until such development takes place is now the focus of several clinical psychologists.

Other ways to Stop Emotional Eating

1. Identify Your Triggers
There are a Lot of Possible causes for emotional eating.
A number of the most Frequent causes Include feeling lonely, nervous, tired, or perhaps just exhausted!

Take some time to spot the Various emotions which are causing you to reach food.

If you have identified emotional Ingesting as a problem you want to tackle, then you will probably spot patterns that you are able to tackle head-on with these hints.

2. Locate Alternative Resources of Pleasure

As Soon as You've identified the possible Activates of your emotional eating, you can produce strategies to help prevent these situations in the long run.

For instance

If you are feeling lonely or tired, Consider phoning a friend or family member to catch-up. Sometimes just being in a social environment might also help, such as heading into a coffee shop to work in your notebook instead of sitting in the home.

If you are feeling tired, and It is late at night, go to bed!

If you are feeling stressed or Nervous, consider going for a walk, run, or lifting weights.

3. Just Eat When You Are Hungry

Food scarcity is not a problem. Once was for our ancestors, and also many people have forgotten how to recognize and translate the hunger signals which our bodies deliver us.

Yes, it is much easier said than done. However, before you start your refrigerator door, ask yourself why you are reaching for meals.

Is your tummy grumbling, or can be There something else forcing you? Stop for a minute and make yourself aware of your own motivation.

Are you craving some Particular food, or Can you eat a plate of white broccoli and fish you are that hungry?

4. Avoid Temptations

You are more likely to produce poor meal Choices in case you've got unhealthy and tempting foods in your kitchen cabinets.

Were you aware that willpower is a Finite source, which it depletes over the course of this day?

Maintaining a jar of biscuits around Wastes valuable willpower, you may be used to operate on important life objectives. And do not just place the snacks from perspective, as your brain knows they're still within easy access.

Instead, Eliminate the biscuits Completely -- as in throw them in the garbage!

As Opposed to deprive yourself of Snacks altogether, attempt and save your favorite foods for particular events and stick mainly to healthful snacks such as fruit, vegetables, and protein-rich choices.

5. Hire a Coach or Trainer

A personal trainer may supply Training on healthful eating habits and responsibility -- you are not as inclined to give in to cravings should you have to compose it on your food journal!

While this (and also the tips outlined Above) can certainly help, should you believe emotional eating is getting a Serious problem, then we strongly advise talking to some more formally qualified nutrition counselor.

CHAPTER TWELVE

A NEW LIFESTYLE

I want to provide you with positive affirmations in this audio guide. You have come a long way, and I want you to confirm these affirmations with yourself frequently. Remember to choose a comfortable space to sit in. Perhaps a space that allows you to speak out loud now. Keep your breathing exercises in mind, always maintaining an even rhythm in your breathing. This is a fun exercise, an exercise that will reassure you of your worth. Now, allow me to guide you.

I want you to participate in this section by repeating my words. Please do repeat these words out loud because it's essential to hear your own voice. I will pause briefly after each affirmation, and you will have the time to repeat the sentence. Shall we begin?

I acknowledge my own value, and my confidence continues to grow each day.

I strongly believe in my own abilities and skills to attract a positive outcome.

I am fully capable of reaching any target I set for myself with my newfound confidence.

I will aim to make memories I treasure because I refuse to live a robotic life.

I will walk into the spotlight with my head held high because I no longer fear the crowd.

I'm not afraid of meeting new people because I'm interesting and have so much to offer.

I don't need to compare myself to another person because I'm unique.

I have the confidence to speak to anyone because my voice is a powerful tool.

I'm confident in my knowledge and refuse to doubt my own words.

I will take some brief time off now and then because life can become hectic for anyone.

I will finish my tasks one by one and not become overwhelmed.

I will own my mistakes instead of punishing myself.

I'm a powerful force, and nothing in the world can shove me off track.

I will not allow myself to take on more than I can handle.

I acknowledge the fact that I cannot control everything.

I acknowledge that I'm not perfect because no person is.

I won't allow my fears to control my thinking and prevent me from living life to the fullest.

I have complete control over negative emotions that plague me at night.

I will create what is best for me because I control my imagination.

I am strong enough to defeat any addiction or pain.

I'm a strong, confident, kind, and loving person who is capable of anything I set my mind to.

Thank you for repeating these affirmations. It's important to hear something out loud before you can accept it

So, what else does hypnotic gastric banding take into account? If you want to make your body a fat-burning tool, refined sugar must be avoided to prevent carbohydrates like bread, kinds of pasta, and pastry. Starch turns quickly to sugar. The body can store fat only if there is insulin and sugar in the body only if you have consumed carbohydrates. The most successful way to make a slimmer body is, therefore, to eat the food that nature has given to you: lean protein meat, fish, poultry, eggs, fruit, vegetables, etc. You do not need to limit the amount because your body can not store fat unless there are carbs. A gastric band, therefore, discourages you from eating foods that burn fat and encourages you to eat the very foods that make your body fat. Yet weight loss almost always plateaus with a very disheartening gastric band. Vanessa Feltz's gastric banding recently reported this problem.

Here's the confirmed reply.

The hypnotic gastric band system changes the size of your stomach but also helps you to get comfortable and enjoy healthier food. Hypno gastric banding is a healthier, long-term, non-evasive choice. Changing your body physically cannot give you long-term results, but you can enjoy healthier alternatives by addressing the main problem causing over-eating.

All the best!

Rapid Weight Loss

Hypnosis

INTRODUCTION

Weight loss hypnosis in this dynamic and fast-moving weight loss industry isn't yet another modern fad. No doubt, new products in this multi-million dollar weight loss industry come in all sorts of shapes and sizes to help people with their weight problems. You've got pills, exercise books, or diet programs that appear to keep popping up on your local bookstore, and some have even made it to the bestseller list. Americans spend millions of dollars on such items every year, and America remains one of the countries in the world with the highest levels of obesity. And how does hypnosis weight loss vary from all other patterns of exercise and diet? Is weight loss hypnosis the magic weight-loss treatment that anyone who has weight issues is waiting for?

In the weight loss industry, hypnosis for weight loss is not exactly a new thing. In addition, weight loss hypnosis methods have been used for years to help people deal with their issues with smoking, memory problems, pain management problems, and, of course, weight loss. Throughout the years, these techniques used to treat weight problems have been continuously refined and perfected, and many forms of research have been done to enhance their effectiveness in the treatment of individual weight management problems.

Weight loss hypnosis also helps lots of people from all walks of life with their weight control problems. In reality, some very popular movie stars work with a professional hypnosis therapist for weight loss to maintain their weight and appearance. And how do you respond to this? Oh, such weight loss hypnosis services are now readily accessible to everyone. There are various ways to get started on a given program.

First, you should try a professional hypnosis consultant for weight loss and work with him or her on your weight loss goals. Nevertheless, make sure the doctor you are seeing has proper credentials and positive results that help other people lose weight. Second, you can buy and listen to the hypnosis for weight loss CDs. This form of self-hypnosis technique is very effective and very inexpensive to lose weight. With these audio CDs, the biggest benefit is that you can listen to them anytime, at any time. Please don't listen to them when driving, of course, as the suggestions in the CDs can induce you to a deeply relaxed state. In tandem with your sessions with your weight loss specialist, you should also use these hypnosis CDs for weight loss for better results, as the secret to having the most gain from a weight control hypnosis program is to repeat the advice given. The more ideas are replicated, the quicker they get implanted into your subconscious brain that will have a beneficial effect on your diet and exercise behavior.

Is hypnosis of weight loss the magic pill everyone was waiting for? Well, Yeah, partly. Going through a system doesn't mean you can just trigger your thoughts, and all of a sudden, the extra pounds will go off. You'll still have to watch your diet and practice your exercise routines. What you'll get from hypnosis services, however, is the added advantage in overcoming your weight problems. The ideas embedded in your subconscious mind will slowly circumvent your old eating patterns, and you will automatically begin choosing healthy foods and feeling full longer and faster even while eating less. Hypnosis services for weight loss also trigger your inner motivator to get you to the gym to workout without pushing yourself like you used to. In reality, after going through these weight loss hypnosis programs, you may be looking forward to going to the gym and exercising.

In a supersized world, people have plenty of opportunities to eat and drink WAY too much, but usually what's behind obesity is more than just craving a large order of fries. A major diet industry in America has grown around obesity and forces overweight people to pay a high price for trendy diets, pills, or high-risk and expensive surgeries. By avoiding carbohydrates or fat, by taking pills or injections, by sprinkling crystals on your food, by resorting to surgery, or by consuming miracle diet potions, many dieters temporarily lose pounds-but do not lose the attitude that leads to weight gains. The result is that after all that hard work and potentially spending thousands of dollars, the majority of dieters are getting back their weight and feeling even more discouraged.

Hypnosis of weight loss can help you change how you feel, and control your bad dietary habits.

Weight Loss Hypnosis Breaks Down Why You Eat

Hypnosis Preparation has helped people lose weight sustainably by improving their eating habits, minimizing stress and pressure, and learning how to relax. Eating too much has nothing to do with hunger, but instead has everything to do with high stress, racing thoughts, and other negative emotional feelings which allow a person to escape from feeling.

Like all hypnosis, the hypnosis of weight loss uses persuasion power when people are in a comfortable state as long as the suggestions are compatible with what the person WANTS to do first. Part of the focus is on changing attitudes and desires for better food choices and resolving the cravings for food. As many dieters have poor thought habits that allow them to use donuts and cheesy bacon bowls to improve their emotions, weight loss hypnosis often helps you to see yourself as a powerful person who doesn't need food to fix something. You learn to see changing eating patterns not as suffering but as rewarding and simple because, in the first place, it is what you want to do.

Does Hypnosis Weight Loss Work?

Hypnosis can be seen as a technique-a method that people use to relax, adjust their attitude and emotions in a better, more optimistic, and more effective way. All hypnosis is "self-hypnosis," and the individual is 100 percent responsible for how it works and what the results are. The hypnotist is like a mentor who advises the individual and directs them in a calm and simple way to learn what they need to succeed. Of course, this is all based on the DECISION to lose weight in the first place the person makes-hypnosis is never a replacement for a personal decision. Neither the hypnotizer nor hypnosis itself can do anything to "make" a human. The person will decide to lose weight, so hypnosis will help the decision, and sometimes, they never have to be on a different diet again.

Why Is Hypnosis A Perfect Solution to Weight Loss

Positive weight loss relies on motivation. They seem to get fired up when people go on diets before they go out. They may lose weight, but they may become frustrated when progress slows down. For someone who has at some time lost a large number of weight plateaus when the body battles weight-loss.

Discouragement makes it easier to rationalize slipping off the wagon when you work hard to lose, and you don't lose much. You think, "I'm not losing anyway, so I might as well have that hot fudge sundae." Or, "I haven't exercised yet, so just forget it-it's ruined the week." Hypnosis in weight loss teaches you to think like thin people, make food choices like these people, and eat like thin people. Naturally, slim people are not that way, contrary to some belief, because they still eat chicken and salad with no dressing. Alternatively, they know what's going to feel good in their stomachs BEFORE they eat, so they can consume in moderation what they want, and know when to avoid eating based on how they feel, and look at treatments as occasional little indulgences, not a constant requirement of fast food that they then feel mentally and physically crappy about consuming.

Hypnosis of weight loss supports healthy weight loss. It keeps your outlook optimistic, even though weight loss is often slow, and while weight loss will still fluctuate from week to week, the other benefits of hypnosis such as increased self-esteem, relaxation, inspiration, and a relaxed state of mind continue to increase. Hypnosis is shifting the link between food and feelings as it re-creates normal eating states of mind. Since the plan does not rely on medications and there are no diets of any sort, hypnosis is a safe weight loss strategy that will leave you slimmer, more comfortable, and with substantial improvements in how you handle food and your emotions.

As with all hypnosis, most people are able to respond to suggestions when they are in a very comfortable state. A successful hypnotist should determine whether you are a good candidate for weight loss hypnosis based on the strength of your desire to improve, and your willingness to embrace training and obey instructions.

How do you pick a hypnotist who is weight-loss?

Weight loss hypnosis is most effective when conducted by practitioners who have a great deal of experience with hypnosis in general and hypnosis, particularly for weight loss. Be sure to inquire about their experience and their achievements in practice working with a lot of people who lose weight. They should be able to show plenty of favorable outcomes and have real comments and results given by people.

If you're ready to stop eternally dieting and create a healthy, easy attitude towards food, the hypnosis of weight loss may be right for you.

So weight loss hypnosis is a powerful tool that can help you achieve your weight management goals. Whatever exercise and dietary routine you've chosen for yourself, weight loss hypnosis gives you control back into your life and empowers you to lose weight and achieve all of your weight loss goals in a safe and quick way.

CHAPTER ONE

The History of Hypnosis and Hypnotherapy

Hypnosis in ancient times It is as old as man himself to use hypnosis as a therapeutic device. We will find the history of hypnosis used to cure and create progress so long as it can be traced back over time. Over the ages, hypnosis has been used under several different names, and the use of hypnosis for healing can be traced back to around 3000 BC in Egypt. Both the Bible's new and old testaments talk of what might be called hypnosis, and the ancient Greeks and Romans had temples of sleep in which those seeking healing would be put into a trance-like state. The Priests would describe their dreams. The Shaman of today can still create catalepsy of the body by rhythmic drumming and monotonous chanting along with eye fixation, and this helps give the shaman the appearance of possessing supernatural powers just as they have done for centuries. Most of what the village witchdoctor, shaman or wise woman has done in the past can be attributed to cultivating deep confidence, faith, hope, and creativity in the person who is being cured and chanting and singing also take the form of what we would call suggestion. After all, if you tell the most powerful and magical person you meet that you're going to get better, you're very likely to do just that. Obviously, in many cases where such an individual was given to a sick person, they would ultimately have healed regardless, so this action has only intensified the healing process.

The mind-body link

Many healers have long believed the body, thoughts, and emotions can affect each other. And it is possible to manipulate a physical illness by focusing on and understanding individual feelings and modifying thoughts and patterns of behavior.

"Mens Sana in corpore Sano," the Romans wrote, good mind in a healthy body. This saying seems to suggest that physical and emotional health has been believed to have an impact on one another for several centuries. To put that in perspective, it's just important to understand how our wellbeing declines after periods of stress or as a result of revolutionary events.

The separation of body and mind in medicine, with Newton's scientific advances, is something that only took place about 1750. Since then, it has been known that mind and spirit are under the jurisdiction of the church and the body under the jurisdiction of science. This is also why non-Western types of medicine see the human being as a whole made up of body, mind, and soul.

Traumatic experiences are stored not only on an emotional level but on a physical level too. The emotional stress of the multiple traumas will impact our immune system and health conditions. It is possible to find tools inside us through the retrieval of old traumas and the emotional charges that are linked to a certain illness that might help us start the healing process.

Modern hypnosis The hypnosis of modern times started in the 18th century with Anton Mesmer (1734-1815). Mesmer was a medical graduate from Vienna's famous medical school and became interested in magnetism after studying as a Jesuit priest. Mesmer became the leading expert in magnetic healing in Europe, where magnets passed over the body to heal. His results were fantastic, and he became incredibly popular. Mesmer claimed that all living things emitted a kind of magnetic 'fluid,' and they would be safe if a person had enough of that fluid. Hence the term 'animal magnetism' comes from. One day Mesmer lost his magnets, and so he only made passes with his hands over the patient and was shocked to find that they were getting better. From there on, he felt the remedies were getting enough magnetic fluid in himself.

The terms hypnotism and hypnosis were coined by the early pioneers James Braid (1795-1860) in 1843. He was a Manchester-based Scottish Surgeon. He found that if there were eyes fixed on a bright object like a pocket watch, for example, some people might go into a trance. He acknowledged that there was a psychological mechanism involved and that the mechanism could be very useful because there was no biological basis for a person's condition.

Another Scottish surgeon working in India, James Esdaile (1808-1859), would use eye fixation to brace a patient for surgery and slow sweeping movements, bringing them into a deep hypnotic trance, inducing full body amnesia.

James Braid and James Esdaile were among the first in their study and use of hypnosis to be considered 'scientific.' Such pioneers separated hypnosis from the realms of mysticism and started experimenting with what could possibly be done to support people with their disorders. Many pioneers in science include Liebeault, Bernheim, Brewer, and Freud. Unfortunately, the great man himself, Freud, was responsible for several shelving hypnotherapy for a while until he abandoned its use.

Acceptance of hypnosis as a therapeutic art By those individuals who have been central to the present perception of hypnosis is Milton Erikson, Ormond McGill, Charles Tebbetts, and Dave Elman.

Ormond McGill was a stage hypnotist, but he held the public interest in hypnosis, but then the great Charles Tebbetts was interested with stage hypnosis in the early part of his life; however, these were different days than those we live in today, and stage hypnosis contributed to a desire to learn more about this mysterious art and thus attracted many of the people who followed the therapist.

In 1958, the American Medical Association's Council on Mental Health approved the use of hypnotherapy; Dave Elman gave some level of recognition of hypnosis from the medical profession in the USA.

The great-grandfather of hypnotherapy-Dr Milton Erikson-was, perhaps the most influential contributor to the recognition of hypnotherapy as both an art and science. Dr. Erikson was a psychiatrist and hypnotherapist with excellent clinical credentials, and he had prestige within the medical community due to his strong medical experience. Many people worthy of notice for their contribution to the development of hypnotherapy as therapeutic art and as a science in the 20th century are Rosen, Abramson, Menninger, Shenk, Magonet, Wolberg, LeCron, Bordeaux, Wetzenhoffer, Erwin and Simonton, who continue to do incredible things with cancer patients using mental imaging and focusing, among other things, on values and belief systems.

Hypnosis and Hypnotherapy

Some people dread the possibility that I may have full power over their minds and bodies and pursue hypnosis with great trepidation while others genuinely hope for the contrary, that all they have to do is lie down, close their eyes go to sleep and wake up with all their struggles, bad habits and miraculously transformed neuroses. The fact is, none of those hypnosis beliefs are right.

The truth is, hypnosis is a normal state which we all practice on a daily basis. Every morning, we are in a hypnotic trance a few seconds before sleep and before we awaken. Many people have encountered what is widely known as "highway hypnosis," whereby you get into your car, start driving to such a familiar home or work location and find yourself at your destination with no clear recollection of the journey and a feeling that time has passed really fast. Others undergo hypnosis while involved in an activity they find all-consuming or very pleasurable and unexpectedly realize that they have lost all track of time once again. This condition is very typical for runners and joggers, musicians, high-performance athletes, and others who frequently participate in activities that involve high attention rates and often concentrate in conjunction with a series of repetitive motions.

Anyone may be hypnotized, but this is another essential part of the hypnotic process, only if they wish. No one may be compelled at any time to participate in any behavior they find morally or ethically repugnant. One retains one's sense of right and wrong in hypnosis, and the basic self is always very much present. Sometimes in a show with a stage hypnotizer performing and making people do crazy things in front of the crowd, a screening procedure took place in which the hypnotizer secretly measured the suggestibility and motivation of the participants through different rates of exercises until the only people left on the stage were those who were extremely suggestive, i.e., they joined the hypnotization.

And that's why many hypnotists and hypnotherapists are trying to say that all hypnosis is "self-hypnosis" because the basic truth remains that if you don't want to get involved with it, you won't, but if you want it to happen, it does. It's really that easy, and it raises the question of why does anybody want to be hypnotized first if it's a normal state and if the hypnotist or hypnotherapist can't make immediate psyche changes

The response is very easy, and we feel enjoyment in the first place while in hypnosis. That's right; being hypnotized feels amazing. Hypnosis can actually be assessed by looking at brain waves, and we know that the longer, slower brain waves we call Alpha or Theta brain waves are correlated with increased development of "feel good" neurotransmitters like serotonin and dopamine in the brain and endorphins throughout the body. Hypnosis creates sensations that contribute to peace, relaxation, and enjoyment in the body. When our brain waves register in the low Alpha or Theta range, we are in hypnosis and therefore access all of the "feel good" neurotransmitters. By the way, brain wave patterns are called Beta for usual daily activity, and Delta brain waves are called those for sleep. These are objectively observable findings, which have been proven time and time again by validated scientific means. It should also be remembered that each and every person's experience with hypnosis is different and special to them, ranging from feeling as though they have fallen asleep to finding no perceptible changes in themselves whatsoever, challenging

259

whether hypnosis has been accomplished for anything in between. The other important thing to note is that the aid of a trained hypnotist or hypnotherapist is required for most people to reach a sufficiently deep level of hypnosis to experience the beneficial effects of certain neurotransmitters and to begin any successful job. This being said, many go on to practice self-hypnosis techniques without another person's assistance and obtain amazing results on their own.

It is also important to note that we have direct access to the subconscious mind while in hypnosis. The subconscious mind is much like the hard drive on a computer; it retains all that has ever happened in your life, has sorted and stored all the information required for daily functioning, governs the body's reflexes and movements and processes information at a rate of four billion bits per second! When in hypnosis we are able to bypass the normal filtration mechanism that exists between the conscious and the subconscious mind, also known as the "essential faculties," and gain direct access to the vast store of memories, feelings, perceptions, ideas and other knowledge in the subconscious mind to help discover what may impede healing, learning, development or the removal of outdated ideas, unhealing As many people still believe, this is not a loss of control, hypnosis is actually a process through which greater self-control is achieved by tapping into the natural resources that already exist in the subconscious mind!

In hypnosis, we are also much more open to suggestion, so it makes it easier for positive suggestions for change to be embedded in the subconscious mind to produce better results in conscious living. Put simply, because of the direct exposure to the subconscious mind; we learn more, we learn faster and with much greater results.

Indeed, children from birth to six or seven years of age are in a normal state of hypnosis almost continuously due to the large amount of learning that happens in terms of motor skills, language, actions, cultural and social norms, etc. during that period. That process has absolutely nothing to do with intelligence at all. Many doubters believe that only the weak-minded can be hypnotized when it is often the ones who find hypnosis an easily attainable condition that is actually capable of great focus, concentration, and attention. In addition, hypnosis can be used as a method for enhancing attention and concentration where there is a deficit, such as in ADD and ADHD.

The key points to note about hypnosis are; that it is a normal state that we are all able to experience on a regular basis, that it feels nice and finally that hypnosis can be a secure, useful resource for achieving greater knowledge, learning better self-control and accessing information stored in the subconscious mind otherwise inaccessible to the conscious mind for the purposes o

Myths About Hypnosis and Hypnotherapy

Why are some people frightened by Hypnosis? Around hypnosis, there are many misconceptions, and these misconceptions are questioned every day. While stage hypnotists and television shows have destroyed the public reputation of hypnosis, an increasing body of clinical evidence supports its benefits in treating a broad range of conditions like pain, stress reduction, depression, anxiety, and phobias, as well as behavioral modifications!

"Hypnosis works, and the scientific evidence in this respect is unambiguous. It also benefits people," says Michael Yapko, Ph.D., a psychologist and member of the American Clinical Hypnosis Society. For decades hypnosis has been used for pain management, including during the Civil War, when Army surgeons hypnotized injured soldiers before amputations.

Hypnosis allows the person to seek relaxation in different areas of their lives to promote a highly comfortable state of inner concentration and concentrated attention. Hypnotherapy Professionals can better serve their clients by also encouraging them to hypnotize themselves at home to relieve chronic pain, improve sleep, or alleviate any depression or anxiety symptoms. This is usually called Self-hypnosis. Many hypnosis practitioners would teach their clients about the idea and philosophy that "all hypnosis is self-hypnosis." What this means is that the client is in full control of their hypnotic state experience.

One of the most common hypnosis misconceptions is that the client is under the Hypnotherapist's influence, and they may make you do things you do not want to do. In reality, the complete opposite is true;

262

the consumer is in the driving seat. The hypnotherapist gives a number of suggestions to the client during a hypnosis session, and the client has the full right to either consider or reject the advice being given. If a recommendation goes against the moral or ethical values of the clients or is in conflict with the interests of the clients, then the particular recommendation can be easily rejected by the client.

Many people have refused the opportunity to explore the advantages of a structured hypnotherapy session because of misconceptions, and what is shocking is that, in fact, we all encounter various types of self-hypnosis on a daily basis. It's similar to daydreaming or being so totally absorbed in a book or television show that you could miss someone speaking in the same place. Basically, that is what hypnosis is. Here's one more proof. We're going through a phase that's very close to hypnosis just before we fall asleep each night. Therapeutic hypnosis is usually an enjoyable sensation of relaxation.

Since 1958 the American Medical Association has accepted clinical or therapeutic hypnosis, in particular as a method for pain management. Medical hypnosis is becoming increasingly popular as a tool for battling a host of problems, from nicotine addiction to chronic pain. Consumers have spent more money on alternative or integrative medicine, including hypnosis, in the past few years than on traditional treatments, said Dr. Thomas Nagy, a staff psychologist at the Stanford Center for Integrative Medicine. Why not try hypnosis? It is safe, and it can be a very gratifying experience.

Hypnosis and its use in hypnotherapy have long been recognized as an effective way to help people. Whether used to treat an addiction or simply to help build trust, hypnotherapy is a useful tool for sure.

Changing negative models into positive ones is a quick way of simply explaining it.

However, many myths about it have led to the entertainment industry and the way hypnotherapy was presented there. It has become so severe that hypnosis is considered a fraud or a dangerous practice that can have dire consequences on one's acts. Such speculations have generated a variety of misconceptions about hypnotherapy that should be clarified and debunked: it is not possible to hypnotize all people-some studies have proposed the possibility that certain people can not be hypnotized. In reality, hypnosis is a state that comes very similar to what people feel when they fall asleep and wake up. In addition, the effects of television have long been studied and found to a large degree 'hypnotic.' Often the mind wanders off, causing people to miss a turn while driving, which is again a light hypnosis state. All of these examples demonstrate that anyone can be put under hypnosis; it's just that often the technique will take a different form. Professional hypnotherapists use a variety of methods that can be used to great effect when placing a patient into a state of hypnosis; it is simply a matter of finding the right approach for a specific person.

Hypnosis is used to manipulate you to act against your will-a hypnotherapist's main function is to serve as a facilitator or guide, i.e., they will in no way make you do something you don't want to do. As a matter of fact, during a hypnotic session, you are completely conscious of all that happens, and you are in complete charge. With that said, if you are not happy with where they are leading you, it is important for you to ignore the therapist's suggestions. The reason this theory is so common is that different stage shows the hypnotist pose as a powerful individual, able to influence others. The reality is that you can hypnotize a person to do things they wouldn't do otherwise, but it never happens against your will. During a hypnotic session, there's always one aspect of the client that prohibits them from doing something that contradicts their moral and ethical values.

During the hypnosis, you can share personal information-people can lie under hypnosis. In reality, these lies can be more inventive than ever because they have access to otherwise unconscious capital. In addition, a person under hypnosis is in complete control of what they are revealing and what they want to keep a secret, and there is no real danger of sharing information that should be kept confidential.

Another theory is that hypnosis will keep you trapped. Well, that's not true because there are so many ways to show this that I don't have enough paper to write all of them.

Second, if it were true that you might get trapped in hypnosis, wouldn't there be cases of people all the time getting trapped in hypnosis? Will there not be protected in the world of hypnosis for families left by loved ones who are forever lost? Hospital wards may provide special therapies for patients who are trapped in hypnosis. They'd teach nurses how to manage those cases. Okay, I'm jesting, but I just want you to know that you can't get caught in hypnosis.

Hypnosis is a normal condition we all get into many times a day. This is a very deep state of hypnosis from which you do not recall everything that the hypnotherapist said, but you're not going to sit there forever. The very worst thing that could happen is you're going to go into a deep sleep.

Your subconscious mind is still involved when you go into a very deep hypnotic state, and certain hypnotherapists tend to operate in such a deep state. You return to normal consciousness while you are being "counted up." Remember, your subconscious mind is always looking after you. If you go deep into hypnosis and do not come out when told to do so, a gentle reminder to your subconscious mind from the hypnotherapist that you are paying for the time you spend in that cozy chair can typically get you out of hypnosis without any problems.

Some people claim that when under hypnosis, they can be forced to do things against their will. This is a fallacy that needs to be washed away. The founders of this theory are media and stage hypnotists "making" people do crazy things in front of everyone on stage. Or in movies when someone gets the evildoer to rob a bank or commit murder.

This theory has got a lot of things wrong. The first being when you move, you bring yourself up and out of hypnosis while you're in hypnosis. The more you come up with, the more movement you get.

The stage shows people dropping, or barking, or quacking is hypnosis exaggerations. When the show begins, the participants may be in a light trance, but after too much jumping and dropping and barking, they are certainly much closer to awakening consciousness than to hypnosis.

As for the evildoer who makes you do his bidding, note well that to defend you is your subconscious mind here. When in regular conscious consciousness, you wouldn't do those dastardly acts, you won't do them while being hypnotized.

You will come out of hypnosis if your subconscious feels disturbed when you are in hypnosis. It is so easy.

On the other side of things, those theories are just as harmful.

The myth that hypnotherapy is magic and will heal you in a single session has people who assume they will leave without it at 2:00 if they come in at 1:00 with a life-long illness.

The reality is that hypnotherapy is very effective in helping people with many issues and has proven especially successful in helping those who want to improve a specific situation in their lives.

With one session, there are several problems that can be solved, but this is not the rule, and the client is a very important element in this equation. For example, when someone is ready to quit smoking, and they've done everything and feel almost helpless, they could get results from a hypnotherapist they couldn't get anywhere.

Yet if anyone goes to a hypnotherapist because they want their partner to quit smoking, the probability is they won't stop because they're not ready.

Similarly, if someone goes to see a weight loss hypnotherapist and has just one session, and then goes out and eats a donut, chances are they won't get anything out of it. Though hypnotherapy has been known to help people stop smoking with one session, it can take up to twelve sessions for things like weight loss.

Weight Loss Hypnosis - Myth Or Miracle?

Weight loss hypnosis has been making headlines in the multi-million dollar weight loss industry in recent years, promoting itself as an innovative way of helping people lose weight and holding off their extra pounds. Such promotions have attracted people from popular movie stars to the average housewife using weight loss methods for hypnosis to assist with their weight loss and hold their figures. With other recent weight loss trends, however, is weight loss with hypnosis an over-hyped theory that doesn't really work as advertised, or is it actually the cure people were hoping for?

No matter what the ads suggest on how the hypnosis of modern weight loss is, the fact is, these approaches have been around for many years. These same methods for weight loss services that are learned in hypnosis are also used to address other conditions in individuals such as drinking, pain management, anxiety disorders, and, of course, weight loss. Strategies employed by many professional weight loss practitioners in weight loss hypnosis are derived from existing and validated hypnosis strategies such as anchoring and association.

To many, the word hypnosis often elicits photos of people performing crazy stunts under a stage hypnotist's instructions. Because of this depiction of hypnosis, for the weight loss methods, people were reluctant to take up hypnosis or seek a professional weight loss practitioner for their weight reduction goals. Although the stage hypnotist uses some of the hypnosis methods, a proper weight loss hypnosis system is unlike a variety television hypnosis program.

A trained weight loss hypnosis practitioner must first understand what your goals are for you during a weight loss hypnosis session. He or she will go over with you what is the present situation you're in, what are the diet and health habits you've got right now, and where you want to be when the plan is over. This stage is critical because it sets goals that you agree with and is sure that you can achieve. This is important because hypnosis can not work if deep down, contrary to common opinion, you don't believe you should do it, or you don't want to. Therefore, you subconsciously become more accepting of the target by carrying out a weight loss plan that you are happy with. The next move will be to bring you into a state of deep relaxation. The hypnotherapist offers you tips for healthy food options and positive words to help you lose weight in this state. These ideas address the subconscious mind. Why Mind Unconscious? Your subconscious mind is a part of your brain's engine. It regulates your thoughts, your emotions, your actions, and your behaviors. By applying these ideas to your subconscious mind, your attitudes and emotions change with regard to food and exercise. Many people have indicated that they don't eat as much as they did before after going through hypnosis for weight loss services because they feel better quicker and faster after a small meal.

A professional weight loss hypnosis practitioner will also include you in setting up a program for yourself, in addition to making recommendations that encourage healthy eating and exercise. Goal-setting strategies will be taught, and you'll know exactly what to achieve, how to meet your goals, and how to evaluate progress. Seeing success during your hypnosis weight loss plan will create a positive feedback loop and help push you to continue on track and achieve the goals of weight loss that you set for yourself.

Therefore, the hypnosis of weight loss is true and is now helping people from all walks of life achieve their goals of weight loss and give them back control of their lives by giving them a simple and easy way to achieve their ideal health level.

Healing the Body with Hypnosis

What does your body tell you in your own life of the need to heal the wound? Every day, the body sends out signals which let you know how safe it really is in general. Aches and pains are usually a warning somewhere deep inside that something are wrong. Some of the origins are a little more obvious than others. It is up to you to take the time to listen to the hints about your overall health that your body offers.

Positive Thought

Nearly every religion in the world states that positive thinking plays a significant role in healing. When it is a necessity for you to heal the body, it is a good idea to spend a little time thinking positively each day. You may just find that in this age-old philosophy, you have made a believer out of yourself in no time when you start to experience the power of positive thinking working inside your body to build a healthier you.

Exercise

It is an exercise that is one of the most neglected factors in healing the body. Over the years, it has been reduced to a fitness role and is equated with the need to keep in shape or assist in that goal rather than a balanced practice in and of itself. Exercise releases endorphins to provide relief from pain and a sense of happiness and well-being at large.

Good diet

A balanced diet is a wonderful resource for healing your body as much as it can cause you to know it. To maintain maximum health, you need other nutrients. Unfortunately, we live in a world of fast food, and very few people get the nutrients required for optimum health. That's why it's important to bear in mind other choices like vitamin supplements-although they're not nearly as successful as getting the nutrients through your diet.

Adopt Healthy Habits

There are some behaviors that you can adopt that will promote improved health. Replace antibacterial soap with your regular hand soap. Often wash your hands and wash them well. Teach your family how to wash their faces, cover their mouths, and use sanitizing hand wipes or liquid cleaners in public to reduce the risk of taking home infections and diseases. Such practices can seem too simplistic but may result in prevention, which is often the best treatment, allowing the body to heal.

Protecting the body with hypnosis Self-hypnosis is just another means of protecting the body from illnesses of all kinds. There are many ways that mastering the art of self-hypnosis can help in your struggle, whether you are trying to reject cancer that is just as hard to take over or ward off the common cold. Hypnosis can help you relax, open your mind to positive thinking, help the nutrients get where they are best served, and help boost immunity, among other great things.

Take control of your healing process. It is time for you to take control of your body and its process of healing. Whether you are using one or all of the above techniques, if you listen to your body and react accordingly-for the best possible health outcome-you can find real help when it comes to healing the body.

Hypnosis is a powerful mode that literally can help your body stop unwanted habits and then start to heal and rejuvenate your body. It's all about the computer device situated within the brain.

After about 5 years, smoking stops being fun, and you realize how reliant you are becoming on that smelly habit. Does anyone really enjoy the desperation and mental obsession with a dried leaf filled with those little white papers that have become your best friend? It's true; it's that bad negative friend you have to take with you everywhere you go. Those "cigs" will be with you 24 hours a day and 7 days a week, and you'll want to press the panic button if by chance you run out. That's how it has been for me. For a period of 30 years, I smoke tons of cigarettes a day. Before the day I was hypnotized and quit smoking forever, I knew nothing about the strength of my subconscious. It's why I became a Hypnotherapist, too.

Stress creates the need to smoke, or does it cause stress? It is very difficult to go cold-turkey in this modern-day world where tension is a daily occurrence. Hypnotherapy is often the last option, and yet smoking cessation is the most successful strategy than any prescription medication designed to quit smoking.

Stress will manifest itself in all sorts of scenarios... Ranging from being depressed to violent. Contrary to common opinion, medications just exacerbate the condition while making huge bucks for the pharmaceuticals. Seek your nearest Hypnotherapist first before you go to get medication to be healthy again. You're going to be happier faster, and it's going to last a lot longer!

Will they hypnotize you? Hey! The condition you strive to achieve is one of absolute relaxation as though you're about to fall asleep. You are still very much in charge because we are enhancing your drive to do what you set out to do.

Hypnosis is essentially a form of deep relaxation that allows the client to take an imagined journey. The imagination is where you build a new, vibrant vision for what you want to be like in your future.

When your critical mind is in a very deep relaxed state, it calms down from that constant thinking that says: "I can't just leave," or "It's just too hard to quit." Side-stepping the critical mind lets you become motivated to accomplish what you felt was impossible before. Not only does it work well with smoking, but it also works well in sports, handling discomfort, and even taking exams.

Old habits of thinking can be replaced quickly and lovingly with fresh, wonderful optimistic thoughts that can make leaving such a positive force in your life. Only imagine if you can avoid obsessing about a question, you can actually do something, be, have anything. You broke the habit, and YOU CAN ACHIEVE ANYTHING SET OUT TO DO. Your level of confidence goes sky-high!

The most popular problem is that after stopping smoking, customers assume they'll gain weight. Luckily, when the body recovers from the smoking effects, the weight would inevitably result in a benefit or loss. It is a positive thing meaning that the body is in the healing process. You can also eradicate the habit with hypnosis, and stop replacing one oral obsession with another. The subconscious mind is already planting the new thought cycle, and when you listen to your private session's mp3, you can really reduce the weight tension.

I suggest that you choose a hypnotherapist who has your mind-rejuvenating your heart and lungs back to an age you feel tremendous strength and energy. A successful hypnotherapist can even get your liver to detoxify your body very gently so that the tar and nicotine or even heavy metals can be extracted very quickly and easily. The body is in the healing process until they leave the workplace and will remain there for a few months.

Hypnotherapy will help move the body into new wellness. Your cells can be ordered to heal through the science of Epigenetics. Hypnosis is the best way to help cancer patients help the body cure at faster speeds, particularly with surgeries. Studies that show hypnosis heals the body have been performed to minimize bleeding, swelling, and bruises, as well as speed up the recovery process 10 times faster. In addition to that, it has been established that 10 minutes of hypnosis actually reduce blood pressure and lower cholesterol.

If you want to quit smoking, eradicate a phobia, help heal cancer or pain, then just use your strong and focused mind to seek it out without medication. It is a lot easier than you could ever imagine. You become a champion, and you'll be shocked by how strong you are.

Burn Calories With Hypnosis

Our habits have taken us to a point where robots do much of the physical labor, and we're supposed to enjoy the benefits of high-tech

276

innovation. How easy all of life's activities have become thanks to decreased physical activity and improved quality of life in terms of the kind of rich food we consume. People in countries of the first world are experiencing ever-increasing problems of obesity, and every approach in the book is tried and tested to counter them; the common ones are fad diets marked by low-fat, low-carb foods and strenuous exercise routines or other types of workouts. Although this seems to work for some, due to their lethargic disposition or helplessness due to stressful, busy daytime schedules, others have yet to find foolproof solutions to their weight problems.

Having a safe, fit body for the long term is a lot to ask off a very hectic lifestyle that men and women are living these days. It takes a lot of commitment and determination to reach the health goals when the weight loss is made a long-term target. That actually has to do more with your mind than with your body. They say that most of the things that happen around you depend on how your mind is attuned to your surroundings, and with the tremendous untapped potential of a human brain that has the right kind of nurturing, one can make almost any task possible. All we need for our minds is the right channeling device, which leads us to the right path of responsible living. While in the World Wide Web's vast network, there are millions of options for instant weight loss services, why don't you give positive, conversational hypnosis a chance to tuning your thoughts for a balanced long-term life?

Conversational hypnosis is about engaging with the subconscious mind in a comfortable state of the trance of a specific person concerned and inculcating high levels of suggestibility in that person so that the positive suggestions relating to successful weight loss become well absorbed in mind and are slowly put into practice in a safe and secure way. The main goal of the hypnotizer is to substitute the subject's appetite for overeating with a willingness to eat well. This form of positive, conversational hypnosis can be combined with a program of behaviors that gives guaranteed weight loss. One-on-one counseling sessions are recommended because listening to tapes and CDs would not be as successful as customized and regularly administered multiple hypnotherapy based sessions of weight loss. You can also try to practice conversational hypnosis and mind management techniques and apply them to yourself with a lot of confidence and will be able to achieve the goals of weight loss you like.

Review Of The Effectiveness of Hypnosis

Hypnosis has been practiced in different ways for over 100 years. There has been much debate about the current state of hypnosis, however, and whether it is effective in helping people conquer anxiety and various disorders.

In 1892 the British Medical Association (BMA) had a group of physicians evaluating the effects of hypnotherapy. This group concluded that the hypnotic state was a true condition and that hypnotherapy's efficacy was apparent in relieving sleeplessness, anxiety disorders, and pain.

In 1955, Professor T. Ferguson Rodger was approved by the BMA Psychological Medicine Community to lead a Subcommittee to publish a more comprehensive study on hypnosis and its efficacy. To learn more about the efficacy of hypnosis, the Sub-Committee interviews several experts on hypnosis from different fields.

After a two-year study period, it concluded that there was ample evidence to show that hypnotism can be successful in treating such conditions and "psychoneurosis," as well as recognizing and resolving unrecognized motivations in subjects. The Subcommittee agreed that hypnosis would help alleviate symptoms and alter very serious habits and/or negative thoughts.

The American Medical Association (AMA) ultimately agreed with that subcommittee in 1958, agreeing that hypnosis has its place in the medical community and can be a useful tool in the treatment of certain diseases and disorders if properly used by trained medical personnel.

It is important to note that hypnotherapy was considered by the AMA as an "orthodox" or standard treatment (not a treatment considered unusual or alternative). This report had been accepted by the Sanitation, Public Safety, and Industrial Safety Reference Committee.

The U.S. In 1995 National Institute for Health (NIH) organized a conference on technology evaluation, which released a detailed study on the treatment of insomnia and chronic pain through behavioral and relaxation approaches.

The overview of the study suggested there was clear evidence of the efficacy of hypnosis in alleviating chronic cancer-caused pain.

There was also evidence that hypnosis could help minimize the pain caused by conditions such as stress headaches, jaw pain, mucous membrane pain and swelling, and irritable bowel syndrome (IBS).

The British Medical Journal (BMJ) published a Clinical Review in 1999 on the state of existing medical science surrounding hypnotherapy and relaxation therapy. There were some positive conclusions drawn in that study of how hypnosis and relaxation could help relieve the cancer-caused pain, nausea, vomiting, and anxiety.

Hypnosis and relaxation in conjunction with cognitive therapy approach (such as sleep hygiene) to treat insomnia, panic disorders, and phobias have also been shown to be effective. There was also evidence showing that hypnosis had some benefit in treating asthma; the analysis also noted.

One argument the analysis couldn't support was that hypnosis could prolong life, a suggestion some hypnotists have made.

In the "American Health Journal" issue of Monday, February 12, 2007, it announced the following results from a recent study: there was a recovery rate of 38 percent in 600 psychoanalysis sessions.

There was a response rate of 72 percent in 22 behavioral therapy sessions.

There was a recovery rate of 93 percent in 6 hypnotherapy sessions.

It is clear that there has been much research and discussion about the efficacy of hypnosis in treating different medical conditions, from anxiety and panic disorders to cancer-caused pain and nausea.

Over the past 120 years, there have been several research and commissions showing clear evidence that hypnosis provides significant relaxation and advantages for people seeking hypnotherapy to relieve pain and specific conditions.

Continuing support for such facts is possibly a big explanation of why hypnosis is nowadays a common practice in our culture.

Proof That Hypnosis Works

There are several divergent views regarding the efficacy of hypnosis as a method of therapy. Scientific research, however, seems to have fallen squarely in the hypnosis camp, is not only a valid method of treatment but also highly successful.

It is only normal that they will want to be presented with evidence that it really works before anyone attempts an alternative therapy, including hypnosis. Over the past few decades, there have been a variety of experimental studies, and they all seem to point to the same conclusion, hypnosis does indeed work. In this article, I'll write about only a few of the hypnosis experiments and how they provide evidence that hypnosis works.

I'd like to understand how the hypnosis works before I start, though. People who weren't hypnotized always think it's a type of sleep where you can be forced to do things against your will. This idea comes about through stage hypnosis in which the hypnotist "controls" their volunteer. The keyword was a volunteer in that last paragraph. A stage hypnotist may call for volunteers, so they're already willing to do what the hypnotist wants them to do only by volunteering. It's easy to hypnotize someone on stage to dance around, but if the hypnotist told them to go and rob them of a store, do you think the volunteer would? Of course not because the volunteer is there to have fun, not to commit a serious offense.

Hypnotherapy is also somewhat distinct from stage hypnosis (the term for hypnosis as used for medical reasons). Before the hypnotist starts a clinical hypnosis session, and the client must discuss the client's expectations and decide on the areas the therapy must focus on.

The hypnosis is believed to function first by opening the subconscious mind to suggestion. The hypnotist will insert ideas from here to help the client achieve their goal, whether it is to lose weight, stop smoking, or something else altogether.

You should now have a fair idea of how hypnosis works, and now I'm going to provide proof that hypnosis works.

Hypnosis and Recovery

The Harvard Medical School dealt with the influence that hypnosis has on the recovery rate of broken bones in 2003. The research took 12 people with broken ankles and used medical care on half of them, as well as hypnosis on the other half alongside standard treatment.

The findings were impressive because, in six weeks, those who had undergone hypnosis had healed as much as eight and a half years of those who had not. Here the proof hypnosis works are self-evident. Only by incorporating hypnosis to their recovery individuals with broken bones healed more than twenty-five percent faster than those who used the standard care only.

This research can be seen as of special interest to athletes who want to improve the healing process so that they can return to training and competition.

Cromie, J.W. (2003) Hypnosis Helping to Recover. Gazette to Harvard University, May 8, 2003.

Hypnosis on pain management

Scientists at the University of Iowa Health Science Relations fMRI are testing to discover the impact of hypnosis on pain management. The study showed that there was less heat discomfort in people under hypnosis than in those who were not hypnotized. This finding also appeared on brain scans, as the volunteers under hypnosis displayed substantially different brain activity patterns than those who weren't. It definitely means that hypnosis somehow filters out brain pain signals.

University of Iowa Health Science Relations, 5135 Westlawn, Iowa City, Iowa 52242-1178

Hypnosis Reveals On Brain Scans

Researchers at Hull University in 2009 noticed that when scanned, hypnosis had a significant effect on brain function. This shows that hypnosis is not just a placebo treatment, like some critics say it is.

Dr. Michael Heap, a study-engaged psychologist, concluded that hypnosis is priming the mind for the suggestion. This research has not only shown evidence that hypnosis works, but it has also thoroughly clarified how it works.

When a hypnotist is prepared for advice, he will then help his client accomplish their goals. I've only touched on three of the numerous hypnosis experiments, but they've been a lot more. There's evidence that hypnosis works for weight loss, relief from IBS, skin disorders, increased fertility, and more.

Maybe the best evidence that hypnosis works is to try it out for yourself. Anecdotal evidence also comes down to the operating side of the hypnosis. And celebrities like Matt Damon and Ellen DeGeneres went on record as saying hypnosis has helped them stop smoking.

So if you're talking about using hypnosis, please do so honestly, because all the data suggests that hypnosis actually works.

CHAPTER TWO

Hypnosis Weight Loss - Does Hypnosis Work?

The word hypnosis never fails to conjure up images in the minds of most of us of something mysterious, shady, or even downright occult. Be told the word hypnosis, and the image of a black-hatted man shaking his pocket watching back and forth in your mind's eye. That enigmatic hypnotizing figure popularized in movies, comic strips, and television. It's not hard to understand why most people tend to question the efficacy or otherwise of weight loss from hypnosis.

Although many people believe otherwise, it is true that subjects are not really enslaved by a master under a hypnotic spell, who can then take control of their actions. They may seem passive and look like an onlooker is asleep, but in fact, they are in a very attentive state. It is in this highly attentive condition that they become extremely open to suggestion. This explains the effectiveness of weight loss techniques for the hypnosis to a very large extent.

Remember the last time you were so exhausted and lying in bed, and you had the wonderful feeling of being comfortably overwhelmed. Then you wished it could stay this way forever. Well, the fact is-with your cooperation, of course, a qualified hypnotherapist can help you achieve the condition very easily. He will then help you imagine yourself being healthier, happier, wealthier, more comfortable, a non-smoker, or whatever.

So the therapist can also induce in you, during a hypnosis weight loss session, the mindset you need to lose weight, control your food cravings, regular exercise, and so on.

The reasoning behind therapeutic hypnotherapy is that the body and mind are closely interlinked, and one never fails to affect the other. If you say that the body is free of pain or illness to the subconscious mind, it will eventually bring about the change. This is why thousands around the world have experienced weight loss from hypnosis that they never imagined they could.

There's a huge amount of evidence to support the idea of weight loss for hypnosis.

Thanks to the power of hypnotic suggestion, it has been achieved by countless women from birth without pain and discomfort. It has helped countless patients with cancer to control the pain of chemotherapy. And several ex-patients simply owe their recovery to hypnotherapy. Hypnotherapy's effectiveness is overwhelming, and doctors, at last, accept today that hypnosis weight loss works.

Many people don't believe in a weight loss of hypnosis. And there are so many others who do not even think hypnosis is possible.

They confess, however, that they have drifted away while thinking about a loved one, forgotten large parts of a car ride (commonly known as highway hypnosis), or "going far away somewhere" while reading a book. There are examples of trance states in nature. Hypnosis weight loss is just as harmless as all of those, and without any harmful side effects.

Ex-smokers and drug users swear by it. It has repeatedly contributed to fixing marital problems and rectifying criminal behavior.

Hypnosis was also widely used in cases where lie detector tests failed! And thousands have also gained from weight loss on hypnosis.

Smoking, drinking, and over-eating (the leading cause of weight gain and obesity) are poor habits of malformed or misguided thought. Proper counseling or even better, hypnotherapy with the aid of a qualified hypnotherapist will aid you to alter or remove certain mindsets completely and encourage you to improve your life for good.

Wanting to lose weight? Starving, vomiting, and pills would only eventually destroy your health. Find out how to make things safer and more appealing today from

Hypnosis Weight Loss - A New Approach

Hypnosis Weight Loss is perhaps the most effective way of keeping fit in the modern-day. This procedure has been scientifically proven to work quicker and better than bad diets, costly liposuction, and so on. Hypnosis Weight Loss was first introduced back in 1957 by members of the ASCH who included physicians, psychologists, psychiatrists, and several other medical branch members. The ASCH members tested the system on two women's teams, the group that got it ended up losing 17 pounds! Meanwhile, the party that did not undergo hypnotherapy lost just a total of 0.5 pounds.

Hypnosis Weight Loss is essentially a technique in which doctors use mental hypnosis to facilitate losing pounds. The process is and has been proved entirely secure. Some said they were scared that they were going to get brainwashed and maybe even make them lose control because they were vulnerable to set-ups. Most people believe this approach is just like normal hypnosis, which will allow you to influence the brain and behavior of the subject, but this is not true. This uses visual imagery to assist the mindset of the patient in managing their weight.

Hypnosis Weight Loss has been shown to work at its best when the patient has a deep commitment and ability to get fit. If the patient does not want this, the procedure may become more complicated. Tested studies say the procedure is showing patients losing up to 97 percent more weight than they would normally.

You may wonder how this miraculous treatment might work without the patient personally being guided by the hypnotherapist. The reality, though, is that the hypnotist only guides the patient through repeated comfort and encouragement, which strongly affects the mental image of the patient. Therefore it is a secure technique that works to cut your weight efficiently without you losing your sense of control or consciousness.

In addition, courses on Hypnosis Weight Loss are stress-relieving, pleasurable, and successful. It's also shown that if you start the courses after outcomes have been shown, the percentage will double! Helping you to give up the extra pounds in just about no time. Did you ever feel like your weight was in the way of your success? Well, no longer, you can restore your self-image with this process, improve your confidence, but, most importantly, help you lose weight. Hypnosis Weight Loss always works so you can always apply for some more sessions and keep the weight off if you ever regain a few unwanted pounds.

An Example of a Weight Loss Session

One of the most common concerns a hypnotist would tackle revolves around weight loss. There are many reasons why people ultimately become overweight. And the hypnotist weight loss is private to many of the reasons that people who are overweight and obese have for being obese. Here are some examples of what some clients on hypnosis had to eat when they weren't hungry.

Arial sought to lose 15–20 pounds. She was a very attractive young professional woman in search of meaningful living. When she called the hypnotist, she initially wanted to improve her relationship with food. She wanted to see food as the nourishing and fuel source it really is. Unfortunately, she had gotten caught up in using food to alleviate stress, or some other emotion, like so many other overweight people. She got involved in eating too much, eating the wrong foods, and eating at the wrong times. Then these became habits that became happenings every day. You can probably see how that could get out of control very quickly.

Arial has been really good about visiting her dilemma with a hypnotist. Acting in a trance with the subconscious, she and the hypnotist were able to understand the sensation she perceived as hunger. Once that feeling became known, the hypnotist's changing of the meaning of that feeling was a simple process. Rather than interpreting the feeling of hunger, she has now come to realize that feeling means success in gaining control of food. And she was conditioned to feel relaxed and confident with that sense of success.

She has confirmed after just two sessions that she has changed her habits and eats less, and is more relaxed with food. And she announced a substantial amount of weight she'd already lost.

Another overweight person, Jennifer, has recently begun to see a hypnotist change specific behaviors that have resulted in her earning 10 pounds. Jennifer ate really fast, made poor decisions, and did a lot of lazy eating. That's the kind of thing that happens when you sit down to watch television, and you end up eating a whole lot of something. As ice cream chips, cookies, or tubs. You most definitely know what I'm thinking about.

Using any substitute programming, she could only wish to drink water while she was in front of the Tube. Whenever she was interested in feeding, she was focused on their food. She was more aware of how fast she was eating, and she was experimenting and becoming comfortable with slower food.

And she began losing weight by changing her behaviors. These are only a couple of ways to help you reach your goal weight by using hypnosis for weight loss. And because it's a change of behavior and is now a conditioned habit, it is a change of lifestyle forever.

Are you sick of dieting yo-yo, and ready to forever change your food relationship? You are, of course! Take the time to get some free tips on how to use your mind for weight loss by hypnosis to remove junk food from your diet so that you can alleviate extra weight and feel better about yourself. Visit my website, HypnoticState.com, to get your free self-hypnosis course or ebook on how to correctly use your mind to learn how to lose weight through hypnotherapy weight loss to regain control and set yourself free to enjoy life.

Hypnosis for Change

We want to adjust. We are afraid of transition. Hypnosis provides a solution to the problem. How does that work? Hypnosis achieves so by recognizing that the mind is so much stronger than you believe it is and by revealing it to you. But of course, as you don't believe your mind is so strong, you have to distract the doubting side of your mind. This Intentional Interruption disturbance is granted a special name- trance. Yet trance sounds a little eerie and somehow otherworldly, and so theories and irrational fears have arisen about trance and hypnosis. I will discuss these misconceptions and fears and, in so doing, show that hypnosis is the use of a perfectly normal environment to your advantage.

What is it, then?

Hypnosis is definitely not what you imagine it to be. Hypnosis is a state of complete naturalness that we all felt at some point. The space between being completely awake and dormant is probably the best way to explain it. Just imagine, in the days when Sunday was special, lying in bed all warm and cozy, quilt tucked around your chin, not having to stand up, no pressure and huge chunks of time just ceasing to exist as you drift in and out of wakefulness and dreams-yet you're aware of where you are and who you are, and if someone walked in with a steaming cup of tea for you, you'd be fully aware of that.

Many of us driving and traveling frequently would have encountered the somewhat alarming realization that we've just covered a portion of our journey and have absolutely no recollection of it. Were we sleeping? What went wrong? Aliens Kidnapping? Nothing more than slipping into a hypnotic state caused by boredom, which is peacefully conscious. The brain thrives on stimulus and heeds the fresh feedback. Something that remains continuously the same is no hazard, and therefore is not taken into consideration. But if this had happened, another motorist cutting in front, braking unexpectedly, we would have been completely in the present, fully alert, coping with the situation and with no knowledge that we were actually not recording what had happened up to that moment.

In therapeutic hypnosis, the use of phrases and suggestions that inspire you and lead you into this calm, relaxed state will guide you into this trance position. The hypnotherapist then retains the condition when there is a therapeutic intervention.

Will that support me?

If you just want to be free from the dilemma (and I'll write about secret reasons to keep problems again) and you're inspired enough, then there's great chance hypnosis will help. But it's not like surgery where someone makes you unconscious, cuts you open, takes out the bad part, sews you up, wakes you up and sends you off to finish the healing alone. They're two men who work together.

Imagine, your fantasy is to visit the jungle and spend some time in it. The jungle is a potentially dangerous area, so it would make sense to employ this guide if there is a guide available who knows the territory, knows what is safe to eat, and the best places to go to have a very nice time-then. The presence of the guide does not lessen the pleasure of your dream fulfillment-yes; he can even improve it by taking you to beautiful places you have not even heard about.

In my mind territory, I see myself as a guide ... And previous consequences ... And unfitting belief systems ... And take the best way to live your life to the fullest. The hypnotic trance is merely a tool to facilitate fast, safe, and protected entry into this area. What area is this? This area is the unconscious mind, and the unconscious mind holds the key to altering behavior, for this is where such patterns reside-behaviors such as overeating, smoking, addiction, anxiety, phobia, emotional distress, fear of intimacy, inability to sustain a fulfilling relationship, knowledge of poverty, etc.

Does that hurt?

Many people may benefit from hypnosis or may have their problems solved or eased considerably, but they do not take advantage of it. And why are they not profiting from it? They don't call a hypnotherapist for an appointment because they: * don't want to be a chicken (i.e., made to appear foolish) * wrongly assume that traditional medicine is the only remedy and doctors have all the answers * feel that they can't be hypnotized and thus don't see hypnotherapy as a remedy * have been taught to believe that doctors are responsible for their safety-they don't think they can't.

Personal details coming from the past that they don't want to disclose feeling powerless and under someone else's control 'magic,' i.e., a simple, effortless answer to a problem when they've been taught that it requires loads and loads of effort for anything worthwhile.

Will I get hypnotized?

Some people have met a hypnotherapist and thought that they were not hypnotized because they still understood where they were; they could hear noises other than the voice of the hypnotherapist, and they remember everything that was said. These individuals were possibly hypnotized because they encountered all these things in a trance. I also blame the use of the word 'trance,' it conveys the impression that somehow 'not there' is a hypnotized person, sent somewhere else by the hypnotherapist who then works his magic unseen by the hypnotizer. What happens is a hypnotherapist-directed shift of focus. Perhaps a better word is 'Altered State.' Conscious diversion also could suit the bill to encourage the unconscious shift.

An anesthetic is not hypnosis. The patient is not 'magically' switched off anyhow. All that is being used are phrases, but the phrases are being used in a way that attracts attention. The way to determine whether you've been hypnotized or not is by whether or not a transition is taking place. Since visiting a hypnotherapist to quit smoking, more than one patient said to friends, "I wasn't hypnotized. I heard every word he said. I just wanted to stop smoking anyway ..." If there is a difference, hypnosis will be the same.

If I were to say 'don't think about chocolate,' you may have chocolate on your mind at the very moment you read those words-even though I told you not to think about it. If I went on to ask you, please do not even mind the sumptuous velvety smooth chocolate texture of the finest Swiss chocolate as it gradually melts in your mouth and covers your tongue, and under no circumstances to worry about any chocolate supplies you have in the house, and most importantly not to eat some chocolate today ...

You may find that you have the odd thought in your mind about chocolate now. If you're a chocolate, then these recommendations can have a greater effect than whether you can take or leave chocolate. You've been guided to chocolate thinking by being told not to think about chocolate. And I wonder how long it will be before you find yourself eating some chocolate, recalling those words, and then deciding to eat the chocolate openly ... Or maybe you're going to fight the urge just to prove you can't be easily influenced ... But that didn't matter.

If I asked you to imagine holding in your hands a ripe, juicy lemon and bringing it under your nose and smell, scrap the skin and inhale the zest, feel the skin's waxy texture and the fruit's deep yellow color, then slice it open and squeeze a few drops of lemon juice onto your tongue ... I'd be very shocked if there weren't any salivary activity in your mouth right now. There was a transition in you that you had no power to prevent, and when you became aware of it, it had already happened-by which time it is too late.

Have I been hypnotizing you?

I certainly put in your mind thoughts that produced a physiological response. But what I was really doing was demonstrating what hypnosis is all about using the imagination's ability to affect how the body, or mind, is behaving and responding. And if I can do that with salivary glands, maybe I can do it with lymphocytes to help you fight the mechanisms of disease. Or maybe I can change your response to something you're afraid of.

Words are powerful, and they have a power you might not be aware of. A skilled hypnotherapist will use language to bring about the changes you through in your life. And it doesn't really matter whether you're in a deep trance or a light trance pretending that nothing else is happening, because the words are going to work their magic, seeds are going to be sown that will germinate later, changes will take place immediately; you can even get 'permission' in a trance to choose for yourself when the transition can take place and then you remain in control.

Out of Check?

Loss of control is one of those areas of fear which prevents people from enjoying hypnotic intervention. There is a presumption that the hypnotist may have some control over you to prevent you from being helpless and that the hypnotist is obviously in a position to exploit your helplessness. That's one story. I am nothing but an ordinary mortal. I can't make you do something that you don't want to do, at least by making suggestions to you no more than anyone else does. It's just that I'm making suggestions that aim to help you and enhance your quality of life. Others who try to influence you through the power of suggestion tend to have their own best interests at heart.

Another part of this lack of control that causes people to stop having a hypnotherapist's support they need is their fear that a hypnotherapist would make them share all their deepest secrets, or make them relive any of the forgotten traumas of the past. Or even that any of these potentially very humiliating things that have happened to them will need to be seen and exposed to someone.

If you go to a hypnotherapist to quit smoking, or lose weight, or have a healed phobia, or minimize stress rates, or stimulate the immune system to reverse a cycle of illness, then it is extremely unlikely that the therapist will see any value in certain issues you choose to keep private. If you're trying to 'fix' a common issue, so that's what's based on. It will only be looked at where the past is relevant to the problem, and it is more likely to be asked about in waking conversation than in a trance. Trance is used when it would be worth learning to reach the secret and overlooked causes of problems, but in most situations, recovery is about improving the present.

... Three times a day, meals after.

In my experience, orthodox medicine comes from the perspective that an organism is the sum of its parts. There are bits of plumbing (cardio-vascular and digestive systems), bits of wiring (nervous system), scaffolding (skeleton), along with all the tissues, such as muscles, organs, and skin that's also in there. Oh, oh! And it has a computer (brain) system that regulates it-consciously (holding the key, reading from the screen) and unconsciously (beating the heart). In my own experience of this View, I, the one who lives, feels, thinks, and hurts in the body, either have nothing or very little to do with the body's problems. These issues are curable by surgery or drugs, or made tolerable by surgery or drugs, or made less intolerable by surgery or drugs, according to this view.

Now this is all well and good and if you have a broken bone then what you need is plaster, not hypnosis (although hypnosis may help relieve the pain after the plaster has been put in place) and if you have a burst appendix then what you need is a hospital with skilled surgeons and sharp knives and people dedicated to helping you recover quickly-again, not hypnosis (although it might just help accelerate your recovery)

There is no suggestion here that we should all stop visiting doctors and begin hypnotherapist looking. But there is a problem, and that is that the existing opinion is that the mind has no role in medicine and that medicine is about the body alone. Fortunately, the perception is shifting. Many physicians use hypnosis to support their patients or encourage hypnotherapist seeking help. Unfortunately, far more physicians are unaware of the effects of hypnosis and how hypnotherapy can be used to promote accelerated recovery alongside or instead of more traditional therapies.

The Wellbeing of You?

So who's responsible for your safety, then? All of us are brought up with the belief that when we get sick, we need to see a doctor who is going to prescribe our medicine to make us better or send us to someone that can help us.

If you believe that the Medicine Men are responsible for your safety, then you only follow orders and hope that the result will be a cure. If you want to be responsible for your health, then you simply use the Medicine Men as one of many sources of experience to pursue the most appropriate treatment for your illness. Or maybe the cure, which leaves you feeling whole and inviolate. Being responsible doesn't mean running your own project. It means determining for yourself that the surgery is the one out of all the choices available that will leave you feeling better about yourself and your health. Being responsible means doing some research, finding out what psychotherapy can do, finding out what hypnotherapy can do, finding out what healers can do, finding out how your mind can affect your body, finding out what medication can do, finding out what drugs have positive effects and what adverse effects they have-before making a decision.

... And eventually, Hypnosis is a method that makes positive change easier. Often the result is magical; sometimes, the transition takes longer to bring about. Magic isn't science, though, and so there may be opposition from the scientific community. I saw the magic, and I don't need research to prove it's true. Hypnosis is capable, in my own experience, of erasing the effects of a trauma that seriously decreases the quality of life. And it's able to do so in less than 60 minutes-where medications and more advanced methods have had little impact over months or years. I haven't seen a clear empirical reason why this is the case, but it still works.

Let Hypnosis Control Your Eating Habits to Lose Weight, Even Permanently

Controlling your eating habits is really a duty and a challenge. But if you decide to slim your body down because you're overweight, you don't have the option, but to suppress your appetite, raising the amount of food you consume.

If we look at some of the traditional diet programs ways, there are many that are technically true, and may even be successful if we're only vigilant in doing their operation.

The need to manage your diet properly is essential to weight loss. But that requires a lot of effort to do and maintain, as you have to endure abstaining from eating what you wanted to eat. In fact, taking the diet program is directly contrary to your eating habits. It's the primary reason the diet program won't last long, and eventually, the need to lose weight would fail.

If you could maintain the habit of abstaining from eating too much, could you survive to subject yourself to the process? How long? How long?

The diet system is already successful if it is just continued. You should extract fats and cut them down to healthy body shape. Yet you have to make an effort and hang on to maintain the negative behaviors and poor eating habits you're used to denying yourself.

But losing weight with hypnosis by regulating eating habits, the poor eating habits, will just go fast, and will really be far from what we might expect from our discussions above. Both of these weight-loss plans will transform into an easily easy workout approach and diet plans, and you will finally be used to it the easy way.

Study reveals that in hypnosis, you are not taken straight from your unhealthy eating habits to the real abstinence, or are simply observing the diet programs. Hypnosis is a process that first goes to a person's mental faculties. Hypnosis requires a mental manipulation that will gradually create a behavioral disposition and change the physical condition and behaviors of which we are accustomed, based on the set of specific directions and suggestions given to the mind about whatever physical condition or habit or action it is intended about.

With the hypnotic approach of weight loss program, such as the above, a person's behavior is already set in mind, and the physical characteristics and patterns used are adjusted and modified to consistently follow and sustain weight loss plan, exercise, and diet, in a natural way, just as easily as the person's normal lifestyle path.

Losing weight by managing eating habits with hypnosis is much more successful, being a normal, established, and practiced habit, with long-lasting stamina, good health, and a body shaped, trimmed, and appealing.

Interrupting Negative Eating Patterns

There are a number of nuanced explanations why people in their everyday lives establish unhealthy eating habits. When it comes to actively and positively altering these behaviors, weight loss hypnosis operates by interrupting unhealthy habits and replacing them with new motivational ones. From how the mind affects the body, how fat and toxins are removed by consuming nutritious food and drinking clean water, how deep breathing stimulates the metabolism of the bodies, and how continuous personal growth helps to achieve success. The basic principles and methodology for weight loss hypnosis will be discussed in this article.

To make a drastic shift in a body of people, changes must first be made within their minds. The subconscious mind still works to keep you safe and in line with your daily actions. That's why dieting alone sometimes isn't enough to lose the last extra pounds. Since thoughts in minds have a powerful impact on the body, and yet healthy weight loss and improved metabolism require new behavioral habits. That this occurs because it shakes the old thoughts and habits.

The number one explanation for overeating is to prevent mental distress or mask it. We need to learn to forgive ourselves and practice self-love for this purpose. Weight loss hypnosis allows one to accept a new self and unlock the old overweight habits by interrupting them and training them in new safe, and supportive ways. If the old pattern is consuming sugar and fried foods, then a routine of eating fresh vegetables, nuts, seeds, berries, and clean water needs to be the new trend. That is the first step on the journey.

They say you are what you eat, and you finally are what you think about most of you. You begin by forgiving yourself with weight loss hypnosis, and then affirm your new ideal slim self with optimistic thoughts, positive emotions, healthy new eating habits such as eating steamed vegetables, salads, and soups with every meal. Lack of sweets you software to snack on nuts, seeds, and berries. The eating plant produced foods, and drinking plenty of fresh foods would allow your body to quickly remove the fat and toxins that are accumulated in the tissues of your body. The aim is to remove the old addictions to food and sugar and give the body what it needs.

There is one other thing the body needs and desires, along with balanced foods and safe drinking water. Deep rhythmic breathing is a long-lived secret to success with hypnosis in weight loss and safe life. You fill the blood with oxygen by breathing deeply in and breathing out absolutely. When you exhale toxins, you activate the lymphatic system, the way the body removes waste. By developing a ritual of deep breathing for yourself, 5-10 minutes, 3 times a day, you can naturally increase your metabolism and your strength. That one habit will alone change your life. Hypnotists consider these principalities and the following method the magic recipe in weight loss hypnosis.

The Three-Step Pattern Interrupt Technique

If you feel a hunger pang sometime during the day, whether you are about to sit down to a meal at any moment, or if you are tempted to eat fast food, follow the steps outlined here to disrupt the old routine and re-program your mind.

Start by taking five deep breaths where you inhale deeply, and then fully exhale. Know, when you do, that you are in charge and just eat for food, and only as much as you need for energy and wellbeing.

Close your eye, and look out for your body. Imagine your perfect self, and feel lean, safe, and desirable to yourself. See other people around you, and imagine how they view you differently. Visualize yourself in a variety of different circumstances and scenarios as slim and sexy, and really enjoy it.

Drink a full glass of beer. This final phase is important because it has been shown by several research studies that people frequently equate hunger with thirst. But if you've had a big glass of water, there's less risk you'll over-eat during a meal.

They are only a couple of deliberate ways to disrupt your unhealthy eating habits, as you can possibly tell by now. The most widely used weight loss hypnosis techniques are designed to be programmed directly into the subconscious mind using suggestions and orders while a person is deep in trance. However, when you emerge from the trance, you should always note why we overeat, give our bodies what they really need, and use the disruption of the three-step pattern frequently. You will still eat this way.

Ways for Self-Hypnosis to Help You Lose Weight

If none of the normal and conventional weight-loss strategies has succeeded for you, then maybe you need a little self-hypnosis boost to get you in the right direction.

Understanding hypnosis is neither art nor science, or at least it is not right now as scientists and doctors are still debating its use and efficacy to a large degree. However, what's a good concept for hypnosis is that it's a method of thought that may help you accomplish those goals based on a number of factors such as your physical environments and your emotional and mental state.

4 Ways to help you lose weight Self-Hypnosis You can use one or a combination of the following self-hypnosis methods to help you lose weight.

VISUALIZATION-You should be very good at generating visions in your mind while using this self-hypnosis technique to lose weight. In imagination, you have to visualize how you will look in the future and when you have shed the extra pounds in your body effectively. The more thorough and vibrant your dream is better, as it means that one day you are absolutely sure that you will attain that condition.

At daybreak, spend a couple of minutes of your time recreating your dream. The position where you hypnotize yourself should be quiet and calm so that there is no external interference to keep you from recreating your dream.

Keep the dream in your mind for many moments, and convince yourself you're already doing something to make it happen. With utmost trust, tell yourself that it will soon become real. If you work hard enough and believe it, your dream is sure to become a reality!

SUBLIMINAL MESSAGES-This method of self-hypnosis is possibly the simplest to adopt since it allows you to make the least effort. All you need to do is pick the recording of self-hypnosis you think best fits your goals. Afterward, all you have to do before you sleep is play it every night. The subliminal messages from these recordings will go into your brain and get your mind absorbed. Such signals will automatically come into play when you wake up, and you will find it easier to lose weight without even realizing it.

STRESS MANAGEMENT-Some people are having trouble losing weight due to stress. For stress management and reduction, a self-hypnosis technique can be used to make your weight loss techniques finally successful.

A diet and exercise often don't work the way they should-which are to help you lose weight because you're too concerned about the outcome. You think so much about the number of calories that you're eating with every step you take in weight loss.

Using a stress management self-hypnosis technique, you'll finally learn to relax and just let go. You will understand that you no longer have to put pressure on yourself because you are already doing your best. You'll learn to wait comfortably and patiently for the recognition of the fruits of your hard work.

Often suitable for people who have gained weight because of comfort eating is self-hypnosis for stress management. Self-hypnosis will make you know eating isn't necessarily going to help you fix your problems. If anything, it would only make your situation worse.

POSITIVE Thought-Often, what you need is to think about your goals positively in order to be real.

In Rhonda Byrne's bestselling book and video The Key, numerous proofs were provided to support the effectiveness of positive thinking. It's also clarified the rule of attraction how it helps you achieve your goals.

If you want to lose weight successfully, you can use self-hypnosis to persuade yourself that Everything is going according to plan. If you can even persuade yourself that you already lost weight, then that's even better!

There must be no negative terms for a positive argument. Instead of thinking, "I'm not going to eat anymore," you should think more along the lines of "I'm going to be slim" or "I'm going to actually exercise."

In the end, it's always best not to use purely self-hypnosis to help you lose weight. Using self-hypnosis as a supplementary method for optimum outcomes which may improve the effectiveness of the traditional weight loss technique you are currently practicing. Self-hypnosis should not be used as a reason for avoiding medical and wellness therapy.

How to Use Hypnosis Right Away

Self-hypnosis is an effective device, but it is a double-edged weapon, too.

That means it can be extremely helpful, making it much easier to do things that might seem unpleasant or even terrifying at first.

For instance, after doing some self-hypnosis, either self-generated or by listening to some mp3 hypnosis, things like talking to girls, making money, learning new skills can become pretty simple and very enjoyable.

Imagine what it would be like to walk up and start talking to ANYBODY easily and naturally, with so much confidence and self-assurance, they immediately think, "Who is this guy? I LIKE him!" On the other hand, self-hypnosis can be horribly restrictive. Many guys are so stuck on

ONE GIRL, sometimes a girl they've never really spoken to, that they're Ignoring all the other girls around them, only waiting, who is sometimes MUCH BETTER.

That ONE GIRL has that guy in his mind, even though he knows NOTHING about her, imagining her as the perfect girlfriend.

All because he has hypnotized himself to think of her as the ultimate divine angel who can magically fix all of his problems.

You come across a girl like this, with some self-hypnotic fantasy of who she is, and look at her as if she's your world's queen, and she'll probably run for the hills ...

That attitude is rather unattractive, to say the least, in a guy she is NEVER Known.

Yet self-hypnosis, the SAME mental technique, is responsible for either creating amazing desire, or terrible and off-putting neediness.

The reality about hypnosis is that you would do far better to find ways to un-hypnotize, rather than hypnotize yourself.

Most people are hypnotized by their issues and believe the solution is to put more layers of hypnosis on top of that.

Yet trance comes in many respects, and not always better than trance. But understand what kinds of trance are in operation in your life is going to go a long way that just looks for more.

And it's easier to remove stuff when it comes to people, rather than put more stuff on top.

One is programmed (the one that generates need), and the other is self-generated, deliberately selected and will program the programmed behaviors and attitudes of that guy inside you who can speak to Anyone easily and comfortably with so much self-assurance and trust that they won't be able to get enough of you.

Here, it's not a magic pill, and it won't happen immediately, but these methods and hypnosis treatments will literally change your life with everyday practice.

How to Detox Tips - Emotional Detoxing

It's not just toxins from the atmosphere and food that can kill us-we're all familiar with the awful feeling of chewing away unpleasant feelings inside. Feelings such as envy, resentment, dissatisfaction, and unexpressed rage can become internal toxins that eventually damage our well-being and quality of life unless resolved.

More and more scientific studies and trials are showing that a positive outlook and emotional contentment have a beneficial effect on our physical health, while those with a pessimistic view of the world do less well in terms of health. Why not use the time you clean your body during detox to try a deep cleaning of your emotions too?

Emotional detoxification involves getting rid of all those emotions and habits that can ruin your life and distract from your happiness.

What is on the train?

Get a piece of paper and ink, and draw the outline of a six-carriage train. Write the names of the people in the front carriage who are most important in your life. Write out the names of those who are next most important in the second carriage. Go through the carriages, including all the people who are playing a daily part in your life, be it friends, family, or colleagues at work. If it's 10 or only one, it doesn't matter how many you put into every carriage.

Have a look at your train once you have finished. You may be shocked to find out who you wanted to have in the first carriage. Maybe you didn't knowingly realize how much other people meant to you.

Conversely, somebody, who would presume to be right up there may have been demoted.

One question that scares some people when they take their carriage at the front is: did you bring yourself in? If not, then why not? The most important person in your life, aren't you? If you are not, then you need to be. If you don't trust yourself enough, your relationships with other people never run smoothly. Put in now, right in the middle of the front carriage.

Build a mind map

You'll need a large sheet of paper and a set of colored pens or pencils for the next step of this exercise. You must construct something which is known as a mind map. Start by writing your own name right in the center of the paper piece, then write the names of the first train carriage occupants around you, like an inner circle of planets circling your Sun.

Now draw a line between you and each of these men, selecting a color for each one that reflects the state of your relationship in some way-just pick the color that feels good to you. When you've done connecting them to you, draw in the ties where these exist that connect them to each other. Your boss may not have a relationship with your mom, but your partner's going to. Yet again, pick the best colors.

Once you have finished connecting the occupants of the first carriage, write down the names of those in the second carriage, a little further away but still circling around you, and draw in the colored links, first between you and them and then between them and all the others. Do the same for the third, fourth, fifth, and sixth carriages, drawing a colored relation for each carriage and you, but omitting the links to each other, unless they are really important or your mind map is too messy.

You're already aware of what's next. Just sit back and consider the colors you selected for each connection, and what you meant when you selected them. Look at those who have negative connotations for you, to continue within the inner circle. Are you upset with him? Can you understand fully why you're upset with them? Or are you jealous, or do you feel hurt or resentful?

This point, where you're trying to find the cause of your feelings, is at least half the fight. Go deeper than tell 'I'm angry because he hasn't done the washing-up this morning.' Are you the one who does the housework all the time? Does that make you feel, on a fundamental level, taken for granted? Putting the finger on why we feel the way we do about others can sometimes be very tricky, as toxic feelings sometimes come from circumstances in our history rather than directly deriving from the current scenario

5 Ways to Release Toxic Emotions

Have you ever felt sad, depressed, angry, or even a purpose-loss? Of course, you've felt or may experience certain feelings at one point in your life or another. They are part of daily life, but should not be. If you don't know how to deal with toxic feelings, you can do more damage to your body than health. An emotional detox will help you get the right cure you need.

It's not uncommon to hear about detoxifying your colon for optimal health, but what about detoxifying your emotions? You should detox your mind just as you detox your body. It's no secret that there is a connection between mind and body. In fact, research has proven it can cause physical symptoms when the mind is under stress. Not only that, but elevated stress rates have been related to other conditions such as heart disease & high blood pressure because of a believing mechanism. That's why so many doctors and spiritual counselors advise you to watch over your mind. Toxic emotions could kill you, literally! Fortunately, you can do a few easy things to clear your mind, regain your health, and bring your body back into shape.

Start with a Colon Cleanse- Many colon hydrotherapists may respond to the fact that their clients feel better after a colon cleanse following successful colon cleanses. Some clinicians believe intestinal matter helps to keep back negative emotions. Thus it purges toxins as well as harmful feelings when a colon detox is done.

Perform a Healing Ceremony- A healing ceremony may be simple as a day-to-day practice of walking, dancing, breathing, praying, or something that makes you happy and calm. You may conduct a healing ritual alone or with someone you love and trust. The goal is to accept your negative emotions and release them. Once you start the process of healing, you start to feel more alive in your body.

Get a massage— Most definitely, a massage would place you in a serene condition. However, a lot of blocked emotions will be released when pressure is exerted on tense areas throughout your body. If you're on a budget once a week or once a month, it would be nice to get a regular massage, though.

Yoga exercise-Yoga is more than just bending and stretching. You become conscious of your breath and body as you perform yoga. You are also strengthening the muscles, organs & joints, releasing suppressed energy, and calming emotions. You should practice yoga every day, or at least 3 to 5 days a week. If you can't commit to regular yoga sessions, try 5 minutes of deep breathing a day.

Get in Tune with Nature- Go on a brisk walk in the morning sun or stand before the gentle ocean will raise your endorphins and make you admire nature's beauty. Some studies have shown that gardening significantly affected the release of negative emotions. All you need is a pocketful of sunshine, and under any conditions, you'll see how wonderful life can be.

Nothing could be more empowering and energizing than detoxifying the emotions.

-Watch your thoughts; they turn into sentences

-- Pay attention to your words; they become acts.

-Watch out for your actions; they are customs.

-Watch your customs; they are your personality.

-Watch your character; it is your destiny- Frank Outlaw

And when volatile feelings begin to surface, you know just what to do to keep you in good health and comfort. Follow these tips every day, and see how your life can be fulfilled.

Detox Your Mind, Body, and Soul With Positive Affirmations

What are these toxic social and emotional components that have arisen in us? An alarming percentage of the world's population is ignorant of the fact that, in this diseased life, they walk around, burdened by contaminants that leave their mind, body, and soul in a state of spiritual deterioration. One look at today's world and why should anyone be shocked at the endemic which affects the human race.

We live in a world fraught with bad news, tragic incidents, future wars, nuclear cold wars, conflict, and hatred between nations, acts of terrorism, and worse-and they are imposed upon us whenever we turn on the television and watch the news. This is a world built upon the base of suffering and catastrophe, and we can do very little about it. We breathe in an air that is packed with deadly toxins, at the turn of a CFC contaminated spray can have a potential for a global meltdown.

And we are witnessing only recently the collapse of the very economy that regulates the lives of every customer in the world today. The foundations of our life crumble gradually as the days go by, and the impact it has on the mind, body, and soul is very frightening. It's a three-pronged attack that both weakens, and the worst thing is that we don't even know about it. It's this' gloriousness; it's gradually creeping into our minds and throwing a shadow on everything we think about, storms bearing on our goals, expectations, dreams, attitudes, and outlooks in life.

It is this darkness behind every sense of despair, fear, hopelessness, and the trigger that magnifies our lifelong pressures and traumas. There has to be something done, and it has to be done early. Spiritual and mental depression are dangerous factors that can quickly and readily affect the body as well. Depression will cause us to lose appetite, to lose health, and to lose our will to live. Stress can cause migraines, high blood pressure, and in some worst cases-vision loss and temporary mania. On the horizon, we need something bright, a rainbow after the storm, a silver lining in the cloud to give us hope, to give us back our life happiness and to give us joy in the universe.

These are not TV cliché goods but very real solutions to a very real problem with these contaminants in our skin, body, and soul. Positive affirmations have been around for a very long time, and they are exactly what you need to hold the light in your life, and the tale signs of stress and depression are telling sidestep. Never recognize what the world looks like, just see it through a lens of positive thought and joy, and you'll be shocked at the sights you'll see and the things you'll learn in life.

Affirmation for weight loss

Welcome to Weight Loss Affirmations. Below you'll find regular affirmations about weight loss, which can help you lose weight if used regularly.

Statements are a pillar of the New Age theory. In reality, the book "You can heal your life" by Louse Hay, which has several statements that allegedly helped people to change their lives through affirmations and visualization, gives us a powerful tool in the search for weight loss. Whether you believe in them or not, affirmations sure do seem to work.

What are such assertions? They are basic statements that, if possible, you repeat to yourself, out loud, gazing into a mirror. They are tense statements starting with "I"-" I lose weight easily and effortlessly, "for example. They seem to 'come real' with unprecedented frequency over time.

Be prepared at first to feel a little dumb - even a little 'fake,' if you like. The trick is to keep on telling them how it feels. Luckily you don't have to believe in affirmations to make them lose weight, or change something else you like to do in your life. As such, they are very useful instruments. Affirmations will also help you get over a mental barrier and continue your weight loss by speeding or jumping.

Of course, the mystery is why they work. Our best guess is they're close to hypnosis - except, of course, you're 'hypnotizing' yourself, and you're staying in charge of the whole thing. Affirmations are likely to circumvent the conscious mind and communicate directly to the subconscious, which is much more effective at 'getting things done' than the conscious mind of daily life. Many of our weight loss hurdles often reside in the subconscious mind, after all. Therefore the subconscious is the only area they can be altered and developed in.

What is more, why affirmations work is the guess of all. There are many, to be sure, philosophical explications. For example, many people believe that in terms of human desires, abilities, and behavior, thoughts, and beliefs are the most powerful thing in the world. A famous quote refers to this; it is attributed to Henry Ford. The quotation is as follows: "If you think you can or can't, then you're probably right." That is, if you think you can do something, you're most likely right, and you'll be good. However, if you do not think you should, you are right again. The belief prevents your success.

The truth is that most of the causes of the weight issues that people have are emotional or psychological. Nonetheless, they do fall into one of two groups. Some of us have psychological problems which make the carrying of extra weight seem harder. For example, women who have been abused in the past may feel safe if they are overweight and invisible. People don't look at them exactly the same way. The women are feeling stronger physically, and more likely to look after themselves. In a way, all that's fine, but it comes at the expense of one's physical condition. If your psychological desire to maintain weight is at odds with your need to be physically balanced, it has to change something. You have to 'offer' something, in short. Affirmations can be of help over the hump.

The second psychological reason for the problems of people's weight is less profound but no less problematic. This cause is the development of poor habits, which are, of course, all too easy to develop, given the preponderance of fast foods and processed foods, and the mega-portions of high-fat foods that most restaurants seem bent on serving us, whether we want them or not. Affirmations help people to bread unhealthy eating habits very effectively. You might say, for example, "I resist unhealthy food" or "I prefer mostly fresh, safe food" Odds are, you'll see results soon. For first, it will be subtle-you will hesitate to pick up the chocolate bar-but new behaviors will be established very easily, and you will be able to respond more strongly to unhealthy foods.

Permanent weight loss or weight management necessitates a lifestyle adjustment. The affirmations given here will help you improve your lifestyle slowly but gradually.

Make smart and frequent use of the positive weight loss affirmations given below. Weight loss or weight management is, in most cases, a direct result of our lifestyle.

However, the food we consume, the amount of feeding, the way we sleep, the physical exertion we experience, the rest we take, the mental disposition we sustain for a long period of time even for our whole lifespan-defines our weight and/or weight issues. Using an acceptable affirmation about weight loss given below to help with your question.

Most diets just work for as long as you work the diet! The moment dieting ends, all the weight loss gradually starts to come back. It just means you will have weight issues again unless you change your lifestyle. Strong weight-loss affirmations will help improve your lifestyle.

It has been found that our body maintains the weight with which our mind is at peace. When the mind considers it appropriate for some reason, then the body will begin to gain weight, and will soon find itself overweight.

For example, if you found it helpful during childhood to be "big-bodied" for safety reasons, then your subconscious mind will take it upon itself to make you big and then maintain your bigness. It is impossible to lose weight gained in this manner unless the mind is dealt with first.

No type of diet will ever help in these cases. For a real weight loss, our mindset needs to be adjusted. You need to make your mind relaxed with your perfect new weight. Affirmations about weight loss should aid in this mission.

Obesity is often attributed to a certain glandular dysfunction. Diäts or affirmations will not work in such cases. You have to undergo the same kind of medical treatment. When you are excessively overweight, consult your doctor before you start a diet or an affirmation for any glandular problems.

Be careful that the affirmation is worded. Never say, "I'm not fat," because you're focusing on your problem, in this case, that is, being fat. And whatever you concentrate on grows. Concentrate on solving. So say, "I'm thin" or "I'm losing weight every day and becoming slimmer and slimmer." If you're a committed person, then repeating the following affirmations over and over again, at least a hundred times a day, ideally in front of a mirror, for a period of at least six months, will slowly but steadily make you look and live a better life, one that's fitter than fatter. As always, combine two or more of those free weight-loss affirmations or even write your own healthy weight loss affirmation, taking a cue from the following.

Weight loss affirmations are the perfect inspiration for your journey towards weight loss. You can use these positive weight-loss affirmations to help organize your mind with positive behaviors.

We all know it is not that easy to lose weight. Using such affirmations about weight loss may also benefit those who face persistent inner resistance while trying to slim down. This article gives you a rundown of positive affirmations for weight loss and confidence building.

We all have patterns that run within our subconscious mind, beginning at a very early age. As well as our climate, we are strongly influenced by our friends and relatives. If you've been given chocolate repeatedly as a kid to avoid crying, you're likely to have a deep-rooted connection to chocolate and equate it with making you feel better when you're frustrated in adult life.

Generally speaking, the behaviors we develop at an early age are beneficial to us because they protect us and make us special, but some of them may be harmful to our well-being and cause us to undermine ourselves (i.e., emotional food). Affirmations are a perfect way to give optimistic thoughts to your unconscious mind, so you can start thinking and behaving towards yourself in a better way. (Remember my point of first discovering the attributes before weight loss occurs?) Going from negative self-talking to self-love doesn't happen overnight. Using such affirmations over time, however, I found a shift in my thought. And this is the very first move.

1. I trust in my ability to love and embrace who I am.
2. I set myself free from all the shame that I have been dragging around the food I've eaten in the past.
3. I do exercise and take care of my body every day.
4. Healing happens both in my body and my mind.
5. Every time I inhale, my whole being is filled with fresh energy, and every time I exhale, all the toxins and body fat leave my body.
6. Every day my health is getting better and better, and so is my body.
7. Everything I eat cures and nourishes my body, which helps me achieve the ideal weight.
8. With every single day, I am closer and closer to my target weight.
9. I'm so pleased and thankful to be weighing kilograms/pounds now. (Fill in the desired number) I can do it; I do it; my body loses weight right now.

10. I'm letting go of any culpability I'm keeping around food.

11. Eating nutritious foods helps my body get all the nutrients that it needs to be in the best possible shape.

12. With every single day, I am closer and closer to my target weight.

13. I notice my craving for dissolving fat-rich foods.

14. I have a deep desire to consume nutritious foods only, and to let go of some processed food.

15. I am the best version of myself, and I work hard to make myself even better. I'm going to lose weight because I want to, and I got the strength to do that.

16. My body is my temple, and I take care of it every day by consuming only nutritious food that cures and nourishes me. I know my metabolism works to my benefit by helping me reach my optimum weight.

17. I am hitting my desired weight and holding it.

18. I have the ability to control my weight effortlessly by a combination of balanced eating and exercise.

19. I thank my body for all the things it does for me. Every cell in my body is safe and fit, and so I am.

20. Every single moment of the day, I feel my body losing weight.

21. I still properly chew my food so my body can absorb it and flush out the nutrients I need to lose weight.

22. I believe in improving my habits and developing new, meaningful ones.

23. I don't have the need to fill my body with unhealthy food anymore, and I can comfortably handle the temptations.

24. I enjoy life maintaining my target weight and keeping fit.

25. I will meet my weight loss goals, and I won't let anything stand in my way until then.
26. I support my body just the way it is, and I'm still trying to better it.
27. I completely understand that unhealthy food doesn't help me lose weight, so I only eat good, nutritious food.
28. My metabolic rate is at its highest level, and that helps me reach my ideal body weight.
29. I trust in my capacity to love myself genuinely for who I am.
30. I accept the shape of my body and recognize the beauty it holds.
31. I am the maker and pilot of my life.
32. I am letting go of unhelpful behavior patterns around food.
33. I'm encouraging myself to make decisions and choices for my own good.
34. I add to my life the attributes of fulfillment, joy, and contentment as I am now.
35. I'm relinquishing any shame that I carry over food decisions.
36. I accept my body for that shape with which I was blessed.
37. I'll let go of relationships that aren't for my greater good anymore.
38. I believe in myself, and I appreciate my greatness.
39. I'm making myself feel good about being me. I embrace myself for who I am.
40. I hold in my heart the attributes of devotion.
41. I have hope and confidence as to the future.
42. I'm grateful for the body I own, and it all comes naturally for me to lose weight. I'm happy to achieve my goals of weight loss.
43. I'm getting weightless every day.

44. I love doing regular exercise.

45. I eat foods that contribute to my well-being and health.

46. I just feed when I am thirsty.

47. Now, I see myself clearly at my ideal weight.

48. I enjoy savoring nutritious food.

49. I keep an eye on how much I eat.

50. I love the workout; it really makes me feel good.

51. Via workout, I become fitter and stronger every day.

52. I'm easily reaching and keeping my ideal body weight I love and care for.

53. I expect a slim, fit, and attractive body.

54. I'm constantly cultivating more balanced eating habits.

55. Every day I get slimmer.

56. I look and feel just fantastic.

57. I'm doing what's needed to be safe.

58. I am glad to be redefining success.

59. I opt for exercise.

60. I want to eat foods that make me look good.

61. I'm in charge of fitness.

62. I always love my body.

63. I'm patient with my bodybuilding better.

64. I'm exercising happily every morning when I wake up, so I can reach the weight loss I wanted.

65. In changing my eating habits from unhealthy to safe, I devote myself to my weight loss program.

66. In my great effort to lose weight, I am pleased with every aspect that I do.

67. I get slimmer and healthier every single day.

68. I am growing a very attractive body.

69. I am cultivating a lively, healthy lifestyle.

70. I build a body I like, and I enjoy it.

71. Changes in my eating habits are changing my body.

72. I feel amazing now that in 4 weeks I've lost more than 10 pounds, and can't wait to meet my lady friend.

73. I have got a flat stomach.

74. I enjoy getting my own power to make food choices.

75. Happily, I weigh less than 20 pounds.

76. I enjoy exercising 3 to 4 days a week and doing toning exercises 3 days a week at least I drink 8 glasses of water a day.

77. I eat regular fruits and vegetables and mostly eat chicken and fish.

78. I learn and use the intellectual, emotional, and spiritual abilities to succeed. I am able to fix it!

79. I'm willing to develop new thoughts about myself and my body.

80. I love my body and respect it.

81. It's very exciting to discover my special weight loss diet and exercise system.

82. I'm a positive story on weight loss.

83. I'm happy to be the right weight for me. Adopting a balanced eating plan is easy for me.

84. I prefer to accept optimistic thoughts about my ability to make meaningful changes in my life.

85. My body feels fine going. Workouts are enjoyable!

86. I use a deep breath to help me relax and cope with stress.

87. I am a pretty guy.

88. I enjoy being at my ideal weight.

89. I'm a kind guy. I deserve to have love. To lose weight is healthy for me.

90. At my lowest weight, I am a powerful presence in the universe.

91. I liberated my body from the need to judge.

92. I embrace my sexuality and enjoy it. Feeling sensual is Good.

93. My metabolism is great.

94. I maintain optimum health on my body.

How to Get Effective Hypnosis Relaxation Techniques

Stress is a part of daily life for men. Rich or poor, young or old, single or married, male or female ... you will face difficult circumstances in your life, no matter what kind of person you are.

Stress can contribute to so much. It can lead to depression. And depression can lead to somebody committing suicide. Some people often cope with stress by increasing their alcohol, cigarettes, or opioid intake. That's risky behavior that can contribute to addiction. Stress may cause many illnesses in the long term.

That is why methods of stress reduction need to be learned. Relaxation is the secret to soothing tension. There are so many ways to calm your mind: meditation, yoga, calming music, breathing exercises, games, and much more.

Techniques for calming the hypnosis are used to alleviate tension. These have been commonly used for the treatment of insomnia, anxiety, depression, post-traumatic stress disorder, and other stress-related conditions. Such methods were, in turn, often used for less pain during childbirth.

These techniques are like meditation because, during the trance, they teach the individual to concentrate on one point of reference. In relaxation methods with hypnosis, you fell asleep, but in reality, you are awake. The one in charge is your subconscious. A suggestion increases your vulnerability.

Stress is triggered by negative thoughts or emotions. For instance, you unexpectedly lost your job due to the recession. You can begin to think and feel like you're useless or dumb. This can lead to depression. During relaxation with hypnosis, negative or anxious thoughts can be converted into a constructive one. For example, your sense of ignorance or worthlessness can be turned into knowledge about how to improve. That is what relaxation techniques for hypnosis are all about.

Hypnosis calming methods employ hypnosis to modify the actions of an individual. Hypnosis is used to cause relaxation or enhance it. If you can't relax, you should hypnotize yourself into relaxation. Suggestions can be started when hypnotized. Such ideas will help shift your emotions or negative thoughts.

Self-hypnosis is part of methods for calming the hypnosis. This includes using scripts or self-suggestion to put yourself in a trance. Self-hypnosis was also helpful in treating people with insomnia and compulsive disorders. This approach has been of great benefit to people having trouble with alcohol or smoking.

Hypnosis relaxation methods are today commonly used for different forms of diseases because of their beneficial effects. You are initially told to speak with a hypnotherapist about the treatment. You'll need to attend a few sessions with your hypnotherapist to be successful in the therapy. And the hypnotherapist will then teach you about self-hypnosis later on.

Know more about methods for calming the hypnosis. The solution to your problems, maybe these.

Hypnosis Relaxation Techniques to Relieve Stress

Quick, every one of us is familiar with the word stress and what it can bring if it is not handled. Whatever your status, financial condition, nationality, or age you may face from time to time and with the current financial crisis, more and more people find themselves in stressful circumstances. When it comes to relieving stress, we all, of course, have different needs and methods. Some spend time on their own while others attempt to rearrange their busy schedules to eliminate some of their stressors.

There's another approach that can help you with tension, probably; hypnosis. Yet contrary to what might pop up in your mind, the self-hypnosis we're talking about doesn't involve a swinging object or any other device to apply in that regard. To give you a better understanding of what relaxation methods are for hypnosis, here are a few examples: Imagery: you might already have an understanding of what the imagery is. The concept behind the imagery is to use your imagination to recreate a location you find soothing or build for that matter. Whether it's an ocean scenery or a field of flowers, you'll start to feel your tension gradually by focusing on what you're imagining. When you like, you can also use relaxation exercises to complement the imaging to produce quicker and better results. This is a mild type of self-hypnosis that beginners can find especially useful when coping with stress.

Self-hypnosis: As the name suggests, self-hypnosis is when you hypnotize yourself for a deep sense of relaxation to be achieved. But self-hypnosis is by no means a straightforward feat to accomplish. Before beginning self-hypnosis, you'll need to use affirmations (positive words focused on the logical thing you're doing to combat tension, negative emotions, and skills), a calm space free of external distractions, and a deep focus.

Usually, self-hypnosis exercises can last about 15-30 minutes but can be extended depending on the need and preference. This is a practical way of achieving relaxation without the use of any special instruments. You can download hypnosis mp3's for a one-time charge for beginners too. It may have the same effects as self-hypnosis, resulting in the same intense relaxation feeling.

Hypnosis is an incredibly powerful device that can be used for just about anything. From clearly handling stressors to more complex ones. You can also go to a professional hypnotherapist if you still have trouble getting it started yourself. What is important is that you act before stress really begins to wreak havoc on your professional and personal life.

Top Breathing Exercises For Weight Loss

That breathing can help you lose fat is quite an interesting fact. Breathing correctly will potentially help you lose fat and in a better way than the workouts. Deep inhalation can effectively burn 140 percent of calories according to some research. Weight loss is directly proportional to the elevated metabolism rate. Also, in this process, you breathe in oxygen due to deep inhalation, which effectively increases the metabolism and flushes the toxins out of your body.

* **Top Weight Loss Breathing Exercises:-** First, develop a habit of directing the body through the so-called deep inhalation technique. You can opt for walking, jogging, etc. for this method-Secondly, yoga can be the perfect choice to help you follow the right strategies for breathing.

-- Thirdly, the easiest thing one can take is to start properly with inhalation. Seek to take out a few minutes from your busy schedule and practice either in the lying down or standing straight position to properly breathe. Profoundly 'belly breathes' yourself to ensure that substantial quantities of oxygen reach the body. Keep your breath for sometime after that, and then exhale the air through your mouth or a straw.

* Weight loss breathing strategies Stressful conditions rarely give us time to relax to think about what's going on inside our bodies. And we suffer from a dysfunctional mental condition. In fact, our inhalation is the psychological mechanism that gets tremendously affected by the so-called stress. In other words, regular breathing is very important to

increase the rate of metabolism and to cleanse the body's internal systems.

Adequate breathing exercises can be very effective for this:-Deep relaxed inhalation-Calming sigh-Clenched fist-Inventive inhalation-Rolling breath

* Yoga Asans: It is strongly believed that Yoga Asans is very beneficial and encourages good air inhalation and exhalation. Pranayama is one of the asans that has significantly helped people fulfill the criteria for oxygen. These four Yoga stages will help your body get enough oxygen and increase your body's metabolism.

They are -Puraka (inhalation)-Abhyantara Kumbhaka (pause after inhalation) Complete pause-Rechaka (exhalation)-Bahya Kumbhak (pause after exhalation) Empty pause If you just obey the breathing exercises, then weight loss does not occur.

Keep in mind the following tips, too:- Seek to take a balanced diet to ensure the body gets all the food needs.

-- You must also stop consuming water when feeding so that the digestive enzymes do not dilute.

-- Stop desserts and then opt for nuts and berries.

-- You could add even more raw foods to your diet table.

-- Try drinking plenty of water because it helps to kick-start the body's metabolism.

Seek the Weight Loss & Total Body Detox Dynamic Duo!

Deep Breathing For Stress Reduction And Food Health

Will you take for granted the breathability? Care about breathing, ever? Breathing is something most people don't think much about unless they have breathing difficulties. Many people take a very shallow breath. Start paying attention to your breathing, and with each breath, you'll just find that your upper chest shifts slightly.

Breathing performs two essential body functions. One reason why we breathe is to bring oxygen into our body to oxygenate our vital cells. The second function of breathing is the removal by exhalation of toxins and waste products from our bodies.

Shallow respiration results in a lack of oxygen in the cells of your body. Because of this lack of sufficient oxygen, you'll experience symptoms of premature aging, reduced vitality, and your immune system won't function efficiently.

Knowing to take deep breaths has many benefits for the wellbeing. Some of the benefits of deep breathing are: reducing stress, stimulating the lymphatic system (the lymph system is responsible for eliminating contaminants from your body), increasing oxygen to the brain, making you feel more relaxed and clearing your mind, and strengthening and healthier lungs.

Learning how to take deep breaths is easy. It only takes a few minutes of effort a day to concentrate on your breathing and develop a new habit of deep breathing. You've probably breathed shallowly for most of your life, so you might feel a little light-headed or anxious when you first start implementing the deep breathing techniques into your life. You don't get used to fresh oxygen flowing into your body.

If you practice a few days of deep breathing, you'll adapt to the increased oxygen intake and begin to notice all the benefits of regularly practicing deep breathing. Every day take these few minutes to yourself to see how much better you feel.

Simple breathing techniques: Simple Deep Breathing: sit up straight, on the floor with your feet down. Relax your back and put your hands on both sides of the abdomen. Slowly inhale through your nose, first draw your breath into your belly to fill and expand it, then up through your center, and eventually expand your throat. Secure first your belly while exhaling and then your middle and arms. Repeat three-four times. Do this exercise over the whole day many times.

Unlimited Power Breathing by Tony Robbins: This is one of my favorite breathing exercises. I first heard about that Tony Robbins technique. You'll follow a pattern with this breathing technique where you breathe in for one count, hold for 4 counts and exhale for 2 counts.

An example of how to follow this pattern is: Sit up straight, flat on the floor with your feet. Relax your back and put your hands on both sides of the abdomen. You will slowly inhale to the count of 5 through your nose, draw your breath into your abdomen first to fill and expand it, then up through your middle, and finally expand your chest. Then hold

343

your breath to the 20 counts, and exhale to the 10 counts. Ideally, you should work up to 10-breathing sets three times a day. You should work slowly to increase the amount of time you inhale, keep, and exhale to improve the lung capacity.

I urge you to try these basic deep breathing exercises to strengthen your mental and physical condition. Deep respiration is a safe, painless way to enhance your health and benefit instantly from this simple procedure.

When under stress, you may also experiment with taking slow deep breaths. For example, if you're stuck in traffic and feel irritated that you're late for an appointment, spend some minutes taking slow deep breaths and realizing how much better you're feeling.

CHAPTER THREE

Hypnotherapy For Weight Loss

You have undoubtedly heard of people who use hypnosis to help them lose weight, and how they say it worked for them-just as many others have been helped to quit smoking. Yet, do you know how it works?

Weight loss hypnotherapy works when a professional therapist creates a patient's ideal mental environment or action to help achieve a desired outcome or goal. This is when hypnosis can become a collaborator in maintaining weight loss with more traditional methods.

The hypnotic condition is usually generated by the process of induction. Although there are a variety of weight loss inductions for hypnotherapy, the majority of them include suggestions for well-being, relaxation, and calmness. There are often instructions included in the induction to remind the person or imagine some experiences that were pleasant to them.

It has been shown that everyone reacts differently to hypnosis. Some people will describe hypnosis as just a normal focus of attention while feeling calm and relaxed. It would appear that most hypnotized people found it to be an incredibly pleasant and relaxing experience.

Part of the reason why weight loss hypnotherapy works are that it focuses on what might cause someone to be overweight in the first place. A professional hypnotist's goal is to tap into a subconscious person and reprogram it to alter whatever behavior originally led to the weight gain. Many hypnotists may work on programming a negative response to a behavior that they want to alter. The hypnotist might use a threat like overeating that will cause you to experience sick or hate chocolate, reprogramming your subconscious mind as a result. If the programming works the way it's supposed to, you'll find that when you've over-eaten, you're not feeling very good or that you're not interested in eating candy. Alternatively, by planting the idea that you prefer healthy options for yourself and don't need to consume fattening foods, the hypnotist could choose to reinforce your resolve.

If you are considering weight loss hypnotherapy, you might want to check out some of the available self-hypnosis CDs and MP3's. Take a few minutes to check out the weight loss options for hypnotherapy that we would like to suggest.

Several people have been found to have a strong response to suggestions given under hypnosis, while others are not as successful reactive. Often fears of an individual may actually hinder their ability to integrate the hypnotic suggestions given to them, usually based on misconceptions. When someone is hypnotized, they are still aware of what is going on and have control of their actions, as opposed to how it is depicted in books, television, or movies. We are usually aware of themselves and their surroundings, and unless otherwise mentioned, they are aware and remember whatever happens while being hypnotized. Hypnosis is meant to encourage people's acceptance of ideas, but it never goes against their will or pressures them to embrace any unwelcome changes.

For treating pain, anxiety, depression, bad habits, stress, and many other medical and psychological issues, several people have found help with hypnosis.

If you're serious about trying weight loss hypnotherapy, there are quite a few excellent therapists online, as well as self-hypnosis tapes and books with which you can operate on your own.

With the exponential rise in the number of people struggling to meet their ideal weight loss targets, there has arisen another possible method of tackling the issue of overweight. Hypnotherapy is reliable, results-oriented, and non-invasive for weight loss. One of the main reasons for its popularity is that the treatment does not require consulting doctors, buying vitamins, undertaking intense physical exercises, or even going on a low-carbohydrate diet, etc. The weight watcher can do hypnotherapy for weight loss-at most he or she can seek assistance from a professional hypnotist, though many can study and practice hypnotherapy at home through various tools of self-help available.

Weight loss hypnotherapy isn't the only place where hypnosis is used. It is considered one of the most promising treatment methods for treating various mental and physical conditions, including pain control, depression, anxiety attacks, addictions, and much more. The effectiveness of the therapy method is corroborated by the fact that even doctors now recommend hypnotherapy for permanent weight loss and refer licensed hypnotizers to their overweight patients.

The weight loss can be achieved in two ways by hypnosis. The first approach is to see a qualified hypnotist, who will lead you through the hypnotism process. However, for others, the cost of care using a hypnotist's services can be an obstacle. You can take the second choice in these cases, which is self-hypnosis. There's no better help than self-help, after all.

Self-hypnosis is not a daunting activity, and there are numerous self-help devices such as MP3 hypnosis, etc., which can be used in the comfort of your home to learn and practice the art. No, you don't have to hit the gym or buy those pricey diet pills to shed those extra pounds. Weight loss hypnotherapy has proven successful, and there's no reason why it shouldn't deliver the desired result for you too.

The reason hypnosis works to lose weight is that it operates at the subconscious level of the mind, the layer from which most of our cravings, phobias, fears, and apprehensions arise. Hypnosis gets to the root of the overeating problem, lack of motivation to do physical activities, cravings for unhealthy foods, etc. by first soothing the mind and then inserting various constructive ideas that the restful mind picks upon. Hypnotherapy for weight loss is so effective because it changes the outlook on food absolutely. You become a more rational person, capable of separating the good and the bad. You are turned into a more optimistic individual who sets and succeeds in achieving practical weight loss goals.

Can something as easy as weight loss hypnotherapy really be the solution you've been searching for in your fight to drop the pounds and hold the fat away forever? Having a hypnotherapist is becoming increasingly common these days for all sorts of health problems such as giving up smoking, overcoming phobias, and being thinner successfully.

348

How does hypnotherapy work to help someone lose weight?

Being able to come off the street and get hypnotherapy done on you is not normal. You usually have to make an appointment first (and sometimes multiple follow-ups, too).

The hypnotherapist will ask you a series of questions, then start putting you into a trance.

The trance has three phases to it. The first is the step of induction, which is close to the counting down often that you may have seen on television before. The second is a deepening level; as the deeper you are in a trance, the more open you are to suggestions you will be. There's the awakening point, at last.

Why is it successful?

You are given a series of powerful suggestions during a hypnosis session. These stay with you when you return to reality but may lose their influence over time.

This is why having multiple sessions to reinforce the desired results is relatively common. The success rate is relatively poor, with only one session.

The hypnotherapist's ability also has a major impact on how effective it can be. Better ones are going to tailor their sessions exactly to you and not just regurgitate the same scripts they are using for all their other clients. This is because you might find the reasons for your

349

weight issue special, and so only tailor-made solutions can work well for you.

The evidence on how effective this approach is is very scarce and can not be believed to be unbiased by the own data of explicit hypnotherapists. Roughly half of those who take hypnosis can expect some form of weight loss success from it with repeat sessions.

How can I obtain access to it?

Hypnotherapists are found throughout the world. The important thing to remember is that medical practitioners are not approved. Nevertheless, you might be able to access it through the national health service or insurance plan for free.

However, most people would have to pay for those programs. Look for qualified accreditations and testimonials from past clients while finding a successful hypnotherapist to give your money to.

You can also listen to digital audio files, which are also a modern way of self-hypnosis if you don't have access to a local specialist. But don't expect quite the same success levels anywhere compared to using a licensed hypnotherapist's services.

Need Motivation to Exercise? Use Hypnotherapy For Weight Loss

You can not maintain a healthy body without having to participate in some form of daily exercise. Our everyday tasks do not take us as long as they did 100 years ago, nor do they involve the physical exercise they did back then, thanks to modern labor-saving tools. We have our houses built ready, we have our food in a supermarket, and we have washing machines for cleaning our clothing. We get in our cars and drive there instead of walking to the corner store or riding our motorbike to work. We achieve more and are more successful in throwing a more positive light on this matter. We're not as physically active as we should be, however, especially when it comes to burning the calories we eat. Physical exercise is a critical component of lifestyle for all individuals. Studies have shown that we have yet to exercise. A modern approach to inspiring people to increase the amount of exercise in their everyday life is by weight loss hypnotherapy leading to improvements in behavior.

Exercising is a perfect way to improve your health. Research at the Mayo Clinic indicates that during exercise, some brain chemicals are released that can brighten the mood of a person. Regular exercise can help you prevent depression, too. Many disorders, such as high cholesterol, type II diabetes, high blood pressure, and osteoporosis, can be managed with exercise.

Today the majority of people living in the United States are overweight. You will become safer, fitter, and lose weight by doing daily exercise. You'll always sleep well if you do routine exercise. Exercising will make it easier to fall into a deep, restful night's sleep. And it actually constructs your resources, directly and indirectly. You are recharging your energy reserves for the daytime by helping you lose weight and rest better at night.

Hypnotherapy for weight loss is a valuable resource for giving you the necessary encouragement if you have trouble working exercise in your everyday lifestyle. Through the use of hypnotherapy for weight loss and a procedure called neuro-linguistic programming (NLP), attitudes and enthusiasm towards exercise have shown to improve. The biggest obstacle for most people is being inspired and finding the will-power to exercise every day. The use of hypnosis decreases low motivation levels and procrastination. (Densky, 66).

If you want to change your lifestyle, you need to change the way you conduct yourself first. Giving yourself a target and keeping track of your progress are excellent techniques for user behavior. You must be motivated and committed to incorporating physical activity into your life. On average, these lifestyle improvements increase people's exercise of about 48 minutes per week. And 48 minutes is a big change when it comes to doing fitness workouts. Through weight loss hypnosis and some lifestyle changes, people don't need to feel nervous about incorporating exercise into their everyday routine.

Reasons Why Hypnotherapy for Weight Loss Works

For so many people, weight loss is the ultimate (and unattainable) goal. There are hundreds of items on the fitness market to sell - supplements, diet plans, exercise systems, and even 'miracle' solutions. Most of these items struggle to achieve the desired outcomes because weight loss is a complex operation.

A viable option is weight loss hypnosis. It offers a holistic approach, as opposed to many of the diet plans and drugs. Hypnotherapy discusses the physiological causes of excess weight gain, which is why it produces consistent performance.

Strong Encouragement

Limitations are all about conventional weight loss. You must learn which foods to avoid, which poor habits to give up, and how to keep your progress constantly in check. In these cases, there would be a lack of constructive motivation.

The emphasis on weight loss hypnosis is on the positive. It changes patterns of thought inherent in it. Instead of thinking burgers can make you fat, you'll discover that carrots can improve your health and provide important vitamins for your body.

Hypnotic positive suggestion "teaches" how to respect your body and enjoy healthy behaviors. It becomes much easier to maintain the system if you are happy and optimistic about it.

Coping with stress

Do you feel like eating more when you're tired, nervous, lonely, or depressed? If so, you have an unhealthy food relationship, and depend on the wrong method for coping.

Hypnosis can help you find out the root causes of stress, anxiety, and even self-loathing. These emotional factors make you overeat, shaping your relationship with food.

Self-consciousness helps you escape the circumstances that make you feel bad. Additionally, you'll learn how to manage these conditions without turning to food. A more balanced coping strategy is always enough to lose weight and start living a healthier lifestyle.

If you can dream it, then you can!

Another pre-condition for successful motivation is a strong picture of your end goal. Weight loss hypnotherapy simplifies visualizing your performance and then translating it into reality.

Traditional weight loss is often synonymous with uncertainty, and sometimes with despair. As a result, a lot of people lose sight of the end goal and get caught up in a vicious loop.

Visualization and optimistic assumptions must work together to make the goal attainable.

Metaphors are also used by hypnotherapists. They'll say the method of weight loss resembles a sculptor's work. The sculptor works carefully on the rock to expose the perfect form contained within. This sort of visualization is easy to manage and use as an inspiration source.

Sustainable weight loss is a slow, complex process. It includes mind and body, a fact about which so many dietitians are unaware. Hypnotherapy offers access to tools and strategies for coping that ease weight loss and make good nutrition / exercising fun activities.

The only way to excel is to take pleasure at the transformation. It is equally important to deal with compulsive eating. The main and most significant requirement for success is to find the reason why you can't lose weight. Hypnotherapy is going to help you do exactly that.

CHAPTER FOUR

Hypnosis Mind Contro

Experts in various fields are using hypnosis mind control methods to get people to do whatever they want.

There is, of course, a question of ethics connected here, and it depends entirely on the individual how he chooses to use control of the hypnosis mind. When using these methods for beneficial work to plant good ideas / pictures in others' minds, it is definitely welcome.

Nevertheless, many individuals with evil motives use hypnosis mind control to acquire other people's sensitive information. The actions are actually illegal and contemptible in those cases.

Often people use hypnosis mind control techniques in their day-to-day lives without being conscious. You should have told an engrossing tale to your tot and watched him listen attentively to it.

At that time, the story affects your child hypnotically, and certain parts of the story could sound so enticing to him that the images will linger forever in his mind.

Similar scenarios arise when someone watches a captivating film or reads an engrossing novel and loses track of time altogether. Experts only fine-tune those skills and use hypnotic stories to take control of the mind of another human.

If you are in sales, you may even use hypnosis mind control to inject optimistic thoughts or ideas into your customers' minds so that they feel interested in and purchase your product.

And those who would have been completely uninterested in your product / service offered should not have been using hypnosis mind control techniques to begin to show interest.

Skillfully the astute salesmen weave amusing anecdotes with customers in their sales pitches. While the prospects can not, in any way, decide whether hypnotic methods are being used.

Also, the salesmen may attend special training programs to learn and master these skills. Initially, planting the need for any product / service is important for the marketers / salesmen.

For example, if someone already has a car and you try to sell him another car, he may instantly reject the offer. However, if you can manage to seed the thought in his mind that his current car is not in good enough, and a car with better facilities is available at the same price, then he may think about your bid.

The best part of mind management methods for hypnosis is that they can be used in different situations. You may want your child to drink a glass of milk but can not.

Or, you may try to sell in formal meetings but without success, or you may be involved in business-to-business negotiations. The methods have proved to be a great benefit in all the above cases.

However, a person needs to be professional enough to consistently and effectively employ hypnosis mind control in each and every scenario. You may find that the techniques do not have their desired impact in certain scenarios, too. It's likely someone or something else has already affected some of your prospects.

In reality, if he already has a preconceived notion or concept, it is harder to plant a new concept into a person's mind. Therefore qualified hypnotherapists are required in advanced psychological cases where the patient can not get rid of a negative idea / dream.

Another situation where the power of the hypnosis mind is used is dependency. On the back of each and every packet of cigarettes is given health warnings. But this in no way has dissuaded addicted smokers from smoking.

A correlation between an unintended outcome and the desired effect, e.g., stopping smoking, will be formed in the hypnosis mind control system. As soon as the addict reaches out for his packet, the hypnotherapist could plant the picture of an ailing child.

If the abuser has a child, he loves dearly, in no way does he want to hurt him. This will cause the addict to stop smoking because his child's love would replace his cigarette addiction.

Experts often use embedded commands to get the people to do what they want. You might tell your prospect that after having purchased one, he would probably not be interested in buying another car.

This comment could encourage him to consider buying another car even though he doesn't really need a different car.

Obviously, you want to learn even more about hypnosis mind control after reading this article.

Subliminal Portion Control

Subliminal Portion Control will help you over-eating in the fight. One of the first things you need to do when you are on a diet is to exercise portion control. We all know that a good weight loss needs more calories to be consumed than you consume. Or you have to consume fewer calories than your body needs, meaning how much you consume is as important as what you eat.

Probably you lose weight as long as you can keep your will power & not overeat. The problem starts when the power lapses, and it is then too late. It could have been a battle with your partner or a rough day at work, it doesn't matter what it was, but it makes you angry, and you feel better eating.

So, when you have an urge to over-eat, what can you do to limit your portion sizes can surprise you with the answer.

Have you learned of subliminal programming before? It's been in there for decades. Subliminal refers to the things that the mind subconsciously handles. Your entire body subconsciously takes in knowledge, that is, without you knowing it. Your mind constantly filters information, some of which you use to consciously manage your day, but most of it is entirely subliminal.

How can subliminal messages help you lose weight? It works by feeding into your brain the portion control messages without the brain simply accepting them as true. No opposition, no misgivings. The messages are very important tools to help you improve unhealthy habits like eating too much.

More and more people are finding ways to keep themselves safer without taking pills and potions. There are no negative side effects in there, one of the best things about using subliminal messages. Dietary, medicinal products can cause diarrhea to heart problems. When there is such an easy and successful way to achieve safe and balanced weight loss, why someone should take them is a mystery to me.

Maybe you're a little doubtful this subliminal stuff could actually work for you. There is no evidence that it works; the research is comprehensive and has been reported and regularly published. Hypnosis is an effective way to stimulate the subconscious with chosen messages. This has been widely used for all kinds of things for several years.

There are hypnotic recordings, which simultaneously have several tracks of the same voice. You may not be able to actively listen to and understand all tracks, but your subconscious mind senses everything and processes it for you. What you have to do is listen and relax, and even though you think you did not fall asleep during the recording. Your brain heard every single word and is ready to act in accordance with the messages given.

You will feel more relaxed and comfortable when you have control over your eating and start losing weight! When you're irritated, and you think you are struggling with your portion sizes, why not try to turn it around using subliminal programming. You have nothing but those extra pounds to lose!

Mind Control for Portion Control

Officially the United States is the fattest country in the world! Not only do we have the largest number of obese people, and morbidly obese people, but it also seems that the pace at which people add all those extra pounds. What could that dangerous trend cause? Many doctors who are at the forefront of the fight on obesity claim that "size distortion" is one big contributing factor.

Have you ever compared the 50-year-old portion sizes to what we call one single portion today? There are advertisements skilfully built wherever you look to tempt you to eat more than you need. Our fast-food mindset encourages "super-sized" portions to complete and give the best "value" to each other. That causes a lot of distortion to the part. We don't know what a typical portion would look like anymore!

Portion proportions were much more modest only 50 years ago. Meals were served on plates smaller in size. Meat cuts were about the size of a regular hand, unlike today, where a steak might be about the size of an NBA player's feet. In the grocery store, I saw huge chicken breasts that seemed to me like double DD's!

Eventually, those super-sized parts would destroy you! The calories and fat add up bite by bite, and soon you'll be supersized too! The list of obesity-related health issues just keeps on getting longer. Begin with diabetes, heart disease, stomach and digestive issues, issues with respiration, and asthma. Besides the mental problems that are linked to treating ill health and low self-esteem.

"I know I have to lose weight, but I've tried it all and nothing works for me." That's almost word for word what everyone who wants to lose weight is saying. Diets don't work, drugs just work momentarily and then much as with shakes and powders, the weight comes back once you're off them! This is really frustrating.

The best way of losing weight and keeping it off is by adjusting your lifestyle. There needs to be a balanced diet and adequate exercise to meet any long-term goals. I am sure this is not really news for you. Neither is the fact that shifts in actions that are embedded deep in the subconscious mind are difficult to create and maintain.

The best way of getting to the subconscious mind is by hypnosis. Hypnotherapy is effective in treating many different conditions such as chronic pain, smoking, and opioid addictions, and yes, even weight loss! Start by looking for a licensed hypnotist and getting a consultation to address your goals and any concerns you have about the program if you want to try hypnosis.

If you know you've got to lose weight and tried it all without success, then it's time to get serious and remember that your only chance is to start thinking differently and making improvements. You should provide regular, 24/7 emotional support for yourself. Start training the brain to suppress images and negative messages. Rely on optimistic thinking and values to meet your goals for weight loss!

Your Stomach Is the Key to Portion Size

Portion size is one of the most significant issues for the consumer who is serious about losing weight. Anyone who wants to lose weight must learn about healthy eating habits, the importance of fresh fruits and vegetables, avoiding highly processed foods, and the value of whole grains. In fact, I require that each client I see investigate proper nutrition or consult with a professional nutritionist. But yet another major obstacle is regulating the portions we consume. Overweight people still just eat too much, no matter how healthy their food choices are. One alternative is to enter a diet system like Jennie Craig that essentially dictates your food preferences as well as your servings.

These programs, for fast weight loss, have a high success rate. The problem, of course, is that change from this form of highly regimented system to a self-regulating regime can be difficult. While for some of us, it might be workable to carefully measure certain servings, many of my weight loss clients are looking for a simpler way to control portion size than just using measuring cups.

And then there's more. It needs us to consider the Stomach's proper function in controlling our eating habits. We need to start listening to the wisdom of our stomach.

The human stomach is an incredibly flexible organ. Our human ancestors have needed a stomach for much of the last two million years of evolution that could accommodate up to two-quarters of food. That's because they may be spending two days chasing a bear on an empty stomach through the plains. So they had to feed really quickly before the saber-toothed tigers chased them off. The ambiguity of food sources and lack of storage options forced our early ancestors to build a suitable stomach for this climate. Early humans lived a life of almost relentless physical effort. And they would only fill their stomachs with food once every few days. It will be a few pieces of leaves or berries the remainder of the time. Our ancestors did not suffer from conditions linked to overweight.

Now the same large stomach does not serve us anymore. If a modern human living a sedentary existence fills the stomach to capacity just once a day, the unavoidable outcome is obesity. That's because the goal was never to fill this stomach in this way every day. Unfortunately, there are several subtle ways we are conditioned to eat beyond full. As the target of a meal, we are trained to experience eating to a feeling of fullness.

Even as a kid, we were conditioned for stuffing ourselves during our mealtimes.

"Come on, Joey, have another slice of pie. Don't you like it? You've got to grow big and heavy. Are you sick? Where's your appetite? Wouldn't you like to be in a clean plate club?" Restaurant portions are always built to fill us with the room, not to mention the joys of all you can eat buffets. It should hardly be shocking, considering this form of programming, that obesity is a national epidemic.

But the same stomach, which causes such a weight loss problem, also offers us a solution to this problem. I advise my clients to eat slowly and stay tuned to the messages from their stomach after every bite, rather than waiting until they feel bloated to listen to the complaints from their stomach. What this means is that when it's no longer churning with hunger, the stomach sends a more subtle signal.

Instead, our stomach is quiet. Around this time, the stomach tells us, "I have enough now to fend off hunger." Although most overweight people are taught to disregard this early warning and keep on feeding themselves, it's easy to use hypnosis to help us feel this subtle warning and stop eating at that stage. Since the food still in your mouth will take up to twenty minutes to hit your stomach, you'll leave the table with a relaxed feeling of satisfaction. But, with a full stomach, you won't feel the sensation of tiredness, bloating or heartburn that is so normal.

Along with tuning in to the signals of the stomach, we can tailor our taste buds for aid in managing portions. We are all conscious that the first bites of a healthy meal are absolutely tasty when we are genuinely hungry. But after a few bites, when the flavor of our hunger is reduced, the taste of the food decreases. After a few more bites, the taste of the food that disappears entirely and we're just shoving the food in because it's there.

Note how this is true for you the next time you're sitting down to a meal. Now, here's the secret: if you tap into the immense joy of consuming those first bites, you'll increase the enjoyment you consume. Enjoy those bites even more by slowly chewing to consume all the subtle aromas. And as soon as this immense enjoyment is gone, as soon as your meal is normal, even boring, just STOP EATING. You can put in the frig the rest of your delicious meal. Those leftovers will carry you a second serving of pure gustatory bliss tomorrow. But the pleasure has gone away for today, and so is your need to eat.

Most of us aren't used to this way tuning in with our bodies. Many of us are conditioned to immediately stuff our faces during the day in response to any feeling of tension, hunger, or just boredom. Many of

367

us are subconsciously influenced by emotional eating patterns that have nothing to do with our taste buds or with our physical hunger. These problems are dealt with in Parts 1-3, Lifelong Secrets of Weight Loss. So at first, it requires disciplined effort and patience to settle for these subtle signals. My practice as a hypnotherapist also allows me to discuss painful mealtimes in memories of my client to rescue their inner child from those situations where they have developed unhealthy eating habits. Hypnotherapy can then be used to help tune in and respond to these messages coming from our bodies.

Note that our eating patterns are processed in the subconscious mind like all other patterns, which can be easily accessed in a hypnotic trance.

When these new eating habits have been put in place, the benefits are massive. Next, we lose weight without having to count calories easily. Second, we're multiplying the benefits of food as we learn to more effectively tap into our bodies. Second, we are gaining control of the common symptoms of heartburn, bloating, and indigestion that are the basic signs of inadequate portion control. Seek to cultivate the new eating style.

You'll soon learn that you can easily regulate portion size by listening to your own stomach and taste buds. Your life then no longer needs to be about regulating your diet. Perhaps you will enjoy a system like Jenny Craig's beneficial external controls or weight watchers while improving those internal controls. But now you don't have to constantly rely on someone to monitor your eating choices.

Food Portion Control

Of the steps taken to lose weight, eating large portions of food is the single biggest hurdle to overcome. As such, managing food portions is an ability dieters need to cultivate if they want to easily and permanently lose those inches in excess.

That being said, the following are some steps you can take that can help you make this undertaking a reality. In preparation for this task, bear in mind that the central component of food portion control is a serving size.

Visual Serving Sizes

Visually become aware of how much a serving size includes Food portion control starts by visually becoming aware of what constitutes a serving size. A deck of cards, for example, can represent a meat serving, whereas a tennis ball can represent a fruit serving. Once you become aware of the visual aids of these serving sizes, you will then be able to make quick judgments as to how much to eat.

Save Large Portions

Learn how to save extra portions for later Most food servings in restaurants are larger than the normal serving. That being the case, you can expect to order a doggie bag or a tub to take home beforehand.

This is also the case when you're ordering in. To avoid overeating, place the food on a plate instead of eating it from the container in which it arrived. The best part about that is that you will later enjoy the rest of it.

Your Serving Size

Decide what a serving size is for you-A serving for a 200-pound athletic man will be quite different from a small woman, so make sure you take that into account before you eat. When it comes to food portion control, remember, it's not a one-size-fits-all proposition.

In addition, increasing or decreasing the visual aids of daily serving sizes is the best way to determine your personal portion size. A deck of cards, for example, represents about 4-ounce meat serving size. Using the deck of cards as a visual aid, if you need more than that, to make a change to get the correct serving size.

Say No to Seconds

Saying no to seconds-We live in a society that finds more to be better. If it comes to food, this is not the case. Learn to say no to seconds to control how much you eat. At first, it may not be easy, but once it is part of your mentality, saying no to more support will gradually become commonplace.

Divvy up the Servings

Divvy up servings before you eat-usually chips, cookies, and the like come in big bags or boxes. Instead of eating straight out of the package, place a serving size in a bowl or tiny plate, and then put away the rest. This way, it's much easier to control how much you eat, rather than relying on self-control to stop your hand from reaching back into the bag.

Tips to Overcome Portion Control

Portion sizes have greatly increased both inside and outside the house. Adults and kids feed their way through obesity.

Distortion of the portion is normal and generalized. Restaurants and fast-food joints are not the only locations where big portions are served. At home, we even represent bigger portions of ourselves. To make matters worse, most of us underestimate our calorie intake. Shape imbalance may be one of the causes of health issues linked to your expanding waistline and/or obesity.

If you suffer from portion distortion, here are 5 ways of regulating portion and holding your calorie intake in check.

1. The consciousness of portion sizes. Be mindful of how much you eat, and what a balanced portion is. If you're dining in restaurants serving big meals, break the food out, and you'll consume a slice that's better for you and take away the rest to eat later. Otherwise, whether he or she does not like sharing, share the meals with someone who is dining with you.

2. Eat slowly. Most of us hurry to complete our meals. You are likely to have over-eaten by the time you're not hungry anymore.

Let the eating and chewing your food gradually become a habit. This gives time to remember when your brain and stomach is full.

3. Eat more low-calorie foods. The illusion will work in your favor if you eat large quantities of low-calorie fruits and vegetables. They're fiber-high and fill you up. You reduce the amount of high-calorie foods eaten by eating low-calorie fruits and vegetables before the main meal. They make good safe, and satiating snacks too.

4. Smaller plate People tend to eat more when they are being served more food. If you've got a big plate, you're probably going to fill it up and stuff it with more food than you can.

If dining at a party or at home, using smaller plaques like dessert plates. A smaller plate means a smaller amount, which stops you from eating mindlessly.

5. Nutrition label Don't be fooled by the calories mentioned on food labels per serving. The serving size is not uniform. Thus, marketers manipulate this loophole by setting serving sizes to trick you into thinking that there are fewer calories as total calories (which is higher) of the entire content are not shown.

Overcoming Food Impulse Eating

If you're like most people trying to lose weight, you probably think that the trick is to find out how to control your diet in some way. The reality is that you should never expect weight loss to work only through will-power and discipline.

When your will-power lacks energy, the problem is that you have little left to prevent you from slipping back into old habits. Will-power is considerably overrated! It's not about making your diet full. Your primary goal is simply to have power over your food choices.

The fact of the matter is that you don't have control over your diet; the most weight gain occurs at isolated stages. Those are what we call "impulse moments." They are usually very brief, but they can easily add up to the extra calories that you eat. If you have been monitoring your diet for a week, you are likely to see when the moments of impulse eating happen. At first, they may seem random, but if you look closely, you can find that there is typically a reason to feed on the compulsion or habit.

You may have a habit of eating after work when you get home and curl up in front of the television. Perhaps it's when you smell those things like baking fresh cookies. Perhaps it is after a difficult dispute with a partner or family member. The main point is you will usually find that snacking, binges, and impulse feeding were rarely from real hunger "out of your regular routine."

I won't advise you that you can focus on discipline because we all know it won't work long-term. Phase one recognizes the binge eating causes first. You can not strategize against consuming urges unless you know what's going to cause them. You won't be able to keep from creating a stressful situation at all times, but you can change how you react to it.

Your goal is to find a way to alter your behaviors or habits when you are likely to be struck by an eating urge. You need a plan beforehand for what you're going to do or for nothing else how you're going to outlast the situation. It's funny how the impulse eating compulsion usually goes away if you give a certain period of time to pass.

Here's a three-step plan for overcoming impulse eating:

 # 1 Identify impulse eating moments. Write down when and what triggers it. Minimize your exposure to situations that you see impulse eating cause. For example, if you get your morning coffee at Dunkin Donuts and there's too much smell of freshly baked donuts to resist, then change where you get your coffee. You're going to have to make some difficult choices but do whatever they take.

 # 2 Improve the behavior by understanding emotional eating cause There are endless ways you can improve the atmosphere or action to let the energy move. Change your routine, for example, to take a shower first thing after you get home, take the dog for a walk, just do something different from your previous habit of sitting down in front of the TV and snacking.

 # 3 Build a mindful eating mentality. That is exactly how it sounds when you prepare your meals and eat with intent. To start seeing food

376

as fuel, stop comfort foods, and change your attitude. Its aim is to provide energy and nutrients for your body and not to overcome boredom or stress.

Recognize the fact that much of all you eat or drink (except water) can affect your hormonal system in a drug-like way.

Ask yourself, "Am I turning on or off the fat storage switches?" If you eat a mixture of natural foods in tiny amounts, you can keep your "fat burning switches" on. However, if you eat high in starchy carbs, processed / refined foods or meals, you can keep the "fat storage switches" switched on.

I still want to teach nutrition and diet according to the 80/20 law. Look to make eighty percent of your diet come from consuming only nutritious foods. The other 20 percent that comes from food or drink that does not help your muscles but serves as a gourmet treat. You don't have to always be fine. Only pursue balance in the 20 percent group of food and drink.

Simply, you're not going to gain weight from eating an occasional pie with dinner. It's non-supportive food choices that are regularly consumed, which cause weight gain. Know, it's all about being careful about your food. Have a strategy, and always be mindful of what you're trapped in your body.

Eating desires is all about thoughts, habits, and routines. Trying to control your feelings is unlikely to be effective, but you can still alter habits and routines. So be careful with yourself; this will take some practice. If you can just bring yourself to relax and think about the implications of eating something, you'll be much more likely to start making healthier choices.

You may be in the habit of snacking at the office from the candy tub, merely because of urges or tension. If you can pause for a second before eating a piece of candy and contemplating the effect, you will be more likely to walk away.

My last piece of advice is to let yourself get inconvenient. We tend to get trapped in a comfort zone, and to bring about change requires strong emotional feelings. Get to the point that you're completely crazy about your current situation and build a deep belief that "enough is enough." It will give you the top-of-the-mind insight you need to shift your relationships with other foods. When the Big Mac is no longer "comfort food," but something you equate with misery, you're going to be right where you have to be. You need to start looking at food in terms of how it will make you feel and how it will affect your strength, health, and weight.

If anything doesn't help you meet your goals of weight loss, it will set you back, or if nothing else will hinder your progress.

With a dedication to understanding causes and modifying behaviors, you will conquer any and all emotional eating patterns. Dream about what you want, and you've got a clear plan for how to get there. Anything that stops you from doing what you want has to be kicked to the curb.

You owe it to yourself to stand up for your safety and your own happiness. You'll be happy at the end of the day!

7 Ways To Eat Right At Fast Food Restaurants

Even though we all say that we "never" eat fast food, after all, it's so unhealthy-filled with bad fat, salt, sugar, preservatives, chemicals, and who knows what else is not good for the you-the real world, the true truth of life is sooner or later, it will happen.

Here at the home of the big burger / jumbo fries / super milkshake / extra topping pizza / crispy fried chicken / best donuts / monster gulp, etc., fast food-cafeteria, you'll be pulling up in line, about to hit the little speaker where you put in your order or get up to the counter, where you'll be asked: "What do you want?" Wise weight loss plan followers tackle this situation with a technique that doesn't involve getting seduced by feel-bad food, mega-buck ads, or just being so hungry / tired / stressed they'll consume nearly everything.

There's no point in post-junketeria shame-life is too short. It's too short to waste in a lumpy, lazy body that doesn't have enough strength or capacity and that you're shamed into staying with. A solid, shapely body that looks good and feels good needs the right fuel (healthy foods) and fitness routine. No news. No news.

Below are some helpful tips about how to eat healthy at fast-food restaurants plan for your realistic weight loss:

1. Eat before you leave home. Here are some options, all of which can be tucked into your tote or briefcase as you head out in the morning to eat half an hour or so before reaching the restaurant: one of the small portions

of low-fat cottage cheese or yogurt (not the fruit bottom, which has added sugar); a small apple or pear; single-serving oatmeal (adding half a cup of boiling water-easy to do in the microwave) or oatmeal (adding to half a cup of boiling water).

2. Have a large glass of cold water before feeding, again about 15 minutes to half an hour. We sometimes equate hunger with thirst-so your body needs more water before your brain receives the signal for thirst. It also helps to restrict how much you consume before each meal if you drink water.

3. One slice of pizza with water or a nutritional beverage (tea or coffee black) and a green side salad (small amount of vinaigrette dressing-half the box they offer you) is a sensitive lunch or dinner weight loss. Vegetarian pizza is your favorite option.

4. Get the grilled (not fried or breaded) chicken sandwich at the burger joint, on whole wheat, if possible-or simply don't eat the bun. If you have a ton of burger, take the smallest one (one patty) and pass the fried cheese, mayo and catsup on. Skip the fries and drink water or diet soda.

5. Were you aware that even the 'low fat' muffins would contain mega-amounts of salt and sugar and equal as many calories as a whole, healthy

meal at the coffee and donuts places? That is real. Your strategy: black coffee or tea with honey or low-fat cream cheese, chicken or turkey sandwich on whole wheat, or a whole wheat bagel or English muffin.

6. What about the problem of fast-food fried chicken? Again, a grilled lean (white meat) sandwich is your perfect option for weight loss. Completely miss the fries and other extras, including the potato salad with heavy calories. Total on the water or a diet. Ask for extra veg (tomato and lettuce) on a sandwich.

7. Roughly none of the barbeque fast-food restaurants are healthy choices if you want to lose weight. My advice (if you have to go) is to use a cheat day, order a sharing platter, and indulge. Eat to enjoy every bite slowly but stop just before you think you've had plenty. Chances are, you're going to have had too much, too calorie-wise-but this is a cheat day, so let yourself enjoy a bit of fast food indulgence one day (per month or so), realizing that you're back on your balanced eating schedule, not tomorrow but today (and every day before the next cheat day allowed).

How to Eat Right For Fitness

Face it, working out on a cold or rainy day can be a frightening experience. In fact, at any time, the idea of slinging weights or engaging in intense cardio may not even appeal to you remotely. But, it's true, many of us enjoy this fitness part. Often, however, getting energized on the concept of eating healthy is harder. Eating right usually means eating just that which you don't like.

It takes time to get used to that. There's no question about that. I have been working in fitness for more than 25 years, encouraging clients to formulate and adhere to a diet and exercise program that works for them, and I still have my own fair share of difficulty and temptation. It's not easy to stave off the temptation when you crave a bucket of ice cream, but sometimes compromise is necessary.

But it doesn't have to be the awful thing you make it out to be, or maybe in the past, you have made it out to be. There's really something very rewarding that comes with seeing the effects of what fitness eating right can do for you.

Here are a few steps to get you going in the right direction:

Eating Whole Foods

Consuming Whole Meals is perfect for eating fitness healthy. It has three advantages that are completely vital to your goals. Whole grains provide more nutrients (advantage one), fiber (advantage two), and need more energy to break down the ingredients for use by the body.

Improve Eating Frequency

You've heard it said consuming fewer meals a day is a great way to increase the metabolism of your body, and then develop more muscle and lose more weight. In reality, this is right, and if you're not doing that at the moment, it's a great time to start now. See, calories are consumed in the body by digestion. You will potentially consume more calories during the day by holding your body on a mission with smaller meals.

But which sort of meal works best? That takes us to the next tip:

Pack on the protein

Calories are required to burn calories. With protein, it can take up to 30 percent of your calories to use this essential fitness element for energy. That means your body will need 45 only to process it for every 150 calories of protein you take in. As protein is a known muscle builder, you can offer the advantage to your body by consuming more of it, particularly before and after a workout.

And those tips don't even consider what carbohydrates can do for you. Carbs, especially in their unprocessed form, do exactly what you want them to do to your body. Your body needs to work hard to remove fiber from carbs, and in its purest form, this type of diet will put your body to work for you in ways that will consume more calories and improve your metabolism. Because metabolism is such an integral part of weight loss and muscle gain, you'll be on the fast track to conquering your fitness and weight issues once and for all.

Simply integrate all these tips, find a good balance, and the rest will take care of themselves.

How to Eat Right for Optimal Health

You need to know how to eat well for good health if you want to lead longer and safer lives. When we grow older, it is increasingly apparent that "we are what we eat." The expression "garbage in equals garbage out" is beginning to become painfully evident. To achieve optimal health, we have to accept the fact that it is the nutrients that power our body and our wellbeing from the food we consume. Therefore, we have to be very aware of how, what, and what we want to bring into bodies.

Let's face the truth; by pursuing our conventional food pyramid, the new fad diet, and replacing fast food with fresh food, the United States is now one of the world's fattest countries.

Hundreds of diets and fads carry the promise to make you slim. They are keeping you focused on food and weight. We deliver simple lifestyle plans that help you concentrate on nutrition and wellness to achieve optimum health. By following these techniques of lifestyle, you will give your body what it wants without being a slave to track calories, grams, points, or the scale.

1. Listen to Your Body. Your body is a wonderful machine that will let you know what it wants if you listen. That means starting to eat with your stomach and not with your mouth. Learn to know when hungry and eat afterward. Do not feed just out of habit, desire, or emotion. Learn to accept not being full when you're done and then stop feeding. Even if there's food on your plate already.

385

2. Drink 8-10 Water glasses. More than 70 percent of our bodies are fat. The vital fluid carries nutrients, hydrates the body, and flushes toxins from our tissues and cells. Not only do we drink large quantities of water every day (6-18 glasses), but more significantly, in our diet, we need high levels of water in the food. Drink little to no water with your meals, as digestion is slowed down by diluting digestive juices. Evite caffeine or carbonated drinks-opt for juices / and tea. (This is especially important for women of all ages because carbonated drinks increase calcium drain on the bones.)

3. Eat small, nutritious meals. You'll probably find yourself eating three or four times a day if you listen to your body and eat only when you're hungry. You'll be fulfilled by consuming meals that have the right amount of protein, carbohydrates, and fat, and your body will get the nutrients it requires. To ensure that each food group gets the right amount, try these guidelines: Protein. Goal portions of your hand size. Lean meat, fish, egg whites, dairy products, and nuts are all healthy sources of protein.

Carbohydrate Cluster. Eat a portion of complex carbohydrates fist size. Good sources include whole-wheat bread and pasta, wild rice, grain cereals, and potatoes.

Fruits and vegetables. Eat a portion of vegetables or fruits and each meal in the fist size. Look for 5 fruit and vegetable portions during the day.

Large. Large. Limit fat intake to what is needed for adequate flavor.

One more rule is to avoid eating 3 hours before bedtime. Sleeping on a full stomach will slow down your metabolism and make your sleep-disordered.

4. Eat Enough Fresh and Live Food.s every day; our body requires carbohydrates, amino acids, and fatty acids to generate vitamins, minerals, and glucose. Not from a bottle / pill / potion should these nutrients come, but from consuming live foods. Live foods such as fruits and vegetables have high concentrations of readily available nutrients contained in natural amounts in nature. These foods need minimal energy to digest in an uncooked form.

5. Reduce the amount of processed food that is high in nutrient content. We can consume it. After all, we eat to fuel and run the gorgeous body. Many foods are calorie high but nutrient-poor. Eating a high percentage of certain foods means taking in too much food to get enough nutrients. In exchange for a little nutrient benefit, our body also needs to spend considerable energy digesting and breaking down these complex foods. Start asking yourself: which foods give me energy, and which foods drain my energy? Eat a high percentage of fruits and vegetables-they require very little energy to digest, and give your buck a great quality bang!

6. Take time to enjoy what you eat. It's not unusual to see people eating while driving to work and talking on the mobile phone in our fast food, multi-tasking country. Eating on the road definitely doesn't add to the eating satisfaction. Relax when it's time to cook and make sure you like what you cook. Eat it slowly and savor every slice. Allow time between every bite, to remove the food from your body. By taking the time to enjoy your meals, you can find that you know that you've had enough before finishing your meal and that your body will get the food's maximum nutritional value with proper digestion.

7. Eat Enough Fiber. Two kinds of fiber are soluble and insoluble. Soluble fiber, present in our foods such as broccoli, peas, and oat bran, can reduce cholesterol levels. Insoluble fiber found in wheat bran beans and celery accelerates the food as it passes through the intestines. This helps avoid constipation and other issues related to digestion. While fiber does not have any calorie or nutritional value, it does help prevent insulin resistance, a disease that affects your metabolism and accelerates aging. Fiber also slows down carbohydrate breakdown in the body, thus avoiding unexpected increases in blood sugar. Lastly, fiber makes you feel complete, and it helps to stop overeating too much. Most experts in medicine and nutrition recommend taking 25-40 grams of fiber a day.

Optimal wellbeing is not an end objective but a path we are witnessing. The seven lifestyle strategies outlined here will provide you with the nutritional basis for a balanced and productive life.

How to Eat Right & Lose Weight

There's a clear, universal rule about the human body: you'll lose weight if you eat right. Length. Yet great weight-loss success doesn't have to come from drastic lifestyle changes or diet changes. For people who fear the change in lifestyle, it may be easier to stick with smaller things over the long term, and that means performance. If you don't stick to that, after all, nothing works!

One of the subtle improvements you can make to the correct eating direction, and weight loss is to reduce the amount of highly refined carbohydrates that you consume every day. Cut pasta, pizza, and other vehicle foods and increase the number of foods that mean something: meats, vegetables, and fruits.

Processing removes essential nutrients from your food, which is one of the reasons why the entire food movement is so successful: it is a vital part of learning how to eat well. Losing weight can really be as easy as making that little dietary change! It may not be a huge (or incredibly rapid) weight loss, but as long as you stick to the shift you've made, it will be permanent.

Hardcore

If you want to go hardcore and want to learn how to eat better and lose weight, keep this in mind: there is a reason people are reluctant to make the leap to a serious low-carb diet. The first phase of every low-carb diet is known as an induction period, and for a few days (sometimes up to two weeks), it requires almost no eating carbs. That means no fruit, minimal veggies variety, and a lot of protein. This can be particularly harsh on someone (almost everyone) suffering from carb addiction.

The goal is to achieve a homeostatic state called "almost ketosis, which simply means that your body is giving up on carbs as a source of energy and instead decides to burn fat. This is an especially good material for people trying to lose weight! Unfortunately, your weight loss will level out after a while, and the only way to break the plateau is to raise your consumption of carbohydrates (rather counterintuitive, isn't it?) for a day or three, and then limit your consumption of carbohydrates, which will cause your withdrawal.

Low-carb problems

Now, a lot of people lately dissolve low-carb diets, claiming it's unsafe not to eat carbs and causing high cholesterol and other issues. The facts are proven: in order to live your body does not need carbohydrates, it can produce every single carbohydrate it would ever need from a proper supply of protein and fat.

Quite controversial, but still proven: High cholesterol is not a detriment to safety. It had never been so. The only point ever made about high cholesterol is that it is somewhat associated with heart disease, but that's like claiming that being tall is associated with basketball playing. There are definitely more tall basketball players than short ones, but it has little to do with the fact that being tall helps you play basketball. Can you see the difference? Cholesterol is a critical material that your body uses for many reasons throughout the body, one of which is maintaining arterial health, so you're probably increasing your risk of getting a stroke by trying to hold your cholesterol down to prevent heart disease!

The argument about low-carb diets is dumb on its face, for one basic reason: mankind lived a low-carb diet for hundreds of thousands of years before we went and invented agriculture and the grain mill. Human beings evolved to eat meat they had hunted, and the fruits and vegetables they had picked, and very little else. Who do we think we have our own past to talk about?

It's OK For You

So if you're going to take things slowly and make positive improvements to your eating habits, or go crazy and jump in with both feet, know that low-carbohydrate diet is the diet that's best for long-term, sustainable weight loss without health risk. That is the absolute basic rule of eating right & losing weight.

How to Eat Right While Pregnant

Pretty as it is, pregnancy puts multiple demands on the body. Your baby starts her life here. The need to take precedence over yours. Your baby needs to grow loads of nutrients. If nutrients required in your diet are not sufficient, some of them will be removed from your body. A lack of nutrients during pregnancy puts both you and your baby at risk. Conventional wisdom advises you to eat for two. Ok, actually not. Yet you need to change your diet. It's best to eat right during pregnancy to make sure your baby grows healthily.

First Things First

You need a healthy diet that provides all the nutrients necessary for your baby's development. This includes electricity, proteins, minerals, vitamins, etc. While preparing your diet, you must pay attention to the following.

Energy. It takes about 75000 calories to have a boy! All during your pregnancy, you need to eat about 300 calories an extra day. Stop empty calories like butter, jelly, jam, and dressings. Opt for balanced calories such as fruit, vegetables, whole grains, protein, etc.

Protein is the main bodybuilding stone. A decent chunk of your 300 calories extra will come from proteins. High protein foods (lean meats, fish, beans, peanuts) should be included in your meals daily.

Calcium. Essential to teeth and bones. During pregnancy, calcium intake significantly increases. You need calcium 1000–1300 mg a day.

Healthy sources are low-fat beef, tofu, green leafy vegetables, broccoli, and sardines. If you are not getting enough, find a supplement.

Iron. Essential to providing enough oxygen for you and your baby. Every day you need about 27 mg. Sources include leafy greens, lean meat, and poultry.

Folic Acid. This is the hardest part. Before pregnancy and during the first 1 month, you need folic acid. It decreases the chance of a baby developing severe brain and spinal cord deficiencies. Although meeting this requirement in an unplanned pregnancy is difficult, it's crucial that you start early. Food sources include leafy greens, veal, and legumes. Look for an extra if you don't get enough (minimum is 0.4 mg a day).

Weight increase

The increase in weight during pregnancy is important for baby development. If you have a typical body type, you need to gain 25-30 pounds during pregnancy. According to the American College of Obstetricians and Gynecologists (ACOG), if you were underweight before pregnancy and if you were overweight, you need to gain 28-40 pounds and 15-25 pounds. However, carrying over 35-40 pounds puts extra weight on both you and the baby. It raises the risk of hypertension, gestational diabetes, and puts the baby at a higher risk of disease in the long term. In the first trimester, a steady weight gain of 2-4 pounds a month and 3-4 pounds a month later is normal.

Tips for maintaining a healthy diet

A balanced diet is the best way to accomplish anything you need. Frequent, small meals (better absorption and decreased bloating) are better than 2-3 big meals a day. You should build your diet plan for the following.

5-9 servings of fruits and vegetables-excellent sources of vitamins, minerals (iron, calcium, etc.), and trace elements. Their soluble fiber helps sustain healthy digestion and prevent constipation.

6-11 servings of whole grains-Provide proteins, electricity, fiber, and essential minerals such as magnesium; Eat whole-grain foods, because most nutrients are in the grain's outer shell.

Protein foods such as beef, poultry, fish, legumes 3 servings-Pick lean meat to limit fat intake. Include fish as it contains Omega-3 fats, which are important for the brain of babies. It also helps to popular the risk of postpartum depression.

4-5 servings of low-fat dairy products-Excellent calcium and protein source.

Monosaturated fats-An An integral component of the house. Stick to safe monosaturated fats in your diet, because you need to limit fats to around 30 percent of your daily calorie intake. Nuts are a prime source.

Fluids 6-8 glasses per day in a colder climate, more when you are exercising or losing sweat fluids-your body needs to build up the required blood volume and maintain a healthy amount of amniotic fluid, apart from its daily needs. Water, fruit, low-fat dairy, club soda are healthy ways to get it. Stop alcoholic, carbonated, or caffeinated drinks.

Avoiding any growing complications

As the baby grows, the body makes some changes. Some of them aren't very accommodating. Following the right diet plan can go a long way to tackling common problems.

Morning sickness. Eat smaller meals, more widely spread over the day. Stop food, which is greasy, fatty, spicy, or fried. It will intensify the morning sickness. Snack between meals, regularly. Try combining protein with fruit / vegetables (peanut butter carrot, yogurt fruit).

Constipation. It allows more soluble protein, so do plenty of fluids. Whole grains, vegetables, and fruits are safe bets.

Hypertension. One frequent pregnancy issue. Limit salt consumption to prevent a flare-up. A healthy diet will give you all the sodium you need (so there's no need to add salt to the food). Consider adding black pepper or lemon juice to your food to improve flavor, to reduce the salt intake without losing taste.

Diabetes. The need for insulin in your body rises 2-3 times during pregnancy. If insulin is not enough or insulin does not function properly (e.g., due to obesity), you are likely to get high levels of blood sugar. Unchecked, it can cause your baby serious harm. To maintain a healthy level of sugar, consume regular, small meals during the day. Avoid unnecessary sugar and alcoholic drinks.

Allergies Pregnancy can intensify allergies already present and cause new ones. If you think food is involved, look out for things that may make the symptoms worse.

Allergy symptoms usually start shortly after eating but within 2 hours at the latest. Which simplifies the recognition of the food in question. Seek to remove any of the identified allergic foods from your diet, and see if they help.

Popular suspects are Seafood. Particularly shellfish such as crab, lobster, shrimp, and so on. Peanuts / peanut butter. They can also contain aflatoxins, one of the most allergenic foods in the world, which rank among the most active carcinogens known to humans.

Arboreal nuts. Fish Peas, almonds, walnuts, etc. Fish often appear to accumulate toxins higher up in the food chain. Several health warnings are issued about high levels of mercury in Tuna.

Food additives, dyes, preservatives, monosodium glutamate (MSG). MSG may have the added problem of becoming a neurotoxin, too. Animal tests have shown its capacity to damage infants' nervous systems.

Fruits. Strawberries and pineapples, aside from tropical fruits like melons, are prime candidates.

Intolerance If symptoms such as stomach pain, cramps, indigestion, diarrhea, and bloating occur more than 2 hours after feeding, you might have a food intolerance and not an allergy. Primary suspects are milk and milk products containing lactose. Try low-lactose foods such as hard cheeses, yogurt, calcium-free milk fortified with lactose. Tofu is also a good substitute, although the amount of soy food you eat should be reduced. They contain phytoestrogens, which, if ingested in excess, can be harmful to you and your children.

Wheat and other grain containing gluten.

Maize products and products containing starch from the maize.

Supplements Consider taking supplements (particularly good pre-natal vitamin) to ensure you get all the essential nutrients you need. Not all add-ons are produced equal. Talk to your doctor about which product suits your particular needs.

Last thoughts Pregnancy is a beautiful and unique period of your life. Not only does it help you prevent complications from adopting a balanced lifestyle and diet, but it also makes it a smoother experience.

Eat right when you are pregnant, lead a safe lifestyle and, above all, enjoy this wonderful time.

CHAPTER FIVE

What Is Gastric Band Hypnotherapy?

 The gastric band (also known as a lap band) has become an increasingly popular surgical procedure for those who want to lose weight during the last decade or so. A band is fitted around the stomach and inflated in a way that significantly decreases stomach ability. This means the patient consumes less food, which leads to a fast and lasting weight loss.

But surgery with the gastric band isn't without complications. With any surgery of something going wrong, there's always the inherent risk, but there are also some issues that the lap band can specifically cause. It involves a slipped band (which can result in too much or not enough stomach capacity), acid reflux, nausea, vomiting, diarrhea, regurgitation, blockages and other problems. And although the findings are unquestionably impressive, there are definitely hidden risks. But wouldn't it be awesome if there had been a way of replicating the gastric band's success without any of the risks?

Yeah, there's definitely away in there. Recently hypnotherapists repeated the lap band treatment solely with hypnotic suggestions with great results. No scalpels, anesthetics, or wounds-pure mind-power. Hypnotherapy has become the latest craze in weight loss due to its safe and impacts the existence of the gastric band. A quick search on Google shows hundreds of happy patients who have undergone hypnotherapy in the gastric band and lost much of their excess weight. But how exactly does it work?

To understand how gastric band hypnotherapy functions, first, we need to look at hypnosis and the mental effect. Although human mental awareness is far from complete, the most welcoming theory is that the mind consists of two major components-the conscious and the subconscious. You should be most familiar with the idea of conscious thinking because this is from where the daily cycle of thought originates. Whenever you think to yourself, "I am thirsty, I should go get a drink" or something similar that is at work in your conscious mind. Your subconscious mind is much deeper and, in a way, stronger. It governs all those instinctive behaviors and responses you're not really thinking about, your routines, your impulses, and your phobias. Hypnosis operates upon the subconscious mind. The subconscious is primed by hypnosis and able to consider suggestions.

Now we understand how hypnosis works; it is a little clearer how hypnotherapy works on the gastric unit. A hypnotherapist can create a hypnotic state within their client and then speak to them as if it were really occurring via the gastric band technique. There is no pain or something really happening physically at all, but it is very difficult for the subconscious mind to distinguish between illusion and reality. This is why very strong dreams can often seem all too real.

If the subconscious mind assumes that the body is fitted with a gastric band, it will behave as though you are fitted with one. That means you'll feel full faster, eat slowly, and consume smaller meals. This obviously results in weight loss, which is very important.

In addition to being safer than surgery, hypnotherapy by the gastric band is also much more convenient-generally ten times less costly than surgery. There are also professional hypnotherapists selling audio packs that have the very same session on CD or MP3 that are even less costly because the hypnotherapist only has to record the session once with certain clients. It will cost inferior to $100.

And if you are thinking of getting surgery with the gastric band, then the normal form of hypnotherapy might well be worth your consideration.

Hypnotherapy Gastric Band Hypnosis

If you're clinically obese-BMI over 30-there's hope with a virtual gastric band placed under hypnosis-sure, hypnotherapy may be the best all-round weight-loss choice.

I have run two successful tandem weight loss programs and so have had great experience supporting other people with their weight issues-both programs have the same philosophies at their heart. Many people on a diet are eating the items they shouldn't eat or go back to their old ways after dieting and losing weight. Some of their diets that exclude certain foods-leaving an unbalanced diet that puts a strain on their liver and kidneys-which are potentially very dangerous.

I think it's important to get people in touch with the joy of eating healthy food and persuade them of the cost-effectiveness of consuming less good quality food rather than cheaper fat sugar and salt-saturated foods-good nutrition really provides greater value for the buck, and after all, you wouldn't put paraffin in your fuel tank? You wouldn't put fuel in the car to take the metaphor further for comfort eaters if the oil light comes on, would you? Yet the oil light is a sign that something is wrong, and putting chocolate in your mouth won't fix the problems. Comfort food fixes little but gives rise to obesity.

Some of these issues are related to anxiety tension or lack of self-confidence or childhood behaviors rooted in bad eating practices as they grew up: "you have to clear your plate"-for example. I say pounds more in the waste bin than pounds on the floor!

Hypnotherapy may tackle these concerns-providing approaches to cope with anxiety and depression and loss of confidence and using methods such as regression to cope with psychological issues that

402

could have contributed to an unhealthy relationship with food. One lady of 21 stones came to me, and after we had dealt with her bullying problems and offered her dietary advice, she immediately started to lose weight-something she should never have done!

Furthermore, the American Health Authority also blames a lot of obesity on fast food-which you can also call "junkie" food-the food has added fat sugar and salt, and the taste buds are actually addicted to this stuff-if you've ever seen "Supersize me" you know how unhealthy it can be, especially if the eating style is skewed to junk food.

The food diary is another valuable tool-to remember what you eat but also when and why you consume those foods?

When obesity hits a BMI point of over 30 then for some the option is strong: if they don't lose weight, they'll have serious health problems-they'll have tried all the diets and pills and found them to fail because they haven't solved any of the underlying reasons for overeating. Often they are left with a Gastric Band's only option-the the operation will cost about £3,000-£ 7,000-in some situations the operation can be risky-I just had a client who had several strokes and two of them extreme-the risks are too great for her.

Combining good nutritional advice with learning to properly enjoy food and dealing with underlying psychological problems can result in permanent weight loss. Alternatively, putting the Virtual Gastric band under hypnosis, using something called the HypnoGastricBand system, makes weight loss even more probable. The machine works with most people, and consumers have mentioned not only being able to see and observe the procedure without discomfort but also being able to feel it when it's installed. The discomfort passes quickly, and people find that they start eating smaller portions and, like my other customers who lose weight, they eat less and exercise more and start enjoying the food again.

The procedure of the gastric band is spoken about under hypnosis, and because it is keyhole surgery it is relatively easy-wrapping a band around the higher part of the stomach-the band can be tightened or loosened, and the golf ball-sized portion of the stomach created by the band means that the hypothalamus, the appetite regulator, informs you that you are complete-the food passes about naturally. The hypnotic stomach band placed under hypnosis works the same way as a real stomach band. There are also weight reduction plans that do the same but skip wearing the gastric band if you have a BMI under 30.

And if you have tried the others and it has failed, try hypnotherapy. My experience is, it's a practical option for most people.

Do Hypnosis Gastric Bands Really Work?

Lately, there's been a lot of press reports about the virtual hypnotic gastric band, but does that work? The vast quantity of websites out there would have you believe it works, and it is successful.

Such websites will just tell you what they want you to know and will not show you the absolute truth. Yeah, there have been reports in the press, but are they not just press releases sent to their publications to improve this procedure's credibility?

There won't be any newspaper publishing an article saying the hypnotic gastric band doesn't work, so who will read it? It would be as if they were writing an article stating that children do not like eating vegetables; no one would read it. But if they released an article that says a new technique was discovered that would make kids enjoy vegetables, then it would be a different story.

Indeed, peer-reviewed scientific journals are the only outlets that can talk authoritatively about whether a technique works or not. Since this technique was on the market, there were no scientifically validated studies demonstrating the effectiveness of the virtual hypnotic gastric unit.

This weight-loss strategy is no different from the conventional weight-loss methods that want you to believe they have the solution to your weight problem. We want you to believe their treatment will instantly turn off the mental and physiological factors that generate the weight issue right now. No treatment can do that, particularly if it doesn't tackle the real reasons why you're having a weight issue.

Having done one of those procedures is just like cutting off the head of a plant. At first, you think it's gone, and you start making progress, but those roots begin to crave the light underground. Then gradually, they start breaking the surface of the soil, at which point the old patterns of actions begin to take over again. You could then say to yourself that you deserve this chocolate bar because you were so good. Finally, those weeds start flowering and start taking up more of your lawn, at which point you give up trying to lose weight completely.

The hypnotic band may help some people temporarily lose weight, but over time people may start stretching out the limits of this procedure, as some do with the actual surgical version. The one thing about overeating mental and physiological factors is that if they aren't treated, they will come back again. This may be during one of those times a person undergoes emotional stress. The person can then use the food as a comfort either consciously or even unconsciously.

The individual then goes back to believing after this event that they have a gastric band fitted but that one little slip up has now undermined the confidence. The next time the person goes through some emotional stress, then it's even easier for them to use food for comfort because they've done it in the past already.

Finally, the individual then no longer believes that they are fitted with a gastric band and resort to the emotional and physiological dimensions of overeating that have never really been discussed first. The individual will then want to fork out another £1200, which will charge some places to get it done again.

To be genuinely competitive with your weight, the mental and physiological factors that lead to your being overweight need to be overcome not just in the short term but in the long term. There is, therefore, no need to go through some kind of actual or imaginary process by solving these problems since the origins of the problem are no longer there.

"The Hypnoband" - Myth Or Reality?

A gastric band operation is a technique used to make the stomach size smaller so that the volume of food required to "tell" the brain that the patient is complete is considerably smaller.

The patient thus eats less and can lose weight with little to no effort.

While the benefits are self-explaining, there are many drawbacks, including the fact that this procedure carries risks, like many others. The side effects of post-surgery result in a significant amount of discomfort, swelling, bruising, and cost varies between £5 K and £8K.

Hypnosis provides a wonderful and significantly cheaper alternative to the gastric band procedure; the "HYPNO-BAND" or "HYPNO-BAND" is essentially the method of using hypnosis, misdirection and persuasive power to make an individual believe that he or she had actually undergone a gastric band procedure when there was no surgery. The client is then forced to forget all about the hypnosis session and preparations and make-believe there has been a real surgery.

How could this be? Very literally, with the associated emotions, perceptions, and physical changes, our unconscious mind is able to manipulate and erase part of reality and construct a new collection of memories and beliefs.

This type of work on hypnotherapy can be implemented with various approaches and settings that give considerably different outcomes. The more practical and accurate the gimmicks are, and the greater the chances of success.

The big question is: What happens if the client finds out that no operation has actually been carried out?

Can the knowledge that no surgery was done immediately neutralize the results?

Well, the fact is, if the client learns there was no surgery, the "programmed" values in his or her mind would eventually shift and begin to accept that his or her stomach is the same size it was before.

Certainly, if the person figures out the truth late enough for the stomach to shrink due to the reduced amount of food eaten, the stomach would shrink. But what are the chances of keeping the truth that long? What are the chances of the client not expecting some sort of physician follow up? What are the chances the consumer won't doubt the lack of scare? What are the chances that friends and family members won't tell the company that no operation has ever taken place? I'm just saying slim, really lean.

Of course, if you have an open mind enough to know that if your appetite has been decreased because you understand that no surgery has been done, or perhaps better realize that your appetite is decreased simply because your mind has been "reprogrammed" to feel less hungry, then you can choose to believe that hypnosis will make you feel like your stomach is no longer able to eat as mucus. And that is a ton possible.

Is "HYPNO-BAND" really working? And when it does, it really does!

Will that work for everyone? Categorically no. Is the "HYPNO-BAND" better than some other treatments focused on Weight Loss Hypnosis? For others, it can be, and not for others.

Recommend this? While the "HYPNO-BAND" would work better for certain people than other types of hypnosis-based treatment, we do believe certain methods of hypnotherapy will work just as well, if not better. The "HYPNO-BAND" can, therefore, be the most suitable solution for a limited percentage of people.

Incorporating NLP, EFT, Nutrition, and Personal Training advice makes the way we apply this type of therapy even more effective. Clients record weight loss of anywhere from 2 to 6lbs a week.

Gastric Band Hypnotherapy - Yes or No, How Do I Decide?

Some overweight people think they will solve all their issues with food, weight loss, and overeating by having gastric band hypnotherapy. This, in many ways, echoes the preconceived ideas sometimes held about hypnotherapy; let someone else take control of it, tell me what to do, and then my mind will be programmed differently, and I will do what I have been instructed to do.

Gastric band hypnotherapy addresses several concerns about having the actual operation, with all the ramifications of a major surgical procedure, but consumers still need to discuss their underlying issues with their diet and overeating relationship. After having had gastric band surgery, people were known to put on weight because they liquidated their food, chocolate bars, ice cream so desperate to fix their food / sugar. In this respect, the procedure for hypnotherapy is no different. Clients must be prepared to work with the therapy and tackle their problems to support and sustain weight loss.

Hypnotherapy and counseling are effective ways to address the underlying reasons for overeating or eating incorrect food. Addressing those causes, and people also find that they start treating themselves better and start losing weight as a result. They resolve the reasons behind their bad habits, low self-esteem, inability to put themselves first, and find that their commitment to eating healthy foods at the right time do so as their confidence improves. They learn that their stomach is their fist size, and appreciate the importance of serving suitable portion sizes. They may begin regular exercise in a manner that improves their fitness levels.

There are often several areas that need to be addressed before gastric band hypnotherapy is considered:-Comfort eating is a problem for many people. Eating in the evenings while watching television, using chocolate, cakes, crisps to ease the stresses of life may provide temporary relief, but the reality is that many unnecessary extra calories are often consumed. This then gives added stress as the realization of what was eaten dawns.

-- Take time to have the right mealtimes. Sit and eat at the dining table, in a more disciplined way. Eat gradually, and concentrate on having fun with every mouthful. Use a smaller plate and make food a pleasurable experience with its appearance, color, texture, smell, all an important part of the experience. Remove any distractions, such as work, television, and reading content. Enjoy food in every mouthful.

-- Poor eating habits can be improved by preparing ahead of time, scheduling yourself so that shopping for food includes buying fresh, nutritious, easy to prepare foods that allow a positive relationship with food. If food needs to be prepared late at night or after a tiring day at work, snacking, ordering a take-off, or consuming pre-chilled meals or quick, high-fat alternatives may be all too tempting. By preparing a weekly menu, maybe with evening meals planned in advance and ready to be taken out of the freezer, and with lunchtime items that are readily accessible meal times, a safer, less stressful choice will create.

-- Low self-esteem can mean people find food to be their one reliable friend. Hypnotherapy should address certain interactions that led to low self-esteem. Some people may have had serious, unforgiving parents, school teachers, brothers, and sisters. They may have been bullied at school and found that their miserable existence provided a temporary respite from food. Hypnotherapy may relegate those earlier experiences to the past, where they belong, and allow for the adoption of increased trust, self-belief, and self-esteem.

Gastric band or no gastric band, food issues, and weight loss never get resolved easily. A third party relying on someone else to address issues, in turn, means relinquishing responsibility for personal choices and decisions. Even though it works overtime, the underlying causes and compulsions still re-emerge in the short-term. It is necessary to fix any underlying issues, not just the symptoms, to learn healthier eating habits and to improve the food relationship. Then, it will solve the problem.

Gastric Band Hypnotherapy, How to Decide

Gastric band hypnotherapy is a treatment that, when addressed, frequently provokes strong opinions. Some people see it as an effective weight loss procedure in favor of the decision. Others claim that it doesn't address the underlying causes for the diet and weight issue, that the treatment alone isn't enough to cope with weight loss.

The truth is, treatment of the gastric band done either surgically or with hypnotherapy does not prevent someone from putting on weight. People can still liquidate food, candy, drink sugar, fatten beverages if they so desire. An individual needs to address their food and eating relationships before considering performing the treatment.

Let's look at what needs to be resolved before we agree to undergo hypnotherapy for the gastric band.

-- Food is a love / hate relationship in the lives of many people, as they fail to have a healthy food relationship. Many people don't schedule their meals beforehand, so they end up eating fast snacks, processed food, unhealthy foods because they're too busy to determine what to eat, where to shop, and then actually prepare a meal.

-- Managing stress can be an aid. Many people lead highly stressed lives with several stress areas. While food shopping and its preparation can be considered stressful, relaxation, warmth, de-stressing is often associated with eating and drinking and are something to look forward to at the end of the day. Unhealthy or over-eating may have begun as a quick fix, a recompense, a temporary measure until the stress areas are addressed.

A little forward planning will help better manage stress and implement healthier eating habits. Organizing regular healthy meal breaks throughout the day, making nutritious snacks available such as fresh fruit, nuts, crispy vegetables to nibble will make it possible to better manage stressful situations through breaks, and good food.

-- Many people are suspicious about food, particularly when they try to lose weight. In supermarkets, reading the labels; does low-fat mean low-sugar, what about salt, chemicals, preservatives? Getting to learn a bit more about food preparation, taking time to shop wisely, preparing meals accordingly are items that can do the cooking and eating a more pleasurable, enjoyable experience that adds value to your life. The appetizing aromas of food, the different colors, textures, and the way it is served can all make mealtimes a pleasurable, enjoyable experience, and a fun part of the day.

-- Take your time with the food. Feed more slowly, savor the smell, flavor, texture of what you consume. Sit down slowly and eat, putting your cutlery between every mouthful. Let the pressure off by preparing meals for the week ahead. So if you come home, in the freezer or the slow cooker, there is something already prepared, so you don't have to hurry about.

-- Better look after yourself. Drink still more tea. Many people drink too little water, and then think they're hungry when they're a bit dehydrated in fact. Commit to more normal, better sleep. Keep your bedroom cool, airy and tidy, and it will be a relaxing place to relax and sleep. You're less likely to overeat, binge, or break your pledge to healthy eating when you feel better about yourself.

-- Exercise is a vital part of healthy living and is a successful way to lose weight when combined with a good diet. Some people want to use a gym, as they feel obligated to go daily after paying a subscription fee. They may like the structure of daily exercises, fitness classes, or swimming and maybe combining it with a social aspect of frequent mixing and meeting with people. Others like to go out with family and friends for a daily walk or join a tennis club, badminton or golf. Doing something you enjoy, that works for you is the only way to engage in exercise on a regular basis.

Before determining if gastric band hypnotherapy is for you, it's important to look at ways to strengthen your relationship with food and eating. You will then determine whether gastric band hypnotherapy is a viable next step in your dedication to weight loss while adopting a healthy diet, exercise, and food-related behaviors.

Hypnotic Virtual Gastric Band Therapy

Initiated by Sheila Granger, the hypnotic virtual gastric band weight loss device is a groundbreaking weight loss program. The system has been checked and proven to cause no diet weight loss.

The program effectively harnesses each individual's power and helps individuals improve their lives completely. The system's strength is that virtually everyone will join.

Why the virtual stomach band hypnosis works, The virtual stomach band is essentially a non-surgical procedure that uses the power of hypnosis to make sure you're comfortable with just tiny amounts of food. Once you go to the hospital for the operation, a professional surgeon will treat you, who will advise you that your stomach size is smaller, and you need to start eating small amounts of food.

You will also be advised during the procedure that the stomach band will make your stomach smaller, and it will automatically adjust itself to allow you to lose weight slowly and safely. You will also get hypnotic recommendations to dislike mischievous food. Besides this, you'll also be asked how to move your body healthily to make sure you're physically fit.

The treatment basically seeks to reassure you that you are full, so you lack the desire to eat more; thus, you eat only small amounts of food.

A virtual gastric band is associated with flicking a switch in the brain, according to Wendy Hoyle, a Redhill-based hypnotherapist (specializing in weight-loss hypnotherapy without dieting). This is because the band shifts the attitude of a person about food and helps one control the cravings.

Difference between virtual gastric band and actual gastric band

The virtual band is confused with the lap band (actual gastric band) by many. The reality is the two are entirely different. This is because the interactive band deals with the mindset of an individual and their relationship with food, while the real band does not deal with the mind of a person-the band is actually put into the stomach to minimize the amount of food you consume.

The other thing is that you have to consume a pureed diet for a number of weeks before you start consuming regular food when the lap band is implanted into your body. If you overeat, you will break the band, causing you to return to the operating room.

You don't have to think about bursting the band due to overeating with the virtual band. This is because if you know you're over-eating, what you need to do is go for hypnotherapy where you'll get the band tightened by hypnosis.

Virtual gastric band advantages

• It's easy: all you need to do is visit a surgeon who will constantly remind you that the stomach is tiny and that you need to change your eating habits.

• It is affordable: because no surgical instruments are needed, the procedure is inexpensive compared to bariatric surgery and other operations.

• No side effects: this is because the treatment is non-invasive.

The virtual gastric band system is time-tested and has been shown to be successful in causing weight loss. If you're interested in weight loss without any side effects, this is a treatment that you should consider taking on.

Does Gastric Band Surgery Really Work?

In today's culture, hypnosis for all illnesses is becoming increasingly common, but many people are still doubtful as to whether it really works. Whether it's weight loss hypnotherapy or smoking aid, there are plenty of places to get hypnosis in London and around the UK.

Hypnosis is now seen as one of the most successful ways to lose weight and hold it off, with celebrities like Lily Allen and Geri Halliwell using it to help keep their weight down, it's no wonder it's had such a popularity increase.

Hypnosis is when the body is at a calm state of awareness. Gastric band hypnosis uses suggestion and imagination carefully constructed to allow you to subconsciously believe you've had a gastric band installed. This makes it so that you can only eat small portions of food, i.e., just enough for nutritional and energy needs but nothing more. The obvious consequence of this is weight loss.

British woman Marion Cornslost has been reported to have lost more than 44lbs in weight and reduced her dress size from 22 to 14 in four months after being hypnotized into thinking she had a gastric band attached. Marion tried "any other diet and program the world has to offer" before going on this treatment, like Atkins, WeightWatchers, Slimfast, milkshakes, weight loss pills, and even a personal trainer! But none of that was as good as the curriculum on hypnosis.

There are many scam artists operating in this market, so it's understandable that it might not be the preferred choice for everyone. But if you want to look at something like that, the difference between success and failure will largely depend on the skill of the hypnotherapist you select. There should be no issue for an ethical health practitioner to provide you with references so you can check his track record.

My view? It's just time to learn. This kind of weight loss may not be the cup of tea for everyone, but keeping an eye on developments in this field may be worthwhile. Of note, the operation has far fewer side effects and health risks than actual gastric band surgery, so are certainly something to remember. Until making any decisions, make sure you talk to the people involved and make sure that whomever you choose to do, your hypnosis is ethical in their practices.

Gastric Band Surgery Versus Gastric Band Hypnosis

So, you're just talking about making your weight issue serious. You are always feeling out of shape and want to start slimming down. In fact, you are so serious that you are even considering a surgical operation to help you take off the weight. Now that we know you're serious let's take your options over.

Weight loss is about getting in fewer calories than you're eating. If you eat 3,500 calories in a week as you would usually consume, you will lose 1 pound of weight. That means you're going to want to lose 500 calories a day for this to happen. You'll have lost 50 pounds over the course of a year. Increase the number of calories you remove from your regular or weekly diet, and the number of pounds you lose over time will increase. These are the fundamentals of weight loss, and even though you choose surgery to assist you in your weight loss journey, those fundamentals don't change.

Your surgical choices include many different procedures, and the one that this article focuses on is the surgery of the gastric band. You will be wheeled into the operating room for gastric band surgery, where you will be sedated, and a team of doctors conducts a laparoscopic procedure. That allows you to make a number of small incisions in your chest and stomach region. The doctors must put very small cameras and surgical instruments into these incisions. The surgeons should be able to cut off pieces of fat while watching their progress on a TV screen and move back the organs that cover the stomach. It is so they can develop a tunnel beneath your stomach bag.

The surgeon will then add a band across the top of your stomach until the tunnel is completed. This band is close to your trash bag, getting a twist closure. This closure has the function of isolating the top part of your stomach and using that to create a smaller reservoir to collect the food you consume. It will then slowly reach the rest of your stomach as it breaks down and can pass through the now very small gap created by the gastric band.

After you have mounted your gastric band, you would always need to eat smaller quantities of food in order to lose weight. Recall that the formula for losing one pound a week is consuming 500 fewer calories a day. That didn't improve anyway. What has changed is that at one point, the stomach is incapable of eating a lot of food. Your stomach has expanded to the size of a golf ball, physically. Eating more than 4 or 5 mouthfuls of food would now place a great deal of stress on your digestive system, and you'll get a very poor physical reaction to eating too much. Those doctors call this dumping.

Gastric band hypnosis is a very interesting way of making use of the imagination. Using the technique of stomach band hypnosis, you will have a mental stomach band mounted and will be directed to follow the smaller portions of the procedure that the surgical patients will follow. Some virtual participants in the gastric band find that they experience a tightness in their stomach after the virtual gastric band is activated. They have the same kind of emotions as if they did actually perform the actual surgical procedure. If this happens to you, you will then be motivated to adopt a fewer-food eating regimen, and you will lose weight.

And I invite you to join one of my free weight loss groups for the gastric band hypnosis. These organizations are actively studying this method to see how successful it can be. It has been attaining a success rate of 90-95 percent, with attendants losing weight. There are also reduced-priced individual sessions available for the New York virtual gastric band, and for the remainder of 2010, you can take advantage of these free and low-cost deals.

CHAPTER SIX

Creating Positive Daily Affirmations to Live Your Best Life

Positive daily affirmations are a great tool to make your dreams come true. Affirmations are words or phrases regularly pronounced to reinforce a single belief. They help to reprogram the subconscious mind from negative to a positive thought. The idea is to take optimistic thoughts on what you want to see happen in your life and repeat them enough to make them part of your thinking. It becomes a conviction afterthought is repeated, and creeds become our reality. Follow these simple steps to come up with your own meaningful affirmations:

Step 1: Decide What You Want to Achieve in Your Life Start by analyzing what you'd like to improve in your life in the next few months or in the year. Want to get a career that's satisfying more? Want to care less about what other people think? Want to be more polite, more understanding? Want to feel more like yourself in all facets of your life? Write down this below. If you have a long list, pick the most significant one, follow all of the steps, and repeat with the others.

Step 2: Create Positive Statements. Once you get an idea of what you want to change, but the idea into a few simple statements representing the truth of that change. Make sure to make it a constructive statement in the present tense when composing an affirmation. For instance, if you want a more fulfilling job, you would think your statement would be: I want a more fulfilling job. But it would be always a more important affirmation: My work is satisfying. These two sentences are similar, but the intention is shifted from wanting a fulfilling job to actually having one by using the second sentence. It's very important to be that precise and constructive when writing your affirmations.

Step 3: Keep Them Practical. Your subconscious mind will benefit from positive statements that broaden and extend your viewpoint, but if you push things too far, your "inner judge" can step in and contradict the statements. So make your affirmation logical, but also optimistic. If you do this, it will work for you with positive affirmations. For instance, "My work is satisfying," affirmation could seem like too much of a stretch, and your subconscious mind might put up a fight. In this situation, you may need an assurance of the "bridge" to help you feel the validity of your argument. Your "bridge" declaration may be: "I am on my way to a satisfying career," or "I am thankful for all the satisfying aspects of my work."

Step 4: Congratulations to them! You have produced affirmations that change a life. Now you're putting them to everyday use.

• Read them aloud every day, either in the morning or before bedtime. Speak in a strong positive voice, when reading them. Reading them out in front of a mirror is also great.

• Write them up and post them anywhere you see them every day, like a fridge or a mirror in your bathroom. Or write them down on sticky notes and stick them all over!

• Record reading them and listen to them by car, by subway, or when you're exercising.

You get the impression. Making your affirmations a part of your daily life can keep you focused on what you want to achieve. You can do exactly that!

Focusing on Your Presence of Mind With Mindful Affirmations

What is Mindfulness?

In fact, the concept of mindfulness has been around for thousands of years. It has its origins in the earliest Buddhist teachings (2500 years ago). Over the centuries, it was used in traditional Eastern contemplative practices such as Hatha Yoga and other practices of meditation. In the utter recognition of their own life, Zen masters taught the mindfulness to enlightened monks.

The way we use the term here, though, mindfulness should not be confused with mysticism or spirituality centered inward. Today Mindfulness refers not only to the acceptance of one's reality but also to what one is doing with that reality. Mindfulness, as we use it, is the ability to live in the moment and to relate to the world in a non-judgmental and reflexive manner as opposed to reactive fashion.

In recent years, Mindfulness has been modified by science and westernization so that it can be practiced every day, used without years of practice, and consistent and useful within almost every modern human activity. Mindfulness is essentially an introspective technique for grounding your feelings, emotions, and actions in the fact you are feeling at the moment, so you can stand back, observe, understand yourself more thoroughly and take care of your own needs.

The act of Mindfulness is the ability to focus your attention on your inner thoughts while allowing past or future concerns to go away. Witnessing your thoughts popping up and then going away without self-criticism will take some practice, but most people can accomplish this without extensive training, just daily practice. Only monitoring your breathing, for example, can have a calming effect on your mind and slowly regain your sense of wellbeing. When you quiet your thoughts about what to do and your instincts decide what to do, your subconscious mind takes over. Here you move gently from dwelling on the past or the future to focus on what you are currently doing right. Being in the state of consciousness helps you to listen to your heart and figure out what you really need. Mindfulness helps you to remember your emotions, observe your thoughts, and to move away from distraction.

We live in an age of constant chaos and transition. Probably most of us get on autopilot through life. Our brain is filled with restless ideas and memories, which are difficult to keep track of, particularly when we get stressed. We tend to "tune out" and just "try to get through the day." Naturally, everybody's mind wanders, but when you practice mindfulness, you are aware of wandering your mind and can gradually redirect it back to the present. Mindfulness lets you quiet all the noise in your head gently. Paying attention to your breathing, monitoring your emotions, or checking for stress in your body are just a few of the many ways to reduce mental chatter. You can learn to avoid the tendency to jump to conclusions through diligent practice, make assumptions and idle decisions, and understand that your negative or positive feelings come from you and not from the outside world around you.

Dr. Marsha Linehan, founder of Dialectical Behavior Therapy (DBT) based facts, says we need to adopt a "Reflexive Mentality" to cope with anxiety and improve. Your mind is conditioned here to behave like Teflon; nothing will stick to it long enough to be attached. Beware

427

of giving calmness and patience to those who follow the practice has been shown. People who practice everyday Mindfulness are not evaluating their material but processing life. Mindfulness, the ultimate state, is mental resilience.

In reality, mindfulness can also help you stay focused and conscious even when you're engaged in mundane activities such as driving, eating, and going. Research has demonstrated its positive effects on immune system boosting, pain management, stress reduction, and personal awareness cultivation.

A beginning Mindful sequence may involve:

-sitting in a quiet and comfortable location

-thinking about where you are and what you are doing right now

-closing your eyes

-allowing thoughts to move out of your consciousness with your unjudging mind and gentle persuasion

-focusing on the sensations of breathing and noticing each breath.

What are Affirmations?

Affirmations are declarative remarks about something you already know, have done, or intend to do. When you use an Affirmation, you are not only aware of your thoughts, but you take control of them consciously. When you speak, write, read, or even think of an affirmation, you actually take action to consider what is good about you.

Studies have shown that much of our day to day thinking is negative. Working with Affirmations makes you aware of how creativity chips away self-defeating thoughts. Affirmations help you construct a new reality and imagine what you want from life.

Negativity will theoretically endanger your wellbeing and happiness. In fact, you are more likely to be pessimistic and not realistic or optimistic when you don't pay attention to your thinking. The more you know what you're actually telling yourself, the more optimistic you're going to sound. Using command-based phraseology, retaining the Affirmation in the present tense, and making it a reality-based phraseology provides more strengthening. Telling yourself constantly that you are, or will be, worthy, safe, and effective, the more the optimistic attitude flows. By using regular Affirmations, you are more likely to see a bounce in your step and a lift in your life.

What are Mindful Affirmations?

"Mindful Affirmations" are not just motivational comments. We use the term as thought-provoking phrases, which derive loosely from the mindfulness ideas of Dr. Jon Kabat-Zinn, who developed Mindfulness's medical and meditative models. He came up with Eight Stations of Mindful Meditation:

-Smile

-Relax

-Arrive

-Attend

-Find the Essence

-Slow down

-Listen

-See things from a new perspective

Mindful Affirmations integrate one or more of those active stations into each passage to help the Mindful notion of having an "open mind" where possibilities have no limits. They are not meditations as Dr. Zinn, and others have used them. Mindful Affirmations take ordinary affirmations such as "Your self-confidence will carry you on," and make them more reality-based so that the reader will slowly understand and accept the truth about their lives. An example of extending the above affirmation into a Positive Affirmation would be, "I never thought of my own self-worth until I saw myself going backward in life. Letting myself go and losing everything I had won me made me feel trapped and dependent. I now see how harnessing my self-esteem will help me not only find my way but also take me through life."

Pain is rising and inevitable. Alas, too many of us have become addicted to pain. Yet pain is facultative! Mindful affirmations make our conscious and subconscious minds look at our suffering and let go of our worries over the unknown. Our subconscious mind inside has a desire for change, but it doesn't know what to change or how to do it. Our outer conscious mind is desirous of relaxing, calming, and embracing our situation. Our two minds eliminate expectations / accusations while working in concert and encourage us to gently analyze our past emotions, thoughts, and actions without concentrating or being judgmental.

When Mindful Affirmations are written in the first person, they can help the reader not only empathize with the writer but gradually begin to accept and support their own suffering, saying within themselves, "I guess I'm not alone." Mindful Affirmations not only break down the self-imposed isolation of the reader but also give them shift choices such as in the passage, "I'm seeing that response rather than being alone." One of Mindfulness' core values is being able to see yourself and the world around you with a "different set of eyes." The emphasis is on embracing, participating, and discovering a new way of living or looking at life (refers to "Play" therapy). Mindful affirmations enable the thought of the reader to remain engaged while encouraging the surrender of old baggage and unmet standards.

Mindful affirmations use positive assertions such as "I feel happy," but allow our present awareness to reinforce the statement that gives us clear thinking to see our options. It's a technique to cope with. For example, the statement "I make myself sit and notice my surroundings when I'm anxious" reflects your inner desire to remain calm and focused, rather than being distracted and scattered.

The book takes Affirmations to the next level by first discussing how "I" (the reader) has arrived at the state of being unable to take control, what has resulted, and how "I" plans to take command of my future life.

Using these three Reinforcement elements not only encourages the desire to do better but also plants the seed more deeply that "I" can improve, and "I" will benefit from my experience. In fact, mental affirmations are cyclical. Any time a negative feeling occurs, the reader has the option to do good or not.

Affirmations to Live By

Affirmations have a long-standing history, and they seem to be around since the dawn of time. Some may call them prayers, while others view them as nothing more than positive thought. All those things are they, and much more. For one thing, I'm sure they're one of the most successful ways to achieve self-fulfillment.

I use regular affirmations. I think we should all live our lives as an affirmation, and in real life, itself is the greatest affirmation of all.

Here are my 10 favorite affirmations for those of you who are new to affirmations.

1. I am getting better and better every day and in every way.

2. Whenever I set a definite target, to build and maintain massive momentum, I take immediate action toward its attainment.

3. I take full responsibility for the truth of the world in which I live, and I make steady progress in building the truth of my deepest dreams and desires.

4. Fear is a great friend to me. I live my life as if my biggest fear — the fear of mediocrity-ruled it.

5. I am grateful for the challenges that I face because the challenges that fulfill my life are overcoming.

6. I am thankful for the richness that flows through my life because I am a money magnet.

433

7. Today I live life to the fullest since the past is ancient history, and the future is never to come.

8. I thank you for my ever-growing wealth, for I can do great good to humanity with great wealth.

9. In my life, I take total personal responsibility for managing my destiny.

10. Public status shows mean little to me; it is my ever-growing wealth and what good I can do about it that is much more important to me.

Those are some of my favorite claims. I have created or adopted thousands more after nearly 50 years in search of self-fulfillment. The main thing to remember is to be continually watchful of your current subconscious state and use the most suitable phrases for your present state of mind. Your mind is in a constant state of change, and the claims that have been important to you in the past may no longer be valid in your present life.

While the "New Age" basis for the "Law of Attraction" is currently based on Quantum Theory, it is the evolutionary process that is really spreading "The Answer." Evolution claims that everything in the world is in a state of flux. Evolution demands either that we grow and succeed, or that we are doomed for extinction. So, as you establish your claims, note that our evolutionary mandate is development and progress. Defeat is not an option. Settle for nothing short of total self-fulfillment.

Affirmation Music Will Transform You

Improving self-esteem: self-discussion = self-esteem

We are bombarded with repetitive advertising, news, opinion, and sensory knowledge every day. In the brain, neuronal pathways form grooves or patterns that result in repetitive patterns of thought. Within our brains, negative perspectives taken from a multitude of sources become crystallized experiences. We tend to assume that these ideas are "our," and they are accepted and cherished by the ego and thereby become an integral part of our belief systems. In addition, our conscious mind interprets this knowledge and processes these signals on the basis of our understanding of family, community, and culture.

If these trends are negative, we will establish negative internal dialogs in the near future, and these recordings will play over and over inside our heads, resulting in low self-esteem, depression, addiction, and a pessimistic world view. Such negative mentalities leave us to think 'in the shell,' trapped, without change or improvement, and our relationships, health, income, and other areas of our lives are starting to suffer.

Groove Control: How to create self-esteem and trust Through Affirmations

Meditation has helped me see that my thoughts are becoming my acts, and I have to be aware of what kind of self-talk I allow my consciousness to enter into. When I control my emotions, then what I do is controlled. I tend to think constructive and useful thoughts,

436

rather than negative and harmful thoughts because we are what we think the most.

The understanding has been of good service to me. I had very low self-esteem as a young man. I started to redefine how and what I felt about myself, and I set out to reprogram those long-held, cherished convictions purposefully with the use of constructive everyday affirmations.

What is Affirmation?

Affirmations are optimistic declarations about your core beliefs, ideals, and prevailing inner interactions with yourself.

Positive day-to-day affirmations will help you sustain a good mental outlook, increase self-esteem, and concentrate on your desired prosperity, performance, health, relationships, or any aspect of your life you want to change. Repeating and believing affirmations will help reprogram the mind from the negative self-talk that holds you away from the achievement, happiness, wholeness, and fulfillment that you deserve.

A New Genre of Inspiring Music: Combining Empathy and Affirmation

I understand the tremendous emotional impact music can have on the psyche as a musician. I'd joke to myself on the dance floor man singing happily all the lyrics to a song he once knew back in his day. He hadn't even thought about it. The music brought back life into the past. I'm sure he can remember where he was, who was with him, and what he felt when he heard that particular song last time.

Then a light went off, "Why don't I combine music and affirmation's tremendous power to build a strong, repetitive emotional re-programming tool to help minimize negative self-talking!" This auto recommendation album, played, for example, on your drive home, would help infuse optimistic statements into the brain. Old beliefs will be reshuffled into fresh, healthier beliefs, shifting the very foundation of the inner dialogue we have with ourselves.

"I'm getting better and stronger every day, in every way" French pharmacist, Emile Coue Mind Power Secrets: How Words Build You Words that we shape in our minds are mini creations that come from the little self, or ego that doesn't exist, and Higher Self that is All That Is. We form our reality together. Words affect our environments, our bodies, minds, and so on. A simple word can have so many meanings depending on how presented it is, and the purpose behind it. Once the word comes out, it brings tremendous strength to it. Words may organize, kill, ease, love, criticize, inspire, or praise.

The words "I am" are powerful phrases. Those clear words say the world you are here, ready to build and focus your energy on your highest good and intentions.

Discover Your True Self Behind the Words

Why are we drawn and repelled by others at those terms? Aim definitely has a great influence. The meaning behind the word propels the word deeper into the minds of our conscious and subconscious. In fact, our attitudes, value structures, motives, and expectations play a role in how the term is understood or viewed.

The Bible says: "The word (OM, Jesus, Allah) was in the beginning, and the Word was with God, and the Word was God" (John 1:01). Yogis claim this celestial sound pulse is heard as a sound of different frequencies, or a combination of sounds. To Hinduism, OM is known as the essential vibration from which all else emerges. OM is the refrain or chant that is often used in meditation and is sung at the start of many Hindu prayers. My beloved author, Paramahansa Yogananda, calls OM the sound of celestial motor vibration.

Thoughts + Beliefs = Reality. If we believe we can ...... we can!

Core values on who we think we are are at the core of our inner dialogue with ourselves. It has to have an emotional impact on you for affirmations to be truly successful. You have to 'know' that they are real. Speaking or singing the affirmation out loud with great conviction ignites the fire of passion within you, thereby magnetizing your thoughts and polarizing them. When your conviction charges the confirmation, energy becomes a movement or e-motion, and your thoughts and desires turn into reality.

"Whatever the mind can perceive and believe it can accomplish." -- The Napoleonic Hill

Mother of Skill: Repetition

The notion of falling into our minds takes daily practice. For optimum motivation, the affirmations should be repeated regularly. When the mind is comfortable and open to fresh ideas, it is best to plant new seeds of improvement into the fertile soil of the mind. It is best to listen to or repeat your optimistic everyday statements after your meditation session. The mind may resist rising above old ideas, hardened attitudes, values, preconceived notions, and conditionings, but with ample time, practice and repetition of affirmations of love, trust, power, or success, you can re-channel the mind to new and more useful ideas about you and your planet.

What is so wonderful about motivational music is that you don't even have to worry about the latest song consciously; you just need to listen to it every day. Soon, the subconscious mind will assimilate the new mode of thought and will take hold of the new belief. The situation you desire will be generated automatically.

The Concept of Self-awareness: As Within, So Without

As I grow as an individual and discover continuous newness about myself and the world I live in, I become ever more conscious of the importance of language, knowledge, and belief as to the major players in how I co-create a life worth living in. I have realized that what we are saying and feeling about ourselves is becoming our reality. And if we are really merely terminals for our Higher Force, we have to be mindful of what we think and speak and how we speak it.

As I dive into consciousness and the role it plays in my transformation from an ego-centered individual to a God-centered individual, I come face to face again with the notion that all life is subjective and that there is a divine solution for all problems. In a sea of energy, there is nothing else but water. The energy is perhaps the sound vibration, and it is the very building block of our life and reality. As a songwriter, singer, and audio engineer, this musical, electric consciousness excites me. But I'm going to save that for another thing.

Becoming and being-The Divine Healing of Everyday Positive Affirmations

What we draw to ourselves must be what we believe, resonate and vibrate too. How we control fine particles of thought, how we set energy in motion by fanning the fire of desire inside, and what we want to concentrate on all helps to build what we end up being.

Every day listen or sing to the music of praise and believe it to be real. Write down your own special affirmations and build the life that you dream of. Control your reflections. Be mindful of your terms, and the underlying meaning. Your strength is limitless by the use of affirmation music, combined with explicitly defined written goals and applied faith.

How To Have Positive Weight Loss Through Affirmations

To get a perfect body, we adopt diet plans or weight loss pills these days. Those methods are unfortunately not very effective. Either they fail, or they are short-term if they do succeed. We are gaining weight in no time, and again, we will follow the same methods to reduce excess fats. Alternatively, loss of weight can be accomplished by a healthy and normal method. The key to achieving healthy weight loss is by making use of affirmations of successful weight loss.

Positive affirmations about weight loss serve as a mind reprogramming app. They change the structure of your inner creed by implanting every thought, whether positive or negative, into our minds in the form of a pattern when repeated several times. Then our subconscious incorporates these behaviors into our daily lives leading to either positive or negative improvement. The reason diet plans don't perform well is that they can change your habits, but they rarely change your patterns of thinking. Strong affirmations about weight loss work in the opposite direction, shifting the values to achieve better behaviors. Coincidentally, the use of affirmations of successful weight loss works far more efficiently in the long term than the easy strategies for diets alone.

The first step toward achieving your target is to get rid of all those negative thoughts, inner beliefs, and habits that contribute to weight problems like 'I'm so fat' or 'I gain weight every day.' These thoughts prevent you from attaining ideal weight. Your subconscious is making your body gain weight because the subconscious is leading you to believe such negative thoughts are real. Start weight loss by maintaining a positive attitude. The less you get to slim down, the more optimistic feelings you get.

Second, and perhaps the most significant phase, is to live in the present. Rather than worrying about past mistakes, you'll learn to live in the moment and be motivated to change what you couldn't do yesterday. Get your self-image better. Gain trust in yourself. Believe in yourself, and keep telling yourself that you are going to lose weight or that today you feel lighter. Create your confidence as much as you can by going out in public places with the strong conviction that you are one step closer to gaining ideal weight, and that you are already succeeding. This move includes initiating the start of affirmations about successful weight loss. By living and behaving in a manner that presumes you've already lost weight, the subconscious will start believing it has already done so, making the task of actually losing weight much simpler with affirmations of successful weight loss.

The secret is the language that you use. For the mind to embrace, you have to use constructive, clear, and correct terms. You have to honestly believe everything you say, and then feel the building of emotions inside you. You have to get your mind to believe that the affirmation of a healthy weight loss you create can be realized. Never think for a moment 'will this happen? 'Instead, consider 'it will happen' or 'it's happening already.'

The confirmation of effective weight loss must be replicated over several times in order to be successful with the 'natural weight loss technique.' You should write down any positive thoughts you have on a note, and check them in the morning and before going to bed, most importantly, every day. Some physiologists have suggested writing it down on a sheet of paper if you have any negative thoughts. Review it later at the end of the day and seek, for example, to come up with a more rational optimistic answer, instead of "I am so fat" you should say "I feel lighter today" Any time you think you're confident you're one step closer to slimming down and achieving your goal. Recall making your own assertion that your mind would genuinely believe to be true. Below are some examples of optimistic statements: I am losing weight right now.

I am feeling better today.

I love that feeling of growth.

I love food, which makes me think.

It's effortless to lose weight.

I love to be safe.

Today I feel very good.

Every day my body gets stronger, slimmer, and healthier.

Stay confident and safely and automatically achieve the desired result. Using optimistic affirmations about weight loss, combined with a healthy diet and exercise schedule, is by far the best and easiest weight loss plan.

CHAPTER SEVEN

Tips To Get The Most Out Of Your Hypnosis Sessions

Do you remember like to try weight loss hypnosis? If it does, then take heart! You're great, and it actually shows you're able to get your health and fitness goals to the next stage.

All hypnosis is to open the "CD-ROM" tray in your brain to allow a better program to run on the "machine" of your brain. For example, if you were rewarded with candy every time you did something that made your parents proud, you probably equate being good-along with the feeling of being the rewarded-every time you eat sweets. Hypnosis for weight loss will encourage you to start changing the plan in your head so that you can balance eating healthy food with feeling rewarded. A good hypnotist will explain all of this to you and ease your worries.

Here are three fast tips to help you irrespective of whether or not you are having a weight loss hypnosis session:

1) Change your vocabulary to what you really want, not what you "don't want." You have to be precise because that's how your brain operates. Say to yourself, "I want to get healthy, so I can run a 5 K race in less than 45 minutes to raise charity money." This is much more realistic than "I want to lose 30 pounds."

2) Turn the attention to what you want to get or achieve. Refrain from what you want to "lose." The word "loss" means something which has been traumatic for most people since they were young. That's why "losing 30 pounds" is a much tougher target than saying to your brain, "I want to gain improved fitness, and I want to maintain a body that's at least 75 percent muscle and no more than 25 percent body fat / retained water."

3) Have a lofty goal to drive your motivations. For example, with a certain weight training program, you would like to be featured as a testimonial before and after. Finally, you may want to enter a bodybuilding contest or a model contest to inspire your transformation. Or you might want to start a sport or a new activity that you've always wanted to try. Such high expectations will motivate you to do the little stuff you need for your fitness goals.

If you may be interested in weight loss hypnosis, bear in mind shifting your vocabulary away from "loss" and concentrating on what you want. From there, you can select a high target that will inspire you and help lock in the optimistic programming that a professional, licensed hypnotist can offer you.

Self Hypnosis Tips For Beginners

People had hesitated about hypnosis in the earlier times because of the thought that it contains evil forces or anything that suggests negativity. It's been related to influencing someone to commit corruption of any kind. Because of this, people are excited to try it out. However, what they did not know is that there are a variety of advantages that can be obtained from this approach when performed correctly and with the aid of the right people.

What Hypnosis Can Treat It can stimulate the functions of a person's body and, among others, can relieve someone from common sleep and digestive disorders. It can build some harmony in one's personality and approach to life, too. For one thing, the right hypnotic therapy will put away one of the things that hinder you from optimizing your procrastination ability.

Hypnosis operates by making the human subconscious focus on something unforgettable or pleasant to provide the body with rhythm. The body may also adjust to a pattern until it usually continues on its own. It's also even more shocking to remember that hypnosis is also an effective weight loss option. But how does one really do it?

Starting out with hypnosis, Here are some guidelines for hypnosis, which could be very helpful. For starters, of course, all the requisite training that correlates with the approach will have to be taken. It should be remembered that while hypnosis offers a person many benefits, it can also pose dangers when performed in the wrong way and without proper planning. Gathering all possible hypnosis tips from different sources wouldn't hurt one.

There are now several books available and write-ups on the subject as well as the site online about the process, so this one should be simple. However, the safest approach is for the experts themselves to demonstrate. An individual may already proceed to actually perform hypnotism when all of this is finished. The first important thing to concentrate one's attention is to evaluate the subject carefully. Anything that annoys an individual needs to be exposed or found. This will serve as the basis for the subsequent acts. For a hypnotic therapist, what you want for your patient is to unload everything first and start with a clear mind if you are doing it for yourself.

This way, it is much easier to focus on it. It's also advisable to take things slowly, especially if you know a person or you are new to this. The body responds differently in some situations when too much pressure is placed on it. You wouldn't want to make the issue serious, wouldn't you?

Relaxation is crucial. Another tip that is useful for most common hypnosis is to just try to let the body relax as much as possible. A stressed mind or body can not absorb the instruction, which is to be given. When the relationship between the therapist and the patient is strong, they will find it much easier to interact with each other and, therefore, to know each other's needs. This is also a clear way of determining the quality of the process to be practiced.

Tips For Choosing A Hypnotherapist

If you've ever decided to see a hypnotherapist for help with a medical illness or maybe a health problem, then rest assured that finding a successful therapist isn't really that difficult. Because of the rise in popularity of hypnotherapy, there are undoubtedly many therapists living in the immediate area, but to feel comfortable during your appointments, it is worth taking some time to make sure the therapist is the right one for you.

Telephone numbers and addresses for nearby clinics will be easily accessible through yellow pages, or through contacting professional organizations via websites or lists.

If you are aware of someone who has already undergone a hypnotherapy session and they have had a positive experience, then a referral from family or friends is the best way to make sure you have a trustworthy individual. If you need to start from the beginning and study the subject, however, it's a good idea to have a list of questions ready to ask the therapist before booking an appointment. That's so you can be as confident as possible that this therapist is the right one for you.

For example: If you contact them, do they seem professional and yet welcoming

- Sound interested in your question, and do they seem confident they can help?

- It may also be helpful to ask them what their success rate is, especially in relation to your situation.
- Ask them about their professional qualifications-it's crucial that you feel confident and comfortable about their ability.
- Ask them how long they've been in practice o It's important to find out how much their fees are, don't be afraid to ask this, as you might need to book a series of sessions depending on your particular requirements.
- An estimate of how many sessions may be required on average would be helpful when planning the course of therapies, when you may need to take time off work, take funds, or plan childcare.
- Depending on how urgent you feel that you need to be seen, ask them when you can get in for an appointment.
- It's easy to feel anxious if you've never been to a hypnotherapist before, so verify that you can bring a trusted friend or family member with you.
- Inquire whether you are being taught self-hypnosis as part of the ongoing recovery process.

Hypnotherapy helps someone who is willing to learn and is ready to fix aspects of their lives that they are dissatisfied with. Simply, it heals into an altered state of consciousness. Experienced experiences are analogous to reaching deep relaxation, and the therapist accesses the subconscious mind where important changes for emotional and physiological problems can be made. To gain even more from hypnotherapy, it helps if the client has faith and trust in the therapist and so it is crucial for the client to ensure that all specific questions are

451

addressed before beginning the sessions, and that will start the treatment correctly.

Tips for Becoming More Intimate with Your Kitchen

It should come as no surprise in a country known for excess that obesity is one of the biggest health problems faced by Americans today. The fact that adults get fatter, our children get fatter, and the prevalence of obesity-related diseases continues to increase is well-documented in scientific journals and popular media.

Are you yourself overweight by a few pounds (or more)? It's not just your fault. Millions of dollars are spent on advertising to keep us hungry, and in our fast-food culture, instant gratification always wins over healthy eating choices. There is a wide range of convenience foods such as frozen pizzas and microwaveable meals, snack foods are more popular than they used to be, and soft drink firms are now offering exclusive deals with colleges.

If you're searching for ways to lose weight on the internet, you'll find more details than you'll ever have time to learn. Exercise programs, diets, pharmaceuticals, hypnosis, and many other options are all there at great expense for you, for some free and for others. Regular exercise will always be important for good overall health, and so is psychological fitness. However, as a consumer society, when one effective solution is just to step away from the living room couch, we spend a fortune buying vitamins and special meals on delivery to our doorsteps. You call it a kitchen!

Just get into your kitchen and eat! You've already won a large part of the fight by doing a little homework, taking the time to pick healthy ingredients, and making an effort to cook a meal yourself. You cut a large portion of fat from your diet, you became less sedentary by getting off the sofa, you know what you put in your body, and you even know if it was cooked safely or not. You have saved money too.

If you're just starting out in the kitchen, or just need a little bit of nudge to get you started, the following tips will make your home-cooked meals more efficient, interesting and enjoyable!

Choose the best equipment for yourself. With a decent pan or two, you'll be much more effective than a whole package of inferior cookware from your local discount store.

Identify the origin of the local produce. Food bought from the farmers' markets is fresher and more affordable in general.

Take the organization. Plan your meals a few days in advance, and if possible, do some of your prep work in advance.

Oh, spice it up! Spend some time in the supermarket's spice row to take the stress out of your meal.

Pick your own cookbook. There are lots of good books available for simple, convenient, and nutritious meals with recipes.

See the series for the cooking. Choose a series that focuses on usability so you won't get bullied.

Brush up by taking a class on your basic skills, or go all out and take an advanced course. A variety of cooking courses are offered by several community colleges and city leisure programs.

Relax. Slow down. You'll soon learn how rewarding the cycle itself is.

Be a little bold. Don't think about trying new ingredients and cuisines.

Join a friend in the kitchen, particularly if a good cook is that friend. Most seasoned cooks are glad to share their expertise with an enthusiastic student.

You will soon be cooking your way to better health with a little dedication and a small investment of time. You'll also have more time to exercise, and you'll definitely lose those cravings for fast food. Very big me? I don't believe it!

Weight Loss Motivation Tips

Motivation to lose weight can be a little difficult when dieting. The relentless process of weight loss, weight loss, weight loss, and weight loss can become agonizing and demotivating.

The following tips come from my workshops and seminars to help you get rid of the weight and find the inspiration for weight loss.

Tip 1-Choose what you want to get rid of Make sure you know exactly how much weight you want. It just doesn't cut any weight, so have an exact figure of what your target weight is, and how much you lose.

Tip 2-Keep off the scales Don't weigh yourself regularly; it will weaken your enthusiasm for weight loss and frustrate you. Instead, choose one day a week when you are going to weigh yourself and weigh yourself at the same time every day (I usually prefer Mondays because you might be at your lowest after the excesses of the weekends!).

Tip 3-Test yourself Most weight loss is not instantly apparent by weight but is more obvious by losing inches. So, weigh and record your arms, neck, hips, and thighs.

Tip 4-Track your progress Motivation comes from seeing results, so track your weight loss and shorten your measurements, and you'll be more inspired to lose weight.

Tip 5-Eat regularly Some dieters believe they can lose weight easily by missing meals. NO!-NO! But it doesn't work. When you miss meals, then your body begins to believe there's a famine coming, meaning your body is piling on the fat to survive the famine. Eat snacks daily.

Tip 6- Don't Deny Yourself Most dieters would deny something sinful like chocolate, cookies, etc. The problem is, if you deny anything to yourself, you want something more. So then choose not to have it, as you would then be in charge. You can want to have this sometimes, which is nice too.

Tip 7-Drink, drink, drink ... And no, I'm not thinking about alcohol. I mean yummy, delicious water Drink lots of it because it will flush out your system's toxins and help you stay safe!

CPSIA information can be obtained
at www.ICGtesting.com
Printed in the USA
BVHW012120050221
599228BV00028B/61